Fifteen Years of Hippocampus Press

Fifteen Years of Hippocampus Press

2000–2015

Derrick Hussey, S. T. Joshi, and David E. Schultz

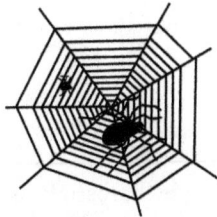

Hippocampus Press

New York

Published by Hippocampus Press
P.O. Box 641, New York, NY 10156
http://www.hippocampuspress.com

Cover design by Barbara Briggs Silbert.
Hippocampus Press logo designed by Anastasia Damianakos.

ISBN 978-1-61498-148-0

Foreword

Derrick Hussey

Five years ago, as Hippocampus Press entered its second decade, I remarked that one measure of our success was the ability to continue our activities and to increase both the size and number of our projects. Now, at fifteen years of Hippocampus Press, it is gratifying to look back and acknowledge that we have fulfilled these criteria. Additionally, we have, in my estimation, largely stayed true to our vision, which was to publish editions of surpassing interest and utility to Lovecraftians the world over, without undue concern over the appeal of these titles to the greater book-buying public. We are Lovecraft specialists who publish books with our fellow enthusiasts in mind. In the 125th year since the birth of H. P. Lovecraft, his global reputation and legacy is at last ascendant, and we are proud to be at the forefront. From modest beginnings, we now have released under our own imprint in very accurate editions an array of titles which, astoundingly, includes all the canonical fiction, nonfiction, and verse written by H. P. Lovecraft, together with a growing number of annotated editions of his letters, as well as a wide range of other material. For our efforts, the press earned the Horror Writers Association's 2011 Specialty Press Award. And there seemed to be not much hyperbole involved when, in 2014, *Publishers Weekly* proclaimed us "the world's leading publisher of books related to horror writer H. P. Lovecraft."

The past five years have seen a continued increase in our pace. In our first year we issued just a single book, and in 2010 thirteen; 2015 seems likely to see no fewer than twenty publications. Through it all, our core team has remained essentially the same. Barbara Silbert, Anastasia, and I are still in New York, David E. Schultz is in Milwaukee; and S. T. Joshi is in Seattle. A few words about these last two. Mr. Schultz, in addition to his almost fathomless knowledge and insight into Lovecraft, is a meticulous and creative designer, without whom we would be lost at sea. Upon his entering ostensible retirement last year, some of his long delayed projects coming to fruition, including *The Book of Jade*; and others, highly anticipated, will see the light of day in short order, including his annotated editions of both *Fungi from Yuggoth* and the *Commonplace Book*. Mr. Joshi, of course, remains an unflagging engine of productivity and brilliance. His energies propel, not only Hippocampus Press, but the entire world of Lovecraft. It is truly a prize beyond price to work so closely with these gentlemen, and to count them as friends.

One very welcome byproduct of longevity as a press is the opportunity to see the field develop, as new stars ignite and burn brightly. The past five years has witnessed our publication of fiction by John Langan, Josh Kent, and Simon Strantzas, among others; in the *Lovecraft Annual* scholarly work by a new generation including Alex Houstoun, Martin Andersson and Juha-Matti Rajala, and in *Spectral Realms* the work of K. A. Opperman, Ashley Dioses, Adam Bolivar and others. Here I must also mention a succession of talented young men: the Hippocampus interns. To date the roster comprises Dejan Ognjanovic, who has gone on to edit an edition of Lovecraft's tales in his native Serbia, and other books; Michael J. Abolafia, now coeditor of item 157 below, and Alex Lugo, entering his freshman year at Cornell. Although we continue to use established Lovecraftian artists for our book covers, including Jason C. Eckhardt, Denis Tiani, Harry O. Morris and Robert M. Price, we have also engaged newer talents, such as Fergal Fitzpatrick, Santiago Caruso, and Daniele Serra, commissioning these luminaries to develop a new visual vocabulary for cosmic horror beyond the traditional (perhaps somewhat over-familiar) iconography associated with Lovecraft. It is not much of a stretch to draw a parallel between the upswing in both the caliber and level of inspiration of modern Lovecraftian art and that resurgence in the aesthetic and technical quality of modern Lovecraftian literary productions that impelled S. T. Joshi to revise and retitle his overview of the Cthulhu Mythos (item 165).

Finally, it has been of real satisfaction to aid in the development of scholarly resources at institutions around the country to benefit Lovecraftians now and in the future. In the past five years, Hippocampus Press has been significantly involved in the establishment of the S. T. Joshi Endowed Research Fellowship for H. P. Lovecraft at the John Hay Library, Brown University; the cataloguing and conservation of the C. W. "Tryout" Smith archive of amateur journals at the New York Public Library; and the Donald Sidney-Fryer Research Fellowship for Clark Ashton Smith, George Sterling, Ambrose Bierce, and their Literary Circle at the Bancroft Library, UC–Berkeley (to be inaugurated in 2017). Doubtless more such projects will emerge in due course of time.

I remain grateful to have been afforded the opportunity to work with all the fine people and agencies mentioned above, together with many other authors and editors; artists, printers, and booksellers; agencies and estates; for the benefit of our readers worldwide. In a blind cosmos, if such we truly inhabit, such a convergence of talent, inspiration, and enthusiasm is fortuitous indeed.

My Years with Hippocampus Press

S. T. Joshi

I t must have been sometime in 1999 when, at a dinner of the "New Kalem Club"—an informal group of Lovecraft devotees who gathered at O'Reilly's Irish Pub on 31st Street in Manhattan once a month or so to shoot the bull and down a pint of Guinness (some of the more faint-hearted members settled for Bass Ale)—that I leaned over to Derrick Hussey and said, "How'd you like to start a new small press?"

I will be frank: my purpose was in some sense self-serving. Marc Michaud's Necronomicon Press was undergoing a certain turmoil because of Marc's personal difficulties, and I felt the need for another small press to take up the slack. By that time, my horizons had expanded from the narrow world of Lovecraft scholarship to the broader study of weird fiction, and I felt that a press that could take advantage of the burgeoning interest in Lovecraft and other weird writers, both "classic" and modern, could serve an important purpose.

Back in 1999, a number of needs in the study of Lovecraft were still unmet. His collected poetry had not been issued (I had prepared such an edition, initially scheduled for publication by Arkham House, then by Necronomicon Press, and finally released by Night Shade Books in 2001), his collected essays had not been assembled, his immense body of letters remained largely unpublished; and, of course, there was the ongoing need to advance Lovecraft scholarship—a task that was being hindered by the virtual cessation of the flagship journal in the field, *Lovecraft Studies*. (Over the next several years, a few more issues of *Lovecraft Studies* did appear—one published by Hippocampus Press—but the journal finally collapsed in 2004.)

In addition, there remained many significant works of weird fiction—both novels and collections of stories—whose intrinsic merit, and whose influence upon Lovecraft's own work, demanded their reprinting. Although such publishers as Ash-Tree Press and Tartarus Press were then engaging in a course of reprinting many weird classics, these were for the most part in the tradition of the Victorian ghost story, which did not influence Lovecraft significantly and therefore would not have any direct appeal to Lovecraftians. (Tartarus Press began as an imprint for restoring the work of Arthur Machen into print.) So the outlook for a new press seemed bright.

In fact, I recall mentioning to Derrick, "If you begin a press, I can guarantee that I myself can supply you with enough titles to keep it operating indefinitely." This was not spoken out of arrogance, or for the purpose of making

Hippocampus Press a private imprint of my own; it was simply a recognition that the press could fill a niche in the realm of small-press publishing that was currently not being met by other imprints, and that, after twenty or more years of research, I was in a position to prepare editions of Lovecraft and other writers that could keep a small press busy for years. Whether such a press could actually keep afloat financially by issuing such editions was a question for another day.

Derrick, who had recently left a position at the New York office of Routledge and seemed to be looking for something to fill up his time, readily assented. I was aware that he had a certain modicum of capital behind him—an essential requirement for a small press, since it was unlikely that our first several titles would be blockbusters. As our first title, I offered my extensively annotated edition of *Supernatural Horror in Literature*—an edition that had actually been assembled all the way back in 1981 (based on an initial expression of interest by Greenwood Press that was subsequently withdrawn). My friend and colleague David E. Schultz had done a preliminary layout of the book, for the purpose of estimating how big it might be, and Derrick felt satisfied that the result was a book worth publishing. So the first Hippocampus Press title slipped unobtrusively into print in the year 2000.

My recollection is that the book was fairly well received; I have no figures on how well it sold, but it did eventually get reprinted. It took us a full year to prepare another volume for the press, and this too was a book that had long been delayed—an annotated edition of the corrected text of Lovecraft's "The Shadow out of Time." The spectacular discovery of Lovecraft's original manuscript, among the effects of a woman in Hawaii, created a furore in 1994. I was the first scholar to be allowed access to the manuscript, and in February of 1994 I prepared a corrected text; but that text sat for years while legal and other difficulties were resolved.

Since then, Hippocampus Press has published books on a seemingly wide array of subjects, but I believe most or all of them can boil down to a few broad rubrics: 1) material by or about H. P. Lovecraft; 2) material by Lovecraft's friends and colleagues; 3) material that may have influenced Lovecraft; and 4) original work by leading authors of weird fiction or by promising newcomers.

It was not long after the publication of the first two Hippocampus titles that I broached the subject of publishing Lovecraft's collected essays. There still remained a few essays by Lovecraft that had not been published at all, while many others were scattered in a multitude of small-press volumes. The framework of what became the five-volume *Collected Essays* (2004–06) was suggested by my edition of Lovecraft's *Miscellaneous Writings* (Arkham House, 1995), where a topical or thematic division of the essays was presented, rather than a strictly chronological arrangement. And yet, this division itself was based upon a provisional arrangement of Lovecraft's complete works that I had devised as early as 1980, as I was working on the first edition of my bibliography of Lovecraft (1981). In that sense, the *Collected Essays* constitutes virtually the final instalment of what I had then envisioned as a 13-volume *Collected Works of H. P. Lovecraft*.

Of course, the last frontier in the publication of Lovecraft's work is his letters. Necronomicon Press had made a start by issuing batches of letters to individual correspondents (Henry Kuttner, Richard F. Searight, Samuel Loveman and Vincent Starrett, Robert Bloch) in the early 1990s, and Hippocampus Press followed up that program by publishing the letters to Alfred Galpin (2003) and Rheinhart Kleiner (2005), edited by David E. Schultz and myself. At that point our horizons expanded, and we wondered whether the entirety of Lovecraft's letters could be issued in book form (as opposed to electronically), with exhaustive annotations. Our first venture in this regard was the massive two-volume edition of Lovecraft's letters to August Derleth (2008), followed—after years of legal and logistical difficulties—with the even more massive two-volume edition of Lovecraft's letters to Robert E. Howard (2009). These titles, in effect, constitute the first four volumes of what promise to be approximately 25 volumes of Lovecraft letters. We have now issued letters to James F. Morton (2011), Elizabeth Toldridge and Anne Tillery Renshaw (2014), and Robert Bloch and others (2015), with the joint correspondence of Lovecraft and Clark Ashton Smith to follow.

Mention of Smith brings to mind that we have engaged in substantial work in Smith studies. My edition of Smith's juvenile novel, *The Black Diamonds* (2002), was again based on work that had been done years ago: in 1979–81, Marc Michaud and I had catalogued Smith's papers and manuscripts for the John Hay Library of Brown University, and among those papers was *The Black Diamonds*. The manuscript was a fearful mess, and it took me some time to ascertain that it constituted a full version (minus a few pages) of the first draft and several short attempts at subsequent drafts (these drafts have not been published); it took still more time to decipher Smith's youthful chirography and transcribe the text. After the book was issued, Dr. W. C. Farmer, a late colleague of Smith's, announced that he had the two missing pages of the manuscript, along with another, somewhat shorter juvenile novel, *The Sword of Zagan*, as well as other material. These texts were issued in 2004. We also issued Smith's *Last Oblivion* (2002), a selection of his best fantastic poetry, which set the stage for the three-volume edition of Smith's *Complete Poems and Translations* (2007–08), an edition that David E. Schultz had been working on since the 1980s. We also published a noteworthy collection of articles about Smith, *The Freedom of Fantastic Things* (2006), edited by Scott Connors, now the leading Smith scholar.

Lovecraft's colleagues have fared well at Hippocampus Press, with editions of the writings of R. H. Barlow (2002), Samuel Loveman (2004), Donald Wandrei (*Sanctity and Sin* [2008], an expansion of Wandrei's *Collected Poems*

[Necronomicon Press, 1988]), Edith Miniter (2008), and a number of others. Hippocampus publications of George Sterling, the California poet who was the early mentor of Clark Ashton Smith, are a result of my own devoted interest in this much-neglected writer. I was pleased to issue a volume of Sterling's weird verse, *The Thirst of Satan* (2003), which set the stage for the massive three-volume edition of Sterling's collected poetry and verse drama that appeared in 2013. Schultz and I also edited the joint correspondence of Sterling and Smith (*The Shadow of the Unattained*, 2005).

Scholarship on Lovecraft has been enhanced by the re-establishment of a journal devoted to his life and work, the *Lovecraft Annual* (2007f.), as well as two volumes of Robert H. Waugh's scintillating essays, *The Monster in the Mirror: Looking for H. P. Lovecraft* (2006) and *A Monster of Voices: Speaking for H. P. Lovecraft* (2011). Hippocampus also reprinted *An Epicure in the Terrible: A Centennial Anthology of Essays in Honor of H. P. Lovecraft* (2011), a significant collection of essays that first appeared in 1991. Within this rubric might be considered the highly innovative volume *Lovecraft's New York Circle: The Kalem Club, 1924–1927* (2006), assembled largely by Mara Kirk Hart (the daughter of George Kirk) with minimal assistance by me. This volume contains substantial literary material by the various core members of the Kalem Club (Rheinhart Kleiner, Arthur Leeds, Frank Belknap Long, Samuel Loveman, Everett McNeil, James F. Morton) and is preceded by the fascinating "Kalem Letters"—a batch of letters by George Kirk written to his fiancée, Lucile Dvorak, which provides an unprecedented first-hand glimpse of the Kalems in New York. Kenneth W. Faig, Jr.'s *The Unknown Lovecraft* (2009) will, I hope, finally bring recognition to this pioneering Lovecraft scholar for the invaluable work he has done over the past thirty years or more.

The NecronomiCon convention of 2013, which attracted an unprecedented 1200 devotees to the Biltmore Hotel in Providence, R.I., set the stage for a number of significant publications relating to Lovecraft, including David Goudsward's *H. P. Lovecraft in the Merrimack Valley*, Steven J. Mariconda's substantial collection of essays *H. P. Lovecraft: Art, Artifact, and Reality*, and an extensively revised version of my edition of Lovecraft's collected poetry, *The Ancient Track*. Even some works of Lovecraftian fiction, from Kenneth W. Faig, Jr.'s *Lovecraft's Pillow* to my whimsical novel *The Assaults of Chaos*, graced the dealer's tables at the convention.

The fostering of scholarship has been an important objective at Hippocampus Press. We are well aware that there are fewer and fewer outlets for the study of weird fiction, as many academic publishers that formerly published this material are now cutting back in the wake of budget cuts. Benjamin Szumskyj's admirable anthology of essays on Robert E. Howard, *Two-Gun Bob* (2006), along with such of my own volumes as *Primal Sources: Essays on H. P. Lovecraft* (2003), *The Evolution of the Weird Tale* (2004), *Classics and Contemporaries*

(2009), and *Lovecraft and a World in Transition: Collected Essays on H. P. Lovecraft* (2014) have been generally well received; and I was pleased to lend some assistance to Rosemary Pardoe in a splendid volume of criticism of M. R. James, *Warnings to the Curious* (2007). Gary William Crawford, Jim Rockhill, and Brian J. Showers edited an exemplary collection of essays on J. Sheridan Le Fanu, *Reflections in a Glass Darkly* (2011); and volumes on Arthur Machen and Robert Aickman are in the works. William F. Nolan's *Nolan on Bradbury* (2013), a compilation of more than sixty years of the author's writings on the California author of fantasy and science fiction, won a Bram Stoker Award. Massimo Berruti and others assembled the first full-length volume of critical essays on William Hope Hodgson, *William Hope Hodgson: Voices from the Borderland* (2014). In a somewhat related vein, our founding of *Dead Reckonings* (2007f.), a review journal devoted to weird fiction—based in large part upon the successful *Necrofile* (1991–99), issued by Necronomicon Press—has resulted in substantive analysis of contemporary work in the field.

The press has also done important work in another area of weird fiction that tends to be given short shrift—weird poetry. The volumes by Barlow, Loveman, and Wandrei, cited above, contain substantial amounts of poetry, and the publication of Nora May French's collected poetry, *The Outer Gate* (2009), connects with the press's interest in Smith, Sterling, and poetry, as does the issuance of *Dreams of Fear: Poetry of Terror and the Supernatural* (2013), the most exhaustive historical anthology of weird poetry since August Derleth's *Dark of the Moon* (1947), and the long-awaited edition of Park Barnitz's *The Book of Jade* (2015), augmented with much biographical and critical information on the little-known poet. The press's first work of original creative writing was R. Nemo Hill's *The Strange Music of Erich Zann* (2004), a poetic extrapolation from Lovecraft's "The Music of Erich Zann." H. L. Mencken's *Collected Poems* (2009) may seem far out of the scope of Hippocampus Press, but it reflects our ongoing interest in poetry and my own personal interest in the work of the iconoclast from Baltimore. And the publication of Donald Sidney-Fryer's immense *Atlantis Fragments* (2008)—a compendium of his three volumes of *Songs and Sonnets Atlantean*, some of the finest weird poetry and prose-poetry written since the heyday of Clark Ashton Smith—represents the culmination of Sidney-Fryer's illustrious career as a creative artist. Volumes of original poetry by Ann K. Schwader (2011), Wade German (2014), K. A. Opperman (2015), and others have generated considerable interest among devotees of this genre. In 2014 Hippocampus initiated the biennial journal *Spectral Realms* for the publication of original weird poetry along with selected "classic" reprints as well as articles and reviews on weird poetry; the journal has proven to be spectacularly popular (among poets, at any rate), in large part due to its exquisite production values.

The publication of my revised edition of *Lovecraft's Library: A Catalogue* (2002)—a third edition appeared in 2012, and there will probably be a need for a fourth revised edition in the coming years—may have triggered the "Lovecraft's Library" series, in which novels and tales that inspired Lovecraft, or in some cases were simply appreciated by him, are reprinted. The series was initiated even before the publication of *Lovecraft's Library* by Stefan Dziemianowicz's edition of A. Merritt's *The Metal Monster* (2002), but got underway in earnest with the issuance of Herbert Gorman's *The Place Called Dagon* (2003). In 2007 we released the first Hippocampus Press "double," an imitation of the format of the old "Ace doubles," where two novels were printed in one book. In this way, several short novels could be issued together, since there still remain numerous titles that Lovecraftians will wish to read for their possible influence on Lovecraft's seminal tales.

The most exciting development at Hippocampus Press—and one that we never envisioned when we first began the press—was the issuance of new creative work by leading contemporary writers and promising new voices. As mentioned, R. Nemo Hill's booklet was our first such venture, but the program gathered steam with the issuance of *The Fungal Stain and Other Dreams* (2006), by W. H. Pugmire, a writer whose Lovecraftian-related work I have long admired. We have subsequently published distinguished work by both veterans (Ramsey Campbell's *Inconsequential Tales*, 2008; Donald R. Burleson's *Wait for the Thunder: Stories for a Stormy Night*, 2010) and newcomers (Philip Haldeman's *Shadow Coast*, 2007; Jonathan Thomas's *Midnight Call and Other Stories*, 2008; Joseph S. Pulver, Sr.'s *Blood Will Have Its Season*, 2009; Michael Aronovitz's *Seven Deadly Pleasures*, 2009). More recently, Hippocampus has issued important new volumes by Richard Gavin (*At Fear's Altar*, 2012), John Langan (*The Wide, Carnivorous Sky*, 2013), Jason V Brock (*Simulacrum and Other Possible Realities*, 2013), Simon Strantzas (*Burnt Black Suns*, 2014), Clint Smith (*Ghouljaw and Other Stories*, 2014), Rhys Hughes (*Bone Idle in the Charnel House*, 2014), and others, while continuing to publish the increasingly recognised work of Jonathan Thomas, W. H. Pugmire, Joseph S. Pulver, Sr., Michael Aronovitz, and others. We are thrilled that most of these volumes have been well received by critics and readers. Our promotion of noteworthy contributions to Lovecraft's "Cthulhu Mythos" began with Robert M. Price's edition of *Tales out of Dunwich* (2005) and continued through Franklyn Searight's *Lair of the Dreamer* (2007), Adam Niswander's trio of novels, *The Hound Hunters* (2009), *The War of the Whisperers* (2009), and *The Nemesis of Night* (2011), Robert M. Price's edition of *The Tindalos Cycle* (2010), Don Webb's *Through Dark Angles* (2014), and several others.

The second NecronomiCon convention, held in Providence, R.I., in the summer of 2015, again triggered the publication of a significant number of volumes, ranging from Lovecraftian or weird fiction (Ann K. Schwader's *Dark*

Equinox; Robert H. Waugh's *The Bloody Tugboat*; Jonathan Thomas's *Dreams of Ys*; Lois H. Gresh's *Cult of the Dead*; W. H. Pugmire's *Monstrous Aftermath*) to works of scholarship (a somewhat delayed edition of selected papers from the "Emerging Scholarship Session" of the 2013 convention; Donald R. Burleson's *Lovecraft—An American Allegory*; a revised version of my *Rise and Fall of the Cthulhu Mythos* under a new title) to what might be the crowning jewel in the entire Hippocampus line: H. P. Lovecraft's *Collected Fiction: A Variorum Edition*. This edition, whose initial work I had begun as a freshman at Brown University in the fall of 1976, was a fully collaborative venture between myself and the two other chief editorial figures at Hippocampus, Derrick Hussey (who meticulously checked the texts of Lovecraft's stories as well as my thousands of textual notes, catching many errors in the process) and David E. Schultz, who not only lent his exhaustive knowledge of Lovecraft to many phases of the venture but applied his formidable skills in design and layout to a work of particular difficulty in terms of formatting. With this edition, Hippocampus completes its publication of the definitive editions of Lovecraft's fiction, essays, and poetry—and with the ongoing publication of Lovecraft's complete surviving correspondence, there will come a day when every word of H. P. Lovecraft's work is available in accurate Hippocampus Press editions.

As Hippocampus Press continues its publications in its several different lines—ranging from my two-volume biography, *I Am Providence: The Life and Times of H. P. Lovecraft* (2010), to original fiction by Jonathan Thomas and Joseph S. Pulver, Sr., poetry by Fred Phillips, continuing editions of Lovecraft's letters, and much other work—I think it can safely be said that the press has established itself as one of the most vital imprints in the field of weird fiction, and can look forward to many years of critical success. But it is the devotion of its many readers that will carry the press into the future, and we hope to continue earning that devotion by the publications we hope to issue in the coming years.

Publications of Hippocampus Press 2000–2015

1. H. P. LOVECRAFT. *The Annotated Supernatural Horror in Literature.* Edited by S. T. Joshi. 2000 (rpt. 2004). 172 pp.

    Contents. Preface; Introduction; Supernatural Horror in Literature, by H. P. Lovecraft; Appendix: The Favorite Weird Stories of H P. Lovecraft; Notes; Bibliography of Authors and Works; Index.

    Notes. Cover illustration by Vrest Orton from the *Recluse* 1 (1927). First printing, 1000 copies plus unspecified overrun, Morris Publishing, Kearney, NE. Rpt November 2004 as a print-on-demand (POD) book. A work Joshi compiled as early as 1981 but for which he could not find a publisher. The text of Lovecraft's essay has been printed accurately here for the first time, as Joshi has collated all previous publications, including the original publication in the *Recluse* (1927) and the serialization in the *Fantasy Fan* (1933–35). Joshi has added extensive commentary and a substantial primary and secondary bibliography for all authors and works discussed in the treatise. A new and updated edition appeared in 2012 (see item 101).

2. H. P. LOVECRAFT. *The Shadow out of Time.* Edited by S. T. Joshi and David E. Schultz. 2001 (rpt. 2003). 136 pp.

    Contents. Introduction; The Shadow out of Time, by H. P. Lovecraft; APPENDIX: Notes to "The Shadow out of Time"; Early draft; Notes; Textual *Notes.*

    Notes. Cover illustration by Howard V. Brown. First printing, 1000 copies plus unspecified overrun; Morris Publishing. Reprint issued simultaneously in 2003 with two competing POD companies, Booksurge and Lightning Source, to compare quality and service. Booksurge POD edition was taken out of print sometime later, and only a handful of this variant state were circulated. Booksurge edition distinguished by matte finish on cover; Lightning Source paperback has a glossy finish on cover. Lightning Source POD and Morris Publishing editions were available simultaneously for a time.

    A landmark publication of the original ms. of Lovecraft's story, which was believed lost until it surfaced in 1994. Joshi was the first scholar to be allowed to consult the text, which he did in February 1994;

but various logistical delays prevented the publication of the edition until 2001. The text, which contains at least 400 textual corrections from the minimally corrected edition in *The Dunwich Horror and Others* (Arkham House, 1984), is exhaustively annotated, with textual variants and a discussion of the finding of the ms. by John H. Stanley, a curator at the John Hay Library, Brown University.

3. *Studies in Weird Fiction 25.* Edited by S. T. Joshi. Summer 2001. 40 pp.

    Contents. From Haunted Rose Gardens to Lurking Wendigos: Liminal and Wild Places in M. R. James and Algernon Blackwood, by Linda J. Holland-Toll; Hawthorne, Hitchcock, and the Fine Women of *Blithedale* and *Psycho*, by Marilyn Knight; Gesturing Toward the Infinite: Clark Ashton Smith and Modernism, by Scott Connors; The Weird Verse of Christopher Brennan, by Phillip A. Ellis; Things from the Sea: The Early Weird Fiction of Frank Belknap Long, by S. T. Joshi; Correspondence.

    Notes. Cover illustration by Robert H. Knox. Back cover photograph of Clark Ashton Smith in 1912 by Bianca Conti. Two hundred copies plus unspecified overrun. A long-delayed issue of a magazine first published (1986f.) by Necronomicon Press. Awkwardly, Necronomicon Press itself issued its own No. 25 (Summer 2003), followed by the final issue, No. 27 (Spring 2005).

4. *Lovecraft Studies 42–43.* Edited by S. T. Joshi. Autumn 2001. 76 pp.

    Contents. Editorial; The Book, by H. P. Lovecraft; The Book of "The Book," by Michael Cisco; H. P. Lovecraft: Reluctant American Modernist, by Steven J. Mariconda; H. P. Lovecraft in Florida, by Stephen J. Jordan; Antique Dreams: Marblehead and Lovecraft's Kingsport, by Donovan K. Loucks; A Note on "The Book," by Donald R. Burleson; The Problem with Solving: Implications for Sherlock Holmes and Lovecraft Narrators, by Deborah D'Agati; The Lurker at the Threshold of Interpretation: Hoax *Necronomicons* and Paratextual Noise by Dan Clore; The Mirror in the House: Looking at the Horror of Looking at the Horror, by P. S. Owens; Review.

    Notes. Cover illustration by Jason C. Eckhardt. Two hundred copies plus unspecified overrun. Another long-delayed issue of a journal first published (1979f.) by Necronomicon Press. The latter published two further issues, No. 44 (2004) and No. 45 (Spring 2005). The journal was succeeded by the *Lovecraft Annual* (items 44ff).

5.   CLARK ASHTON SMITH. *The Black Diamonds.* Edited by S. T. Joshi. 2002 (rpt. 2004). 181 pp.

Notes. Cover and interior illustrations by Jason C. Eckhardt. First printing, 1040 copies: Morris Publishing.

A transcript of Smith's juvenile novel, probably written at the age of 14 (i.e., c. 1907). The ms. consists of nearly 246 pp. of foolscap sheets that had been sent to the John Hay Library of Brown University in 1979–80 by Smith's literary executor as part of the Clark Ashton Smith Papers there. Joshi began transcribing the text at that time but did not finish until years later. The ms. is missing two sheets; shortly after publication, Dr. W. C. Farmer (see item 17) located them in his effects, and they were made available for transcription. The new printing (184 pp.) incorporates the missing text.

6.   A. MERRITT. *The Metal Monster.* Edited by Stefan Dziemian-owicz. 2002. 237 pp.

Notes. Cover illustration by Virgil Finlay. First printing, 1050 copies: Morris Publishing. The first reprint of the 1920 *Argosy All-Story Weekly* serialization of the novel, one of three different texts of the work that appeared in Merritt's lifetime. This is the first title in the "Love-craft's Library" series, which reprints texts that Lovecraft read and was influenced by. Lovecraft read the text in 1934, when it was lent to him by R. H. Barlow. A slow seller despite an abundance of merit, copies were eventually given away free with the purchase of item 21.

7.   S. T. JOSHI. *Lovecraft's Library: A Catalogue.* 2002. 175 pp.

Contents. Introduction; Explanatory Notes; Lovecraft's Library [981 titles]; Weird &c. Items in Library of H. P. Lovecraft; INDICES: A. Names; B. Titles; C. Works by Lovecraft; D. Publishers; E. Subjects.

Notes. Cover illustration by Jason C. Eckhardt. Our first POD title, printed by Lightning Source. Exhaustive revision of the catalogue first published by Necronomicon Press in 1980, with the addition of 60 more titles and listings of tables of contents of many important volumes, along with other additions to the notes. Since publication, dozens of additional titles have been identified; for the third edition, see item 102.

8. CLARK ASHTON SMITH. *The Last Oblivion: Best Fantastic Poems of Clark Ashton Smith*. Edited by S. T. Joshi and David E. Schultz. 2002. 194 pp.

Contents. Introduction; A Note on the Text; Acknowledgments; THE HASHISH-EATER; OR, THE APOCALYPSE OF EVIL; I. THE STAR-TREADER: The Star-Treader; Ode to the Abyss; Nirvana; The Song of a Comet; Lament of the Stars; In Saturn; Triple Aspect; The Abyss Triumphant; The Motes; Desire of Vastness; Shadows; A Dream of the Abyss; After Armageddon; The Ancient Quest; A Dream of Oblivion; Ode to Light; Ode to Matter; II. MEDUSA AND OTHER HORRORS: Nero; Medusa; Averted Malefice; The Medusa of the Skies; Saturn; In Lemuria; Satan Unrepentant; The Ghoul and the Seraph; The Medusa of Despair; A Vision of Lucifer; The Witch in the Graveyard; The Flight of Azrael; The Mummy; Minatory; To the Chimera; The Whisper of the Worm; The Envoys; Nyctalops; Jungle Twilight; Necromancy; The Witch with Eyes of Amber; Cambion; The Saturnienne; Chance; Revenant; Song of the Necromancer; *Pour chercher du nouveau*; Witch-Dance; Not Theirs the Cypress-Arch; III. THE ELDRITCH DARK: A Song from Hell; The Titans in Tartarus; The Twilight Woods; Lethe; Atlantis; The Eldritch Dark; White Death; A Dead City; The Cloud-Islands; The City of the Titans; The City of Destruction; Beyond the Great Wall; Solution; *Rosa Mystica*; Symbols; The City in the Desert; The Melancholy Pool; Twilight on the Snow; The Land of Evil Stars; Memnon at Midnight; The Kingdom of Shadows; Moon-Dawn; Outlanders; Warning; The Nightmare Tarn; The Prophet Speaks; The Outer Land; In Thessaly; *Le Miroir des blanches fleurs*; The Moonlight Desert; Ougabalys; Desert Dweller; Amithaine; The Dark Chateau; Averoigne; Zothique; IV. SAID THE DREAMER: The Castle of Dreams; The Dream-God's Realm; Imagination; The Last Night; Shadow of Nightmare; A Song of Dreams; The Dream-Bridge; Said the Dreamer; Dolor of Dreams; *Luna Aeternalis*; Echo of Memnon; Nightmare; The Last Goddess; Love Malevolent; The Wingless Archangels; Enchanted Mirrors; Selenique; Maya; *Fantaisie d'Antan*; In Slumber; V. THE REFUGE OF BEAUTY: The Power of Eld; Strangeness; The Nereid; Exotique; Transcendence; The Tears of Lilith; Cleopatra; The Refuge of Beauty; Sandalwood; The Last Oblivion; Alienage; Adventure; Interrogation; Canticle; To Antares; Connaissance; Exorcism; Lamia; Farewell to Eros; Some Blind Eidolon; Bacchante; Resurrection; The Sorcerer to His Love; The Hill of Dionysus; Midnight Beach; Omniety; VI. TO THE DARKNESS: Ode on Imagination; Retrospect and Forecast; To the Darkness; A Dream of Beauty; The Pursuer; In the Desert; The Nameless Wraith; To the Daemon of Sublimity; Desolation; Inferno; Dissonance; Remembered

Light; The Incubus of Time; *Laus Mortis*; The Hope of the Infinite; Antepast; Forgotten Sorrow; Lunar Mystery; The Funeral Urn; Mors; September; Ennui; VII. THE SORCERER DEPARTS: To Omar Khayyam; To Nora May French; On Re-reading Baudelaire; To George Sterling: A Valediction; To Howard Phillips Lovecraft; H. P. L.; Soliloquy in an Ebon Tower; Cycles. Glossary. Bibliography. Index of Titles. Index of First Lines.

Notes. Cover and interior illustration by Clark Ashton Smith. First printing, 1650 copies, Vaughan Printing, Nashville TN. The first book to feature color reproductions of artwork by Clark Ashton Smith. A kind of stopgap volume while Smith's *Complete Poetry and Translations* (see items 37 and 50) were being prepared. The basic selection was done by Joshi, with additions by Schultz, who supplied the texts based on his years of work with Smith's poetry mss.

9. R. H. BARLOW. *Eyes of the God: The Weird Fiction and Poetry of R. H. Barlow.* Edited by S. T. Joshi, Douglas A. Anderson, and David E. Schultz. 2002. 210 pp.

Contents. Introduction by S. T. Joshi and Douglas A. Anderson. FICTION: The Slaying of the Monster (with H. P. Lovecraft); Eyes of the God; *Annals of the Jinns:* I. The Black Tower; II. The Shadow from Above; III. The Flagon of Beauty; IV. The Sacred Bird; V. The Tomb of the God; VI. The Flower God; VII. The Little Box; VIII. The Fall of the Three Cities; IX. The Mirror; X. The Theft of the Hsothian Manuscripts; XI. An Episode in the Jungle; The Hoard of the Wizard-Beast (with H. P. Lovecraft); The Battle That Ended the Century (with H. P. Lovecraft); The Fidelity of Ghu; The Inhospitable Tavern; The Misfortunes of Butter-Churning; "Till A' the Seas" (with H. P. Lovecraft); The Temple; The Adventures of Garoth; The Experiment; Collapsing Cosmoses (with H. P. Lovecraft); The Bright Valley; The Priest and the Heretic; The Summons; A Dream; A Memory; Pursuit of the Moth; The Root-Gatherers; A Dim-Remembered Story; The Night Ocean (with H. P. Lovecraft); Origin Undetermined; The Swearing of an Oath; The Questioner; The Artizan's Reward; Return by Sunset. POETRY: I. Poems 1936–1939; [Untitled]; Sonnet V; Sonnet VI; Sonnet VII; Song; [Untitled]; Sonnet; [Untitled]; [Untitled]; R. E. H.; St. John's Churchyard; Dirge for the Artist; Alcestis; N. Y.; [Untitled]; [Untitled]; Altamira; Cycle from a Dead Year; H. P. L.; I. March 1937; II. March 1938; [Untitled]; [Untitled]; H. P. L.; H. P. L.; March; [Untitled]; The Unresisting; Shub-Ad; Who Will Not Know; To Bacchus; [Untitled]; [Untitled]; Winter Mood; Burlesque; Frustration; To a Companion;

Notes. Cover illustration by R. Saunders (from the *Californian*, Winter 1936, illustrating "The Night Ocean"), colored by Barbara Briggs Silbert. An exhaustive edition of Barlow's extant fiction and poetry, including a number of unpublished items derived from Barlow's papers. The fiction was largely edited by Joshi and Schultz, the poetry by Anderson, who also drafted the bibliography.

20

10. H. P. LOVECRAFT. *From the Pest Zone: The New York Stories.* Edited by S. T. Joshi and David E. Schultz. 2003. 150 pp.

Contents. Abbreviations; Introduction; The Shunned House; The Horror at Red Hook; He; In the Vault; Cool Air; APPENDIX: Preface to "The Shunned House" by Frank Belknap Long, Jr.; Little Sketches About Town; Notes; Textual *Notes.*

Notes. Cover illustration by Sean Madden. Interior photographs by Ron Breznay, Donovan K. Loucks, and Steven Mariconda. An extensively annotated edition of the six stories Lovecraft wrote while in New York (1924–26), analogous to the Joshi–Schultz editions of *The Shadow over Innsmouth* (Necronomicon Press, 1994, 1997) and *The Shadow out of Time* (see item 2).

11. HERBERT GORMAN. *The Place Called Dagon.* 2003 (rpt. 2008). 187 pp.

Contents. Introduction, by Larry Creasy; *The Place Called Dagon* by Herbert Gorman; Afterword: Gorman and Lovecraft, by S. T. Joshi.

Notes. Cover design by Barbara Briggs Silbert; interior illustrations by Allen Koszowski. Reprint edition replaced "merman" cover art with illustration by Allen Koszowski. Part of the Lovecraft's Library series. A reprint of Gorman's chilling horror novel of 1927. The Hippocampus staff fortuitously teamed up with Larry Creasy (proprietor of Charon House), who was planning his own reprint; Creasy contributed an extensive biographical introduction, and Joshi added an afterword discussing the novel's possible influence on Lovecraft.

12. JACK MADISON HARINGA. *Drafts from the Moon Pool: The Influence of A. Merritt on H. P. Lovecraft.* 2003. 24 pp.

Notes. Cover photograph of A. Merritt from the collection of Sam Moskowitz. Printed in a numbered edition of 100 copies, the first thirty of which were included in the 30th Anniversary Mailing of the Esoteric Order of Dagon Amateur Press Association. A sensitive essay on Merritt's influence on Lovecraft. Haringa later became coeditor of *Dead Reckonings* (see items 40ff.).

13. H. P. LOVECRAFT. *Letters to Alfred Galpin.* Edited by S. T. Joshi and David E. Schultz. 2003 (rpt. 2004). 287 pp.

Contents. Introduction; Letters to Alfred Galpin; WORKS OF ALFRED GALPIN: Mystery; Two Loves; Selenaio-Phantasma; Remarks to My Handwriting; Marsh-Mad; The Critic; Stars; Some Tendencies of

Modern Poetry; The Spoken Tongue; The World Situation; The United's Policy 1920–1921 (with H. P. Lovecraft); Form in Modern Poetry; Picture of a Modern Mood; Nietzsche as a Practical Prophet; To Sam Loveman; The Vivisector; *Four Translations from* Les Fleurs du mal *by Charles Pierre Baudelaire* (Au Lecteur; L'Ennemi; Remords Posthume; L'Ange Gardien); Scattered Remarks upon the Green Cheese Theory; Department of Public Criticism; Intuition in the Philosophy of Bergson; Ennui; A Critic of Poetry; From the French of Pierre de Ronsard ("Amours"—Livre II.): Aubade; Echoes from Beyond Space; Red; En Route (An American to Paris, 1931): I. New York Harbor; II. On Deck; November; A Partial Bibliography of Alfred Galpin; Index.

Notes. Cover design by Anastasia Damianakos. First edition, first printing issued as POD by Booksurge, taken out of print in 2004 and reissued 2004 as first edition, second printing with Lightning Source, our standard POD printer from then on. Booksurge edition lacked frontispiece (photo of AG). The interior paper stock was changed from cream to white in 2011, at which time slight changes were made to the cover. The first of what was planned as a series of volumes presenting unabridged and extensively annotated editions of Lovecraft's letters to important correspondents; in the event, only one other volume was published (see item 25). Nearly 50 pp. of Galpin's writings were included. Nominated for the 2003 International Horror Guild award for nonfiction.

14. GEORGE STERLING. *The Thirst of Satan: Poems of Fantasy and Terror.* Edited by S. T. Joshi. 215 pp.

Contents. Introduction, by S. T. Joshi; I. THE TESTIMONY OF THE SUNS: The Testimony of the Suns; Mystery; Three Sonnets on Oblivion; Oblivion; The Dust Dethroned; The Night of Gods; Three Sonnets of the Night Skies (I—Aldebaran at Dusk; II—The Chariots of Dawn; III—The Huntress of Stars); The Evanescent; The Thirst of Satan; The Setting of Antares; Outward; The Face of the Skies; Ephemera; Disillusion; The Meteor; The Last Man. II. THE GARDENS OF THE SEA: The Nile; The Fog Siren; The Sea-Fog; Darkness; "Sad Sea-Horizons"; Sonnets by the Night Sea; The Gardens of the Sea; At the Grand Cañon; The Last of Sunset; Caucasus; The Caravan; III. THE MUSE OF THE INCOMMUNICABLE: Memory of the Dead; The Altar-Flame; Ultima Thule; The Directory; In Extremis; Romance; A Mood; The Moth of Time; The Muse of the Incommunicable; "Omnia Exeunt in Mysterium": To One Self-Slain; Three Sonnets on Sleep; Illusion; Essential Night; To Life; To Science; Waste; Amber;

The Dweller in Darkness; Here and Now; IV. THE BLACK VULTURE: The Black Vulture; The Sibyl of Dreams; The Last Monster; "That Walk in Darkness"; To the Mummy of the Lady Isis; Witch-Fire; Song; The Young Witch; Eidolon; The Sphinx; V. THE NAIAD'S SONG: The Haunting; The Naiad's Song; White Magic; The Golden Past; The Revenge; To a Girl Dancing; Flame; The Stranger; VI. A WINE OF WIZARDRY: The Summer of the Gods; Nightmare; A Wine of Wizardry; The Apothecary's; Under the Rainbow; The Shadow of Nirvana; The Wiser Prophet; The Oldest Book; Farm of Fools; VII. THE PASSING OF BIERCE: To Edgar Allan Poe; To Ambrose Bierce; The Ashes in the Sea; The Coming Singer; The Passing of Bierce; Shelley at Spezia. VIII. THE RACK: The Lords of Pain; A Dream of Fear; The Rack; Conspiracy; The Hidden Pool; The Death of Circe; To a Monk's Skull; To Pain; Epilogue: My Swan Song; George Sterling: An Appreciation, by Clark Ashton Smith; Commentary; Index of Titles; Index of First Lines.

Notes. Cover and interior illustrations by Virgil Finlay. A sampling of Sterling's weird verse—the first major reprinting of his poetry since 1969 and a foretaste of our edition of his complete poetry and verse drama (see items 117-119).

15. LORD DUNSANY. *The Pleasures of a Futuroscope.* Edited by S. T. Joshi. 2003 (rpt. 2005 [paper]). 200 pp.

Notes. Cover illustration by Jeff Remmer. Hardcover edition 1000 copies: Covington Group, St. Louis. The first Hippocampus Press hardcover edition, and the first publication of Dunsany's last novel, probably written in 1955 and unearthed by Joe Doyle, archivist at Dunsany Castle. A splendid fantasy/science fiction hybrid about a man who invents a "futuroscope" that allows him to see into the future—where he finds that a nuclear holocaust has reduced humanity to a primitive state.

16. S. T. JOSHI. *Primal Sources: Essays on H. P. Lovecraft.* 2003. 208 pp.

Contents. Introduction; I. LOVECRAFT THE MAN: Lovecraft and the Munsey Magazines; Lovecraft and *Weird Tales*; A Look at Lovecraft's Letters; Lovecraft and the Films of His Day; Lovecraft's Library; II. LOVECRAFT THE WRITER AND THINKER: Autobiography in Lovecraft; "Reality" and Knowledge; *In Defence of Dagon* and Lovecraft's Philosophy; The Rationale of Lovecraft's Pseudonyms; The Dream World and the Real World in Lovecraft; Lovecraft's Alien Civilisations: A Political Interpretation; Topical References in Lovecraft; III. STUDIES ON INDIVIDUAL WORKS: Lovecraft, Regner

Lodbrog, and Olaus Wormius; On "Polaris"; What Happens in "Arthur Jermyn"; "The Tree" and Ancient History; The Sources for "From Beyond"; Lovecraft and the *Regnum Congo*; Lovecraft and Dunsany's *Chronicles of Rodriguez*; On "The Descendant"; Some Sources for "The Mound" and *At the Mountains of Madness*; On "The Book"; Lovecraft's Fantastic Poetry.

Notes. Cover illustration by Robert H. Knox ("Antarktos", 2003), colored by Barbara Briggs Silbert. *Primal Sources* bears the distinction of having been S. T. Joshi's 100th published book. A generous sampling of Joshi's critical essays on Lovecraft, most of them published in *Lovecraft Studies* and *Crypt of Cthulhu* from 1979 onward.

17. CLARK ASHTON SMITH. *The Sword of Zagan and Other Writings.* Edited by Dr. W. C. Farmer. 2004. 181 pp.

Contents. Introduction, by S. T. Joshi; *The Sword of Zagan*; POEMS: The River of Life; The World; The Departed City; Bedouin Song; Zuleika: An Oriental Song; Benares; Rubaiyat of Saiyed; The Isle of Saturn; Temporality; Shapes in the Sunset; Epitaph for the Earth; Night; Rêve Parisien; Averiogne; SHORT STORIES: The Emir's Captive; Fakhreddin; Prince Alcorez and the Magician; The Haunted Gong; The Malay Creese; The Shah's Messenger; The Bronze Image; The Fulfilled Prophecy; The Haunted Chamber; FRAGMENTS: When the Earth Trembled; Oriental Tales: The Yogi's Ring; The Opal of Delhi [I]; The Opal of Delhi [II]; The Guardian of the Temple; The Emerald Eye; [Untitled]; [Fragment of an essay]; [Letter to Munsey's]; Lost Pages from *The Black Diamonds*; Clark Ashton Smith: A Memoir, by W. C. Farmer.

Notes. Cover and interior illustrations by Jason C. Eckhardt. A follow-up to *The Black Diamonds* (item 5), printing another previously unpublished juvenile novel along with other early stories and fragments. All these items derived from the collection of Dr. Farmer, who knew Smith in the latter's final years and was given these mss. over the course of years.

18. H. P. LOVECRAFT. *Collected Essays, Volume 1: Amateur Journalism.* Edited by S. T. Joshi. 2004. 440 pp.

Contents. Introduction by S. T. Joshi; A Task for Amateur Journalists; Department of Public Criticism (November 1914); Department of Public Criticism (January 1915); Department of Public Criticism (March 1915); What Is Amateur Journalism?; Consolidation's Autopsy; The Amateur Press; Editorial (April 1915); The Question of the

Day; The Morris Faction; For President—Leo Fritter; Introducing Mr. Chester Pierce Munroe; [Untitled Notes on Amateur Journalism]; Department of Public Criticism (May 1915); Finale; New Department Proposed: Instruction for the Recruit; Our Candidate; Exchanges; For Historian—Ira A. Cole; Editorial (July 1915); The Conservative and His Critics (July 1915); Some Political Phases; Introducing Mr. John Russell; In a Major Key; Amateur Notes; The Dignity of Journalism; Department of Public Criticism (September 1915); Editorial (October 1915); The Conservative and His Critics (October 1915); The Youth of Today; An Impartial Spectator; [Untitled Notes on Amateur Journalism]; Little Journeys to the Homes of Prominent Amateurs: II. Andrew Francis Lockhart; Report of First Vice-President (November 1915); Department of Public Criticism (December 1915); Systematic Instruction in the United; United Amateur Press Association: Exponent of Amateur Journalism; Introducing Mr. James Pyke; Report of First Vice-President (January 1916); Editorial (February 1916); Department of Public Criticism (April 1916); Among the New-Comers; Department of Public Criticism (June 1916); Department of Public Criticism (August 1916); Department of Public Criticism (September 1916); Among the Amateurs; Concerning "Persia—in Europe"; Amateur Standards; A Request; Department of Public Criticism (March 1917); Department of Public Criticism (May 1917); A Reply to *The Lingerer*; The United's Problem; Editorially; The "Other United"; Department of Public Criticism (July 1917); Little Journeys to the Homes of Prominent Amateurs: V. Eleanor J. Barnhart; News Notes (July 1917); President's Message (September 1917); President's Message (November 1917); President's Message (January 1918); Department of Public Criticism (January 1918); President's Message (March 1918); Department of Public Criticism (March 1918); President's Message (May 1918); Department of Public Criticism (May 1918); Comment; President's Message (July 1918); Amateur Criticism; The United 1917–1918; The Amateur Press Club; *Les Mouches Fantastiques*; Department of Public Criticism (September 1918); Department of Public Criticism (November 1918); News Notes (November 1918); [Letter to the Bureau of Critics]; Department of Public Criticism (January 1919); Department of Public Criticism (March 1919); Winifred Virginia Jordan: Associate Editor; Helene Hoffman Cole—Litterateur; Department of Public Criticism (May 1919); Trimmings; For Official Editor—Anne Tillery Renshaw; Amateurdom; Looking Backward; For What Does the United Stand?; The Pseudo-United; The Conquest of the Hub Club; News Notes (September 1920); Amateur Journalism: Its Possible Needs and Betterment; Editorial (November 1920); News Notes (November 1920); News Notes (January

1921); The United's Policy 1920–1921 (with Alfred Galpin); What
Amateurdom and I Have Done for Each Other; News Notes (March
1921); The Vivisector (March 1921); [Letter to John Milton Heins];
Lucubrations Lovecraftian; News Notes (May 1921); The Vivisector
(June 1921); The Haverhill Convention; News Notes (July 1921);
Within the Gates; The Convention Banquet; Editorial (September
1921); News Notes (September 1921); A Singer of Ethereal Moods
and Fancies; News Notes (November 1921); [Letter to John Milton
Heins]; Editorial (January 1922); News Notes (January 1922); *Rainbow* Called Best First Issue; News Notes (March 1922); The Vivisec-
tor (March 1922); News Notes (May 1922); [Letter to the N.A.P.A.];
President's Message (November 1922–January 1923); President's
Message (March 1923); Bureau of Critics (March 1923); Rursus Ad-
sumus; The Vivisector (Spring 1923); President's Message (May
1923); Lovecraft's Greeting; President's Message (July 1923); [Untit-
led Notes on Amateur Journalism]; The President's Annual Report;
Trends and Objects; Editorial (May 1924); News Notes (May 1924);
Editorial (July 1925); News Notes (July 1925); A Matter of Uniteds;
The Convention; Bureau of Critics (December 1931); Critics Submit
First Report; Verse Criticism; Report of Bureau of Critics; Bureau of
Critics Comment on Verse, Typography, Prose; Bureau of Critics
(June 1934); Chairman of the Bureau of Critics Reports on Poetry;
Mrs. Miniter—Estimates and Recollections; Report of the Bureau of
Critics (December 1934); Report of the Bureau of Critics (March
1935); Lovecraft Offers Verse Criticism; Dr. Eugene B. Kuntz; Some
Current Amateur Verse; Report of the Executive Judges; Some Cur-
rent Motives and Practices; [Letter to the N.A.P.A.]; [Literary Re-
view]; Defining the "Ideal" Paper; APPENDIX: [Miscellaneous Notes in
the *United Amateur*]; Official Organ Fund; [Untitled Note on Amateur Poetry]; [On *Notes High and Low* by Carrie Adams Berry]; [A
Voice from the Grave]; Index.

Notes. Cover illustration (uniform for all five volumes of the series) by
Virgil Finlay. Published simultaneously in hardcover and paperback.
Hardcover 250 copies, Covington Group. One of the most ambitious
projects undertaken by Hippocampus Press—the publication of Lovecraft's complete nonfiction writings, arranged thematically, with extensive annotations. Previously these writings had been scattered
throughout many Arkham House volumes, including Joshi's edition of
Miscellaneous Writings (Arkham House, 1995); but many items remained unreprinted.

19. H. P. LOVECRAFT. *Collected Essays, Volume 2: Literary Criticism.* Edited by S. T. Joshi. 2004. 248 pp.

Contents. Introduction, by S. T. Joshi; Metrical Regularity; The Allowable Rhyme; The Proposed Authors' Union; The Vers Libre Epidemic; Poesy; The Despised Pastoral; The Literature of Rome; The Simple Spelling Mania; The Case for Classicism; Literary Composition; Editor's Note to "A Scene for *Macbeth*" by Samuel Loveman; Winifred Virginia Jackson: A "Different" Poetess; The Poetry of Lilian Middleton; Lord Dunsany and His Work; Rudis Indigestaque Moles; Introduction [to *The Poetical Works of Jonathan E. Hoag*]; Ars Gratia Artis; In the Editor's Study; [Random Notes]; [Review of *Ebony and Crystal* by Clark Ashton Smith]; The Professional Incubus; The Omnipresent Philistine; The Work of Frank Belknap Long, Jr.; Supernatural Horror in Literature; Preface [to *White Fire* by John Ravenor Bullen]; Notes on "Alias Peter Marchall", by A. F. Lorenz; Foreword [to *Thoughts and Pictures* by Eugene B. Kuntz]; Notes on Verse Technique; Weird Story Plots; [Notes on Weird Fiction]; Notes on Writing Weird Fiction; Some Notes on Interplanetary Fiction; What Belongs in Verse; [Suggestions for a Reading Guide]; APPENDIX: The Poetry of John Ravenor Bullen; The Favourite Weird Stories of H. P. Lovecraft; Supernatural Horror in Literature; Index.

Notes. Cover illustration by Virgil Finlay. Simultaneously published in hardcover and paperback. Hardcover 250 copies, Covington Group. The slimmest of the five volumes of *Collected Essays.*

20. S. T. JOSHI AND DAVID E. SCHULTZ. *An H. P. Lovecraft Encyclopedia.* 2004. xx, 339 pp.

Notes. Cover design by Gaile Ivaska. Paperback reprint of the edition first published by Greenwood Press (2001), with a few additions and corrections.

21. ALGERNON BLACKWOOD. *Incredible Adventures.* 2004. 224 pp.

Contents. Introduction by S. T. Joshi; The Regeneration of Lord Ernie; The Sacrifice; The Damned; A Descent into Egypt; Wayfarers.

Notes. Cover illustration by W. Graham Robertson (from the 1916 Macmillan edition of Blackwood's *The Centaur*). Part of the Lovecraft's Library series. A reprint of Blackwood's classic story collection of 1914, which Joshi regards as one of the greatest weird volumes of all time.

22. S. T. JOSHI. *The Evolution of the Weird Tale.* 2004. 216 pp.

Contents. Introduction; I. SOME AMERICANS OF THE GOLDEN AGE:
W. C. Morrow: Horror in San Francisco; Robert W. Chambers: The
Bohemian Weird Tale; F. Marion Crawford: Blood-and-Thunder
Horror; Edward Lucas White: Dream and Reality; II. SOME ENGLISH-
MEN OF THE GOLDEN AGE: Sir Arthur Quiller-Couch: Ghosts and
Scholars; Rudyard Kipling: The Horror of India; E. F. Benson: Spooks
and More Spooks; L. P. Hartley: The Refined Ghost; III. H. P. LOVE-
CRAFT AND HIS INFLUENCE: H. P. Lovecraft: The Fiction of Materi-
alism; Frank Belknap Long: Things from the Sea; A Literary Tutelage:
Robert Bloch and H. P. Lovecraft; Passing the Torch: H. P. Lovecraft
and Fritz Leiber; IV. CONTEMPORARIES: Rod Serling: The Moral
Supernatural; L. P. Davies: The Workings of the Mind; Les Daniels:
The Horror of History; Dennis Etchison: Spanning the Genres; David
J. Schow and Splatterpunk; Poppy Z. Brite: Sex, Horror, and Rock-&-
Roll; Bibliography.

Notes. Cover illustration by Wallace Smith (from Ben Hecht's *Fan-
tazius Mallare*, 1922). A loose follow-up of Joshi's previous treatises,
The Weird Tale (Univ. of Texas Press, 1990) and *The Modern Weird
Tale* (McFarland, 2001), covering authors from the mid-19th century
to the present day, including three chapters (on Les Daniels, Dennis
Etchison, and David J. Schow) that had been scheduled to appear in
The Modern Weird Tale but were omitted for space reasons.

23. SAMUEL LOVEMAN. *Out of the Immortal Night: Selected Works of
Samuel Loveman.* Edited by S. T. Joshi and David E. Schultz.
2004. 244 pp.

Contents. Introduction, by S. T. Joshi; I. POETRY: *Poems* (1911): In Pi-
errot's Garden; Ode to Ceres; Fra Angelico; Song; To P. G.; Lines; A
Twenty-second Birthday; *The Hermaphrodite and Other Poems* (1936):
The Hermaphrodite; River Pattern; Will o' the Wisp; Steener Haa-
konson Dances; Dream Song; Heckscher Building; Euphorion; Aga-
thon; Arcesilaus; Lineage; For a Book of Poems; Ascension; Thomas
Holley Chivers; The Ramapos; Oscar Wilde; John Clare in a Mad-
house; The Minstrel; The Chopin-Player; A Dedication; Vice; Tran-
sience; Dolore; Bacchanale; To Simone's; Ad Fratrem; Isolation;
Remonstrance; Proteus; A Voyage; Legend; The Return; Memoralia;
Forest of Rhododendron; Understanding; Ecce Homo; Ariel; Visitor;
Inarticulate; Madison Square; Contrast; Invocation; Song; Harbour;
Admonition; Foes; Limbo; Interlude; Gates Mills; Wasteland; Amy
Levy; Forest Hill; Andenkung; Dream of Spring; Finis; A Georgia
Garden; Palingenesis; Belated Love; Nostalgia; Becalmed; Mutation;

Dirge; To Dionysus; To Apollo; Quatrains (Poppies; Forgotten Poets; Space; Music; Simeon Solomon; Aftermath); A Chinese Pavilion; Ben De Casseres in Camden; Terminus; UNCOLLECTED POEMS: A Poet; A Sonnet: Lethe; The Birth of Fear; Pierced; A Lily; Lost Youth; Avalon; Hope; The Old Cobbler; Shadow-Land; The Song Unsung; Ship of Dreams; The Birth of Poesy; On Lost Friendship; Peccavi; The Plaint of Bygone Loves; Eventide (I. Sunset; II. Twilight; III. Night); David Gray; An Epitaph; Quatrains; To Alfred Noyes, Oversea; Michael Scott's Wooing; Thomas Dermody; Resurgam; Shadow-Love; Euthanasia; A Burden; A Song of Chamisso's; A Departure; W. E.; On the Passing of Youth; A Triumph in Eternity; Talent; [Untitled]; Adventure; In Sepulcretis; Saturday Evening; A Letter to G—— K——; Ernest Nelson; Heldenleben; Winter; To Satan; Christmas—1923; Genesis; Night Piece (Forest Hill); Monolith; Oscar Redivivus; Unfulfilled; To Mr. Theobald; To George Kirk on His 27th Birthday; Music; Vigil; To a Child; The Dead King; Kin; Episode; Rescue; Transit; An Admonition to the Ladies; Debs in Prison; For the Chelsea Book Shop [I]; For the Chelsea Book Shop [II]; Nepenthe; Quatrain; Reliquiae; Spring at El Retiro; Versailles; [Untitled]; The Goal; John Clare in 1864; II. DRAMA: Oedipus at Colonus; Belshazzar; Nero; Narcisse; Arcady; A Scene for *King Lear*; A Scene for *Macbeth*; The Sphinx: A Conversation; III. TRANSLATIONS: Twenty-four Translations from Heine; Catullus; Translations from Baudelaire: La Musique; Parfum Exotique; Horreur Sympathique; De Profundis Clamavi; La Beauté; Causerie; Chant d'Automne; Le Couvercle; Le Chat; La Fontaine de Sang; Sonnet d'Automne; Ciel Brouillé; Les Chats; Translations from Verlaine: Sagesse; Bruxelles; Romances sans Paroles; Il Bacio; La Bonne Chanson; Vert; Sappho; Sonnet: After Leconte de Lisle; God's Work; IV. FICTION: Antenor; The Faun; The Dog; An Impression; The One Who Found Pity; Christmas-Eve with Sherlock Holmes; V. ESSAYS: Mr. Sterling and Minor Poets; A Keats Discovery; Modern Poetry (An Exorcism); A Note [to *Twenty-one Letters of Ambrose Bierce*]; A Convention Address; The Book of Life; Foreword to *Poppies and Mandragora*; Preface to *The Man from Genoa*; Hubert Crackanthorpe: A Realist of the Nineties; Marcel Proust; Literature and Dry-rot; A Letter on Hart Crane; Howard Phillips Lovecraft; Lovecraft as Conversationalist; Bibliography; Index of Poetry Titles; Index of First Lines.

Notes. Cover illustration by William Sommer (from the 1944 W. Paul Cook edition of Loveman's *The Sphinx*). The product of many years' work by the editors in gathering Loveman's writings (chiefly his poetry) from amateur journals and unpublished manuscripts. All Loveman's known poetry was included, but only selections of his essays, reviews, and amateur journalism. The interior paper stock was changed from cream to white in 2011, at which time slight changes were made to the cover.

24. R. NEMO HILL. *The Strange Music of Erich Zann.* 2004. 51 pp.

Notes. Cover illustration by Joe Werhle, Jr. With audio CD of the author reading his work. Booklet was issued in late 2004, but the CD was not produced until early the following year, hence it bears a 2005 copyright date. A long poem based on H. P. Lovecraft's tale "The Music of Erich Zann" (1921). The first original creative writing published by Hippocampus Press, commissioned by Derrick Hussey following a live reading by the poet in New York City.

25. H. P. LOVECRAFT. *Letters to Rheinhart Kleiner.* Edited by S. T. Joshi and David E. Schultz. 2005. 298 pp.

Contents. Introduction; Letters to Rheinhart Kleiner; WORKS: A. PO-EMS BY RHEINHART KLEINER: Alas!; Dream Days, or, Metrical Musings; Another Endless Day; Motes; At Providence in 1918; Brooklyn, My Brooklyn; Epistle to Mr. and Mrs. Lovecraft; The Four of Us!; After a Decade; H. P. L.; B. ESSAYS BY RHEINHART KLEINER: A Note on Howard P. Lovecraft's Verse; The Kleicomolo; After a Decade and the Kalem Club; Howard Phillips Lovecraft; Lovecraft in Brooklyn; Some Lovecraft Memories; C. RHEINHART KLEINER VS. H. P. LOVECRAFT: To Mary of the Movies [Kleiner]; To Charlie of the Comics [Lovecraft]; To a Movie Star [Kleiner]; To Mistress Sophia Simple, Queen of the Cinema [Lovecraft]; Ruth [Kleiner]; Grace [Lovecraft]; John Oldham: 1653–1683 [Kleiner]; John Oldham: A Defence [Lovecraft]; Ethel: Cashier in a Broad Street Buffet [Kleiner]; Cindy: Scrub-Lady in a State Street Skyscraper [Lovecraft]; On Collaboration; D. POEMS BY H. P. LOVECRAFT AD-DRESSED TO RHEINHART KLEINER: The Bookstall; Content; To Mr. Kleiner, on Receiving from Him the Poetical Works of Addison, Gay, and Somerville; R. Kleiner, Laureatus, in Heliconem; To Rheinhart Kleiner, Esq., Upon His Town Fables and Elegies; [On Rheinhart Kleiner Being Hit by an Automobile]; A Partial Bibliography of Rheinhart Kleiner; Index.

Notes. Cover design by Anastasia Damianakos (uniform with item 13). Complete publication of Lovecraft's letters to Kleiner, including lengthy letters to the Kleicomolo correspondence circle. Includes a generous selection of Kleiner's writings, including his poetry and essays, as well as poems by Lovecraft addressed to Kleiner. This nascent letters series (begun with item 13) was supplanted by the more substantial *Collected Letters* series with the publication of item 54.

26. M. P. SHIEL. *The House of Sounds and Others.* Edited by S. T. Joshi. 2005. 299 pp.

Contents. Introduction, by S. T. Joshi; Xélucha; The Pale Ape; The Case of Euphemia Raphash; Huguenin's Wife; The House of Sounds; The Great King; The Bride; *The Purple Cloud*; APPENDIX: Vaila.

Notes. Cover illustration by J. T. Lindroos. A small number of copies were printed bearing an erroneous price of $15.00. Some made their way into circulation before the error was caught and corrected. Part of the Lovecraft's Library series. An extensive selection of those works by Shiel that Lovecraft read and might have been influenced by, including the 1901 edition of *The Purple Cloud* (substantially different from the revised edition of 1929).

27. ROBERT M. PRICE, EDITOR. *Tales out of Dunwich.* 2005. 302 pp.

Contents. Dunwich Homecoming, by Robert M. Price; *The Thing in the Woods*, by Harper Williams; The Mark of the Monster, by Jack Williamson; The Thing from Lover's Lane, by Nancy A. Collins; Acute Spiritual Fear, by Robert M. Price; Black Brat of Dunwich, by Stanley C. Sargent; The Dunwich Lodger, by Brian McNaughton; The Doom That Came to Dunwich, by Richard A. Lupoff; The Dunwich Gate, by Don D'Ammassa; The N-Scale Horror, by Gerard E. Giannattasio; Dunwich Dreams, Dunwich Screams, by Eddy C. Bertin.

Notes. Cover illustration by Philip Fuller. The illustration has been said to bear a more than passing resemblance to Anastasia Damianakos. A large anthology featuring tales about Dunwich, including the first reprint of Harper Williams's short novel *The Thing in the Woods* (1924), which clearly influenced some elements of Lovecraft's "The Dunwich Horror" (1928).

28. GEORGE STERLING AND CLARK ASHTON SMITH. *The Shadow of the Unattained: The Letters of George Sterling and Clark Ashton Smith.* Edited by David E. Schultz and S. T. Joshi. 2005. 342 pp.

Contents. Introduction; The Shadow of the Unattained; APPENDIX: To George Sterling, by Clark Ashton Smith; To George Sterling, by Clark Ashton Smith; To George Sterling, by Clark Ashton Smith; To the Editor of *Town Talk*, by Ambrose Bierce; The Coming Singer, by George Sterling; Preface to *Odes and Sonnets*, by George Sterling; Preface to *Ebony and Crystal*, by George Sterling; Recent Books of

Fact and Fiction, by George Sterling; Poetry of the Pacific Coast—California, by George Sterling; To George Sterling: A Valediction, by Clark Ashton Smith; George Sterling: An Appreciation, by Clark Ashton Smith; George Sterling: Poet and Friend, by Clark Ashton Smith; To George Sterling, by Clark Ashton Smith; Glossary of Names; List of Extant Enclosures; Bibliography; Index.

Notes. Cover illustration by Philip Fuller (based on photographs of Sterling and Smith). Fifteen interior illustrations from drawings by Smith from his letters to Sterling. Unabridged and annotated edition of the complete extant correspondence of the two writers, who wrote extensively to each other from 1911 until Sterling's death in 1926. Also included are writings by each author about the other.

29. H. P. LOVECRAFT. *Collected Essays, Volume 3: Science.* Edited by S. T. Joshi. 2005. 357 pp.

Contents. Introduction, by S. T Joshi; My Opinion as to the Lunar Canals; No Transit of Mars; Trans-Neptunian Planets; The Moon; The Earth Not Hollow. ASTRONOMY ARTICLES FOR THE *PAWTUXET VALLEY GLEANER:* The Heavens for August; The Skies of September; Is Mars an Inhabited World?; Is There Life on the Moon?; An Interesting Phenomenon; October Heavens; Are There Undiscovered Planets?; Can the Moon Be Reached by Man?; The Moon; [Untitled]; The Sun; The Leonids; Comets; December Skies; The Fixed Stars; Clusters—Nebulae; January Heavens; ASTRONOMY ARTICLES FOR THE PROVIDENCE *TRIBUNE:* In the August Sky; The September Heavens; Astronomy in October; The Skies of November; The Heavens for December; The Heavens in January; The Heavens in February; The Heavens in March; April Skies; The Heavens in May; The Heavens in June; Astronomy in August; The Heavens for September; The Skies of October; The Heavens in November; Heavens for December; The Heavens in January; February Skies; The Heavens in Month of March; Solar Eclipse Feature of June Heavens; Third Annual Report of the Prov. Meteorological Station; Celestial Objects for All; Venus and the Public Eye; ASTRONOMY ARTICLES FOR THE PROVIDENCE *EVENING NEWS:* The January Sky; The February Sky; The March Sky; The April Sky; May Sky; The June Sky; The July Sky; The August Sky; The September Sky; The October Sky; The November Sky; The December Sky; The January Sky; The February Sky; The March Sky; April Skies; The May Sky; The June Skies; The July Skies; The August Skies; September Skies; October Skies; November Skies; December Skies; January Skies; February Skies; March Skies; April Skies; May Skies; June Skies; July Skies; August Skies; September Skies; October Skies; November Skies; December Skies; January Skies; February Skies; March Skies; April Skies; May Skies; June Skies; July Skies; August Skies; September Skies; October Skies; November Skies; December Skies; January Skies; February Skies; March Skies; April Skies; May Skies; SCIENCE VERSUS CHARLATANRY: Science versus Charlatanry; The Falsity of Astrology; Astrology and the Future; Delavan's Comet and Astrology; The Fall of Astrology; [Isaac Bickerstaffe's Reply]; MYSTERIES OF THE HEAVENS REVEALED BY ASTRONOMY: I. The Sky and Its Contents; [II.] The Solar System; III. The Sun; IV. The Inferior Planets; V. Eclipses; VI. The Earth and Its Moon; VII. Mars and the Asteroids; VIII. The Outer Planets; [The Outer Planets, Part II]; IX. Comets and Meteors; Comets and Meteors [Part II]; X. The Stars; [The Stars, Part II]; XI. Clusters and Nebulae; [Clusters and Nebulae, Part II]; XII. The Constellations; [The Constellations, Part II]; XIII. Telescopes and Observatories; [Telescopes and Observatories, Part II]; Editor's Note to "The Irish and the Fairies" by Peter J. MacManus; Brumalia; The Truth about Mars; The Cancer of Superstition; [Some Backgrounds of Fairyland]; APPENDIX: Does "Vulcan" Exist?; Astronomical Notebook; [Astrology Articles by J. F. Hartmann]: Astrology and the European War; [Letter to the Editor]; The Science of Astrology; A Defense of Astrology; Lovecraft's Juvenile Scientific Manuscripts; Index.

Notes. Cover illustration by Virgil Finlay. Interior illustrations by Lovecraft. Hardcover 250 copies, Covington Group. Simultaneously published in hardcover and paperback. Complete publication of Lovecraft's scientific writings, including the first unabridged reprint of his dozens of astronomy columns for Providence newspapers (1906–18).

30. H. P. LOVECRAFT. *Collected Essays, Volume 4: Travel.* Edited by S. T. Joshi. 2005. 300 pp.

Contents. Introduction, by S. T. Joshi; The Trip of Theobald; Vermont—A First Impression; Observations on Several Parts of America; Travels in the Provinces of America; An Account of a Trip to the Antient Fairbanks House, in Dedham, and to the Red Horse Tavern in Sudbury, in the Province of the Massachusetts-Bay; Account of a Visit to Charleston, S.C.; An Account of *Charleston*, in His Maj^{ty's} Province of *South-Carolina*; A Description of the Town of Quebeck in New-France, Lately Added to His Britannick Majesty's Dominions; European Glimpses; Some Dutch Footprints in New England; Homes and Shrines of Poe; The Unknown City in the Ocean; Charleston; APPENDIX: A Descent to Avernus; Sleepy Hollow To-day; Index.

Notes. Cover illustration by Virgil Finlay, interior illustrations by Lovecraft. Hardcover 250 copies, Covington Group. Simultaneously published in hardcover and paperback. First complete edition of Lovecraft's travel writings, including the first publication of two brief travelogues.

31. ROBERT H. WAUGH. *The Monster in the Mirror: Looking for H. P. Lovecraft.* 2006. 302 pp.

Contents. Introduction; PART I: FIRST PRINCIPLES: Lovecraft's Hands; Documents, Creatures, and History; PART II: SORTIES: "The Picture in the House": Images of Complicity; *At the Mountains of Madness:* The Subway and the Shoggoth; PART III: MEDITATIONS ON "THE OUTSIDER": "The Outsider," the Terminal Climax, and Other Conclusions; Lovecraft and Keats Confront the "Awful Rainbow"; The Outsider, the Autodidact, and Other Professions; PART IV: MATERIALISM, THEOLOGY, AND IMAGINATION: Lovecraft and Leopardi: Sunsets and Moonsets; Lovecraft Born Again: An Essay in Apologetic Criticism; Works Cited; Index.

Notes. Cover illustration by Philip Fuller. An extensive selection of Waugh's critical essays on Lovecraft, most of them published in *Lovecraft Studies.*

32. MARA KIRK HART AND S. T. JOSHI, EDITORS. *Lovecraft's New York Circle: The Kalem Club, 1924–1927.* 2006. 240 pp.

Contents. Preface, by Peter Cannon; Introduction, by Mara Kirk Hart; THE KALEM LETTERS OF GEORGE KIRK: Introduction, by Mara Kirk Hart; 1924; 1925; 1926; 1927; WRITINGS BY THE KALEMS: GEORGE KIRK: Book Collecting: The Prince of Hobbies; RHEINHART KLEINER: A Glee; At Providence in 1918; Epistle to Mr. and Mrs. Lovecraft; The Four of Us (Rondeau); Brooklyn, My Brooklyn; Columbia Heights, Brooklyn; [Prisky]; On a Favorite Cat: Killed by an Automobile; To George W. Kirk, Upon His 26th Birthday; To His Peculiar Friend, G. Kirk, Esq.; Your Street; Blue Pencil Anniversary Song; What My Ancestors Were Like; The Great Adventure; If I Had Lived a Hundred Years Ago; H. P. L.; ARTHUR LEEDS: He Had to Pay the Nine-Tailed Cat; FRANK BELKNAP LONG: A Man from Genoa; Come, Let Us Make; The Man Who Died Twice; H. P. LOVECRAFT: Plaster-All; To Endymion; Providence; Waste Paper; Primavera; To an Infant; To George Kirk, Esq.; To George Willard Kirk, Gent., of Chelsea Village in New York, upon His Birthday, Novr. 25, 1925; Two Christmas Poems to G. W. K.; A Year Off; In Memoriam Oscar Incoul Verelst of Manhattan 1920–1926; SAMUEL LOVEMAN: A

Letter to G——— K———; To George Kirk on His 27th Birthday; For the Chelsea Book Shop [1]; For the Chelsea Book Shop [2]; For a Cat; For a Book of Poems; Admonition; Limbo; To H. P. L.; Genesis; Spring at El Retiro; Arcesilaus; John Clare in 1864; EVERETT MCNEIL: From *Tonty of the Iron Hand*; JAMES FERDINAND MORTON: To G.W.K. on His 27th Birthday; From *The Curse of Race Prejudice*; APPENDIX: After a Decade and the Kalem Club, by Rheinhart Kleiner; Bards and Bibliophiles, by Rheinhart Kleiner; Sources and Works Consulted; Index.

Notes. Cover illustration by Barbara Briggs Silbert. An innovative volume conceived and largely executed by Mara Kirk Hart (daughter of George Kirk), in which selections of the writings by the major members of the Kalem Club (George Kirk, Rheinhart Kleiner, Arthur Leeds, Frank Belknap Long, H. P. Lovecraft, Samuel Loveman, Everett McNeil, and James Ferdinand Morton) are reprinted; a few items are previously unpublished. The selections are preceded by an invaluable selection of letters written by Kirk to his fiancée, Lucile Dvorak (1924–27), shedding much light on the Kalems' activities in New York during and just after the period of Lovecraft's residence there.

33. SCOTT CONNORS, EDITOR. *The Freedom of Fantastic Things: Selected Criticism on Clark Ashton Smith.* 2006. 376 pp.

Contents. Introduction, by Scott Connors; The Centaur, by Clark Ashton Smith; Klarkash-Ton and "Greek," by Donald Sidney-Fryer; Contemporary Reviews of Clark Ashton Smith; Eblis in Bakelite, by James Blish; James Blish versus Clark Ashton Smith, to Wit, the Young Turk Syndrome, by Donald Sidney-Fryer; The Last Romantic, by S. J. Sackett; Communicable Mysteries: The Last True Symbolist, by Fred Chappell; What Happens in *The Hashish-Eater?*, by S. T. Joshi; The Babel of Visions: The Structuration of Clark Ashton Smith's *The Hashish-Eater*, by Dan Clore; Clark Ashton Smith's "Nero," by Carl Jay Buchanan; Satan Speaks: A Reading of "Satan Unrepentant," by Phillip A. Ellis; Lands Forgotten or Unfound: The Prose Poetry of Clark Ashton Smith, by S. T. Joshi; Outside the Human Aquarium: The Fantastic Imagination of Clark Ashton Smith, by Brian Stableford; Clark Ashton Smith: Master of the Macabre; John Kipling Hitz; Gesturing Toward the Infinite: Clark Ashton Smith and Modernism, by Scott Connors; Clark Ashton Smith: A Note on the Aesthetics of Fantasy, by Charles K. Wolfe; Fantasy and Decadence in the Work of Clark Ashton Smith, by Lauric Guillaud; Humor in Hyperspace: Smith's Uses of Satire, by John Kipling Hitz; Song of the Necromancer: "Loss" in Clark Ashton Smith's Fiction, by Steve Behrends; Brave World Old and New: The Atlantis Theme in the Poetry and Fiction of Clark Ashton Smith, by Donald Sidney-Fryer; Coming In from the Cold: Incursions of "Outsideness" in Hyperborea, by Steven Tompkins; As Shadows Wait upon the Sun: Clark Ashton Smith's Zothique, by Jim Rockhill; Into the Woods: The Human Geography of Averoigne, by Stefan Dziemianowicz; Sorcerous Style: Clark Ashton Smith's *The Double Shadow and Other Fantasies*, by Peter H. Goodrich; Loss and Recuperation: A Model for Reading Clark Ashton Smith's "Xeethra," by Dan Clore; "Life, Love, and the Clemency of Death": A Reexamination of Clark Ashton Smith's "The Isle of the Torturers," by Scott Connors; Regarding the Providence Point of View, by Ronald S. Hilger; An Annotated Chronology of the Fiction of Clark Ashton Smith, by Steve Behrends; Bibliography; Contributors; Acknowledgments; Index.

Notes. Cover illustration by Frank Kupka ("Resistance, or the Black Idol," 1903). Simultaneously published in hardcover and paperback. The most extensive selection ever published of criticism of Clark Ashton Smith, including both reprinted and previously unpublished essays.

34. BENJAMIN SZUMSKYJ, EDITOR. *Two-Gun Bob: A Centennial Study of Robert E. Howard.* 2006. 233 pp.

Contents. Robert E. Howard: A Texan Master, by Michael Moorcock; Robert E. Howard: A Look at "Two-Gun Bob" 100 Years On, by Benjamin Szumskyj; *The Junto*: Being a Brief Look at the Amateur Press Association Robert E. Howard Partook In as a Youth, by Glenn Lord; . . . From Acorns Grow: Robert E. Howard Revealed in *Post Oaks and Sand Roughs*, by John Goodrich; Sleuths, Secrets, and Grisly Mysteries: The Detective Fiction of Robert E. Howard, by Fred Blosser; Words from the Outer Dark: The Poetical Works of Robert E. Howard, by Michele Tetro; Texas Talespinner: Robert E. Howard's Ways with Words, by Frank Coffman; Robert E. Howard: A Behavioral Perspective, by Charles Gramlich, Ph.D.; The Persistence of the Familiar: The Hyborian World and the Geographies of Fantastic Literature, by Lorenzo DiTommaso, Ph.D.; Bran Mak Morn and History, by S. T. Joshi; "Bitter Pleasures and Swinish Stupidity": Howard's Take on Human Character, by Charles Hoffman; El Borak, the Swift, by Scott Sheaffer; Stars and Strong Men: The Science and Cosmic Fiction of Robert E. Howard, by Martin Andersson; Laudator Temporis Acti: History and Myth in the Works of Robert E. Howard, by Pietro Guarriello; Cimmerian Gloves: Studying Robert E. Howard's Ace Jessel from the Ringside, by Benjamin Szumskyj; About the Contributors; Acknowledgments; Index.

Notes. Cover illustration by Frank Coffman. A generous sampling of criticism of Howard to commemorate the centennial of his birth.

35. W. H. PUGMIRE. *The Fungal Stain and Other Dreams.* 2006. 179 pp.

Contents. An Eidolon of Nothing; Hour of Their Appetite; The Sign That Sets the Darkness Free; Jigsaw Boy; The Fungal Stain; Balm of Nepenthe; Some Darker Star; The Saprophytic Fungi; A Phantom of Beguilement; Stupor Mundi; Past the Gate of Deepest Slumber; His Splintered Kiss; Oh, Baleful Theophany; The Strange Dark Folk; Your Metamorphic Moan.

Notes. Cover illustration and interior illustrations by Robert H. Knox. A volume of Pugmire's recent weird writings, many of them in the Lovecraftian vein. The first Hippocampus Press publication of original fiction by a contemporary writer.

36. H. P. LOVECRAFT. *Collected Essays, Volume 5: Philosophy; Autobiography and Miscellany.* Edited by S. T. Joshi. 2006. 382 pp.

Contents. Introduction, by S. T. Joshi; PHILOSOPHY: The Crime of the Century; The Renaissance of Manhood; Liquor and Its Friends; More *Chain Lightning*; Symphony and Stress; Old England and the "Hyphen"; Revolutionary Mythology; The Symphonic Ideal; "Editor's Note" to "The Genesis of the Revolutionary War" by Henry Clapham McGavack; A Remarkable Document; At the Root; Time and Space; Merlinus Redivivus; Anglo-Saxondom; Amer-icanism; The League; Bolshevism; Idealism and Materialism–A Reflection; Life for Humanity's Sake; [*In Defence of Dagon*]; Nietzscheism and Realism; East and West Harvard Conservatism; The Materialist Today; Some Causes of Self-Immolation; Some Repetitions on the Times; A Layman Looks at the Government; The *Journal* and the New Deal; A Living Heritage: Roman Architecture in Today's America; Objections to Orthodox Communism; AUTOBIOGRAPHY AND MISCELLANY: The Brief Autobiography of an Inconsequential Scribbler; A Confession of Unfaith; [Diary: 1925]; [Commercial Blurbs]; Cats and Dogs; Notes on Hudson Valley History; Autobiography of Howard Phillips Lovecraft; In Memoriam: Henry St. Clair Whitehead; Some Notes on a Nonentity; Correspondence between R. H. Barlow and Wilson Shepherd of Oakman, Alabama—Sept.–Nov. 1932; In Memoriam: Robert Ervin Howard; Commonplace Book; Instructions in Case of Decease; [Diary—1937]; NOTES FOR STORIES: [Notes to "Medusa's Coil"]; [Notes to *At the Mountains of Madness*]; [Notes to "The Shadow over Innsmouth"]; [The Round Tower]; [The Rose Window]; Of Evil Sorceries Done in New-England, of Daemons in

No Humane Shape; [Notes to "The Shadow out of Time"]; [Notes to "The Challenge From Beyond"]; MISCELLANEOUS LISTS AND NOTES; [1] Catalogue of Prov. Press Co.; [2] [Catalogue of Works (1902)]; [3] [Postal Expenses]; [4] Old Farmer's Almanacks Wanted by H. P. Lovecraft; [5] [Notes on Clothing Stores]; [6] [Works Desired by H. Warner Munn]; [7] [Works of Weird Fiction]; [8] Tales by H. P. Lovecraft; [9] Basic Books for a Weird Library; [10] [Remembrancer]; [11] [List of Amateur Papers]; [12] [Possible Collections of Tales]; [13] [Magazine Addresses]; [14] [List of Individuals to Be Sent "The Battle That Ended the Century"]; [15] [List of Correspondents to Whom Postcards Have Been Sent]; [16] Suggested Recipients for Dragon Fly Outside Memb. List of NAPA; [17] Fungi from Yuggoth and Other Verses; [18] [Notable Stories in Recent Issues of *Weird Tales*]; [19] "Little Magazines"; [20] [Worthy Stories in Recent Issues of *Weird Tales*]; [21] [Pronunciation Guide]; [22] Tales of H. P. Lovecraft; Weird &c. Items in Library of H. P. Lovecraft; APPENDIX: [Advertisement of Revisory Services]; [Advertisement in the *New York Times*]; The Recognition of Temperance; [Advertisement in *Weird Tales*]; [Biographical Notice]; Preface [to *Old World Footprints*]; [E'ch-Pi-El Speaks]; Robert Ervin Howard: 1906–1936; Chronology of the Works of H. P. Lovecraft; Index of Titles (Volumes 1–5); Index (Volumes 1–5).

Notes. Cover illustration by Virgil Finlay. Interior illustrations by Lovecraft. Hardcover 250 copies, Covington Group. Simultaneously published in hardcover and paperback. The fifth and final volume of the *Collected Essays*, with a cumulative index to all five volumes and chronological listing of all Lovecraft's work. For the CD-ROM of the set, see item 55.

37. CLARK ASHTON SMITH. *The Complete Poetry and Translations, Volume 3: The Flowers of Evil and Others.* Edited by S. T. Joshi and David E. Schultz. 2007 (rpt. 2012 [paper]). 442 pp.

Contents. Introduction; LES FLEURS DU MAL, BY CHARLES BAUDELAIRE: Preface/Préface; SPLEEN ET IDÉAL: I. Bénédiction; II. The Albatross/L'Albatros; III. Elevation/Elévation; IV. Correspondences/ Correspondances; V. [Untitled]; VI. The Beacons/Les Phares; VII. The Sick Muse/La Muse malade; VIII. The Venal Muse/La Muse vénale; IX. The Evil Monk/Le Mauvais Moine; X. L'Ennemi; XI. Le Guignon/Le Guignon; XII. Anterior Life/La Vie antérieure; XIII. Travelling Gypsies/Bohémiens en voyage; XIV. L'Homme et la mer; XV. Don Juan aux enfers; XVI. To Theodore de Banville/A Théodore de Banville; XVII. Chastisement of Pride/Châtiment de l'orgueil;

XVIII. Beauty/La Beauté; XIX. The Ideal/L'Idéal; XX. The Giantess/La Géante; XXI. Le Masque; XXII. Hymn to Beauty/Hymne à la beauté; XXIII. Exotic Perfume/Parfum exotique; XXIV. The Chevelure/La Chevelure; XXV. [Untitled]; XXVI. [Untitled]; XXVII. *Sed non satiata*; XXVIII. [Untitled]; XXIX. Le Serpent qui danse; XXX. Une Charogne; XXXI. *De profundis clamavi*; XXXII. The Vampire/Le Vampire; XXXIII. [Untitled]; XXXIV. The Remorse of the Dead/Remords posthume; XXXV. The Cat/Le Chat; XXXVI. The Duel/ *Duellum*]; XXXVII. The Balcony/Le Balcon; XXXVIII. The Possessed/Le Possédé; XXXIX. Un Fantôme; XL. [Untitled]; XLI. *Semper eadem*; XLII. Tout entière; XLIII. [Untitled]; XLIV. Le Flambeau vivant; XLV. Réversibilité; XLVI. Confession; XLVII. The Spiritual Dawn/L'Aube spirituelle; XLVIII. Evening Harmony/ L'Harmonie du soir; XLIX. Le Flacon/Le Flacon; L. The Poison/Le Poison; LI. Doubtful Skies/Ciel brouillé; LII. Le Chat; LIII. Le Beau Navire; LIV. L'Invitation au voyage; LV. The Irreparable/ L'Irréparable; LVI. Causerie; LVII. Song of Autumn/Chant d'automne; LVIII. A une Madone; LIX. Chanson d'après-midi; LX. Sisina; LXI. Vers pour le portrait d'Honoré Daumier; LXII. *Franciscæ meæ laudes*; LXIII. To a Creole Lady/A une Dame créole; LXIV. *Mœsta et errabunda*; LXV. The Phantom/Le Revenant; LXVI. Sonnet d'automne; LXVII. Tristesses de la lune; LXVIII. The Cats/Les Chats; LXIX. The Owls/Les Hiboux; LXX. La Pipe; LXXI. Music/La Musique; LXXII. Sépulture; LXXIII. Une Gravure fantastique; LXXIV. Le Mort joyeux; LXXV. The Barrel of Hate/Le Tonneau de la haine; LXXVI. La Cloche fêlée; LXXVII. Spleen; LXXVIII. Spleen; LXXIX. Spleen; LXXX. Spleen; LXXXI. Obsession; LXXXII. Le Goût du néant; LXXXIII. Alchemy of Sorrow/Alchimie de la douleur; LXXXIV. Sympathetic Horror/Horreur sympathique; LXXXV. Le Calumet de paix; LXXXVI. A Pagan's Prayer/La Prière d'un païen; LXXXVII. The Cover/Le Couvercle; LXXXVIII. L'Imprévu; LXXXIX. Examination at Midnight/L'Examen de minuit; XC. Madrigal of Sorrow/Madrigal triste; XCI. The Adviser/L'Avertisseur; XCII. To a Malabaress/A une Malabaraise; XCIII. The Voice/La Voix; XCIV. Hymn/Hymne; XCV. The Rebel/Le Rebelle; XCVI. The Eyes of Bertha/Les Yeux de Berthe; XCVII. The Fountain/Le Jet d'eau; XCVIII. La Rançon; XCIX. Very Far from Here/Bien loin d'ici; C. Le Coucher du Soleil romantique; CI. On "Tasso in Prison" by Eugène Delacroix/Sur *Le Tasse en Prison* d'Eugène Delacroix; CII. The Gulf/Le Gouffre; CIII. The Lament of Icarus/Les Plaintes d'un Icare; CIV. Contemplation/Receuillement; CV. *L'Héautontimorouménos*; CVI. The Irremediable/ L'Irrémédiable; CVII. The Clock/L'Horloge; TABLEAUX PARISIENS: CVIII. Paysage; CIX. The Sun/Le Soleil; CX. Lola de Valence; CXI. La Lune offensée;

Song/Chanson; PIERRE LIÈVRE: Elysian Landscape/Paysage Elyséen [text not found]; The End of Supper/[title unknown; text not found]; STUART MERRILL: A Woman at Prayer/Celle qui prie; ALFRED DE MUSSET: Remember Thee/Rappelle-toi; Song/Chanson; SULLY-PRUDHOMME: Siesta/ Sieste; ALBERT SAMAIN: I Dream/ [Untitled]; [Myrtil and Palemone]/ [Myrtil et Palémone]; FERNAND SEVERIN: Sonnet/Bois sacré; PAUL VERLAINE: IX (Ariettes Oubliées); Il Bacio; La Bonne Chanson; Crimen Amoris; En Sourdine; The Faun/Le Faune; Green; Moonlight/Claire de lune; Song from *Les Uns et les autres*; Spleen [Spleen]; To a Woman/A une femme; TRANSLATIONS FROM THE SPANISH: GUSTAVO ADOLFO BÉCQUER: Invocation/Rimas LII; The Sower/Rimas LX; Where?/Rimas XXXVIII; The World Rolls On/Rimas I (Libro de los gorriones); JOSÉ A. CALCAÑO: The Cypress/El ciprés; JOSÉ SANTOS CHOCANO: The Sleep of the Cayman/El sueño del caimán; RUBÉN DARÍO: The Song of Songs/El Cantar de los Cantares; JUANA DE IBARBOUROU: Rustic Life/Vida aldeana; JORGE ISAACS: Luminary/Luminar; JUAN LOZANO Y LOZANO: Rhythm/Ritmo; AMADO NERVO: Night/Noche; APPENDIX: XXVII. *Sed non Satiata*; LV. L'Irréparable; CXLI. Un Voyage à Cythère; The Peace-Pipe, by Henry Wadsworth Longfellow; Notes; Index of Titles; Index of First Lines.

Notes. Dust jacket illustration by Anastasia Damianakos. Published in a limited hardcover edition of 250 copies (Covington Group). The fruit of many years' work on the part of the editors. This volume, although designated Volume 3, appeared first because it was more convenient for the editors to issue Smith's translations of French and Spanish poetry than to prepare his original poetry (see item 50). Smith's translations (many of them in prose) and the original French and Spanish texts (chiefly from Baudelaire's *Les Fleurs du mal* but also from other poets such as Verlaine, Heredia, and Bécquer) are presented on facing pages. Many of Smith's translations are literal prose renderings that he had not yet versified. Most of the translations were previously unpublished. The recently discovered "The Desire of Loving," a translation of "Le Désir d'Aimer" by Hélène Picard, appeared in Volume 2. For the paperback edition, see item 113.

38. BARRY PAIN. *An Exchange of Souls.* HENRI BÉRAUD. *Lazarus.* 2007. 105 + 114 pp.

Notes. Cover illustration by anonymous (from the first edition of Pain's *An Exchange of Souls*) and by Ralph Fabri (Béraud). Part of the Lovecraft's Library series. The first "Hippocampus double," analogous to the "Ace doubles" of the 1950s, in which two short novels were presented in a single volume. Pain's novel was first published in 1911 and manifestly influenced Lovecraft's "The Thing on the Doorstep"; Béraud's novel first appeared in French in 1924 (English translation 1925) and was an influence on Lovecraft's "The Shadow out of Time." Joshi has written separate introductions to both books.

39. PHILIP HALDEMAN. *Shadow Coast.* 2007. 255 pp.

Notes. Cover illustration and design by Cassie Barden; photograph by David Haldeman. A haunting novel of horrors in the Pacific Northwest.

40. *Dead Reckonings* No. 1 (Spring 2007). EDITED BY S. T. JOSHI AND JACK M. HARINGA. 100 pp.

Editorial; Knowing and Observing, by Paula Guran [David J. Schow, *Havoc Swims Jaded;* Glen Hirshberg, *American Morons*]; Cosmic Chess Games and Halloween Horrors, by Hank Wagner [F. Paul Wilson, *Harbingers;* Norm Partridge, *Dark Harvest*]; From Mr. Hands to Mr. Molester, by Tony Fonseca [Gary A. Braunbeck, *Prodigal Blues*]; Mommy Made Me Do It, by S. T. Joshi [Ramsey Campbell, *Secret Stories*]; Retro-pocalypse Now, by Michael Marano [Cormac McCarthy, *The Road;* James Newman, *The Wicked*]; Judgment Day, by Alan Warren [John Shirley, *The Other End*]; Strange Stories, by John Langan [Neil Gaiman, *Fragile Things*]; Ramsey Campbell, Probably; *Dandelion Wine* Redux, by Jim Rockhill [Ray Bradbury, *Farewell Summer*]; Pay No Attention to That Man Behind the Curtain, by June Pulliam [Brian Hodge, *World of Hurt*]; The Critic as Dadaist, by Richard Bleiler [John Clute, *The Darkening Garden*]; The Thing That Haunts the Dormitory, by Darrell Schweitzer [Alexandra Sokoloff, *The Harrowing*]; A Different Stephen King, by Ben Indick [Stephen King, *Lisey's Story*]; Weeding Out Emotion to Cultivate Violence, by Tony Fonseca [Jack Ketchum, *Weed Species*]; The Sheridan Le Fanu of Humor, by Steven J. Mariconda [T. E. D. Klein, *Reassuring Tales*]; A Remarkable Intellectual Figure, by Donald R. Burleson [H. P. Lovecraft, *Collected Essays*]; A New Dark Age?, by Rob Latham [J. G. Ballard, *Kingdom Come*]; Shades of Blackwood and Elgar, by Mike Ashley [Phil Rickman, *The Remains of an Altar*]; Twenty-First-Century Ghosts, by Stefan Dziemianowicz [Joe Hill, *20th-Century Ghosts;* Joe Hill, *Heart-Shaped Box*]; Books into Film and Vice Versa, by Matt Cardin [Tom Piccirilli, *The Dead Letters;* Tim Waggoner, *Darkness Wakes*]; Metaphysical Labyrinths and Fairy-Tale Archetypes, by John Langan [Tim Powers, *Three Days to Never;* John Connolly, *The Book of Lost Things*]; Lights, Camera, Horror, by Jack M. Haringa [Stephen Graham Jones,

Demon Theory; Mick Garris, *Development Hell*]; A Catalogue of Nightmares, by Robert Morrish [S. T. Joshi, ed., *Icons of Horror and the Supernatural*]; Capsule Reviews.

Notes. Cover illustration by Jason C. Eckhardt (uniform, aside from color, in all subsequent issues). The first issue of Hippocampus's review magazine, designed to carry on the wake of the defunct *Necrofile* (1991–99), published by Necronomicon Press. It was our feeling that the horror field needed a venue for substantial, thoughtful reviews of contemporary publications. Ramsey Campbell graciously allowed the reprinting of his column, "Ramsey Campbell, Probably," originally published in *Necrofile* and subsequently running in *All Hallows*.

40a. LESLIE L. LUTHER. *Moravia and Its Past.* Moravia, NY: Cayuga–Owasco Lakes Historical Society, 2007. 414 pp.

Contents: Foreword, *by George A. Luther*; A Note on This Edition, *by S. T. Joshi*; Preface (1966); Introduction, *by Frederic Luther*; Acknowledgments; I. Local Historians; II. Roads, Streets and Buildings; III. Moravia Schools; IV. Moravia Churches; V. Moravians of Note; VI. Various Local Characters Who Have Appeared upon the Scene, Had Their Day, and Been Gathered to to Their Fathers; VII. African Americans; VIII. Tragedies; IX. Patriots; X. Interesting Letters Received; XI. Miscellaneous Items; XII. Montville; XIII. Town of Niles; XIV. Town of Sempronius; XV. Town of Locke; XVI. Town of Genoa; XVII. Town of Venice; XVIII. Town of Scipio; Further Reading about Moravia; Index.

Notes. A reprint of the 1966 edition. Published by arrangement with Hippocampus Press. S. T. Joshi was at the time a resident of Moravia, and lent assistance in reissuing this highly regarded local history, correcting some apparent errors in the first edition, and recompiling the index to include nearly every name, place and business.

41. S. T. JOSHI AND ROSEMARY PARDOE, EDITORS. *Warnings to the Curious: A Sheaf of Criticism on M. R. James.* 2007. 338 pp.

Contents. Introduction, by S. T. Joshi; I. SOME NOTES ON BIOGRAPHY: Montague Rhodes James 1862–1936, by Stephen Gaselee; Montague Rhodes James, by Shane Leslie; The Strangeness Present: M. R. James's Suffolk, by Norman Scarfe; M. R. James and Livermere, by Michael Cox; II. GENERAL STUDIES: Supernatural Horror in Literature, by H. P. Lovecraft; The Art of Montague James, by Mary Butts; The Ghost Stories of Montague Rhodes James, by L. J. Lloyd; The Toad in the Study: M. R. James, H. P. Lovecraft, and Forbidden

Knowledge, by Simon MacCulloch; III. SOME SPECIAL TOPICS: On Not Letting Them Lie: Moral Significance in the Ghost Stories of M. R. James, by Michael A. Mason; Dark Devotions: M. R. James and the Magical Tradition, by Ron Weighell; M. R. James's Women, by David G. Rowlands; "The Rules of Folklore" in the Ghost Stories of M. R. James, by Jacqueline Simpson; "A Warning to the Curious": Victorian Science and the Awful Unconscious in M. R. James's Ghost Stories, by Brian Cowlishaw; "They've Got Him! In the Trees!" M. R. James and Sylvan Dread, by Steve Duffy; Homosexual Panic and the English Ghost Story: M. R. James and Others, by Mike Pincombe; "If I'm Not Careful": Innocents and Not-So-Innocents in the Stories of M. R. James, by John Alfred Taylor; "As Time Goes On I See a Shadow Coming": M. R. James's Grammar of Terror, by Steven J. Mariconda; "What Is This That I Have Done?" The Scapegoat Figure in the Stories of M. R. James, by Scott Connors; IV. STUDIES OF INDIVIDUAL TALES: The Nature of the Beast: The Demonology of "Canon Alberic's Scrap-book," by Helen Grant; A Haunting Presence, by C. E. Ward; "A Wonderful Book": George MacDonald and "The Ash-Tree," by Rosemary Pardoe; Who Was Count Magnus? Notes towards an Identification, by Rosemary Pardoe; A Haunting Vision: M. R. James and the Ashridge Stained Glass, by Nicholas Connell; A Maze of Secrets in a Story by M. R. James, by Martin Hughes; Thin Ghosts: Notes toward a Jamesian Rhetoric, by Jim Rockhill; Nightmares of Punch and Judy in Ruskin and M. R. James, by Roger Craik; An Elucidation (?) of the Plot of M. R. James's "Two Doctors," by Lance Arney; Landmarks and Shrieking Ghosts, by Jacqueline Simpson; Addendum by Rosemary Pardoe; Bibliography; Acknowledgments; Index.

Notes. Cover illustration by Carl Wilton, from *Ghost Stories of an Antiquary* by M. R. James (London: Pan Books, 1953). The first volume ever published that was devoted solely to James's ghost stories. A substantial anthology, including both reprinted pieces (many from *Ghosts & Scholars*, the leading organ of M. R. James studies) and original works.

42. FRANKLYN SEARIGHT. *Lair of the Dreamer: A Cthulhu Mythos Omnibus.* 2007. 307 pp.

Contents. Tainted Lineage, by Robert M. Price; There Is a Pond; Interlude at the Bridge; The Sorcerer's Pipe; The Innsmouth Head; Armillaria; The Guardian of the Pit; The Closing of the Gate; Mists of Death; Stomach Pains; Lair of the Dreamer.

Notes. Cover and interior illustrations by Robert H. Knox. Substantial collection of the Cthulhu Mythos fiction of Franklyn Searight, son of

Richard F. Searight, a correspondent of Lovecraft. Includes the short
novel of the title, previously unpublished.

43. SEAN DONNELLY, EDITOR. W. Paul Cook: The Wandering Life of
a Yankee Printer. 2007. x, 237 pp.

Contents. Preface; Acknowledgments; ABOUT W. PAUL COOK: W.
Paul Cook: "An Ordinary Printer," by Sean Donnelly; Recollections
of W. Paul Cook, by Arthur H. Goodenough; The Birth of Drift, by
Walter John Coates; The Colossus of the North, by Edward H. Cole;
In Memoriam: W. Paul Cook, by Edward H. Cole; A Bibliography of
W. Paul Cook, by Sean Donnelly; BY W. PAUL COOK: John DeMor-
gan; By and about Ourselves; Inconsequentialities; First Impressions;
A Thought; Howard P. Lovecraft's Fiction; H. P. Lovecraft; Introduc-
ing Vermont Names; More about Names; A Plea for Lovecraft; The
Great "What Is It?"; Jim Morton; A Day in the Life of Willis T.
Crossman; PROTEST STUFF: Introduction; Rhyme; Futility; Paternal-
ism; The Root; Extermination; Parasites; The Plan; Mission; Confi-
dence; Boomerang; The Butt; Fealty; Vacation; Tabloid; "Not
Molested"; Amusement; The Parting; Joy Street; Church; Selections
from Contradictions (Escape; Rootless; Easter; Awakening; Agnosti-
cism); Waters of Lethe; About the Editor; About the Book; The Re-
cluse (cover) (1927); Photograph of Orton, Coates, and Cook; In
Memoriam: Howard Phillips Lovecraft (cover) (1941); Monadnock
Monthly (cover) (November 1901); Vagrant (cover) (Spring 1927); A
Day in the Life of Willis T. Crossman (cover) (1934); Protest Stuff (title
page) (1934).

Notes. Cover illustration by Gale Mueller. A lengthy biographical
study of Cook, the amateur printer and close friend of Lovecraft. Also
includes memoirs of Cook by his colleagues, a bibliography of his publications, and a rich sampling of Cook's prose and poetic writings. A
companion volume to Donnelly's Willis T. Crossman's Vermont: Stories
by W. Paul Cook (University of Tampa Press, 2005).

44. Lovecraft Annual No. 1 (2007). EDITED BY S. T. JOSHI. 160 pp.

Contents. Lovecraft Read This, by Darrell Schweitzer; Lovecraft and
Lawrence Face the Hidden Gods: Transformations of Pan in "The
Colour out of Space" and St. Mawr, by Robert H. Waugh; Memories
of Sonia H. Greene Davis, by Martin H. Kopp; Letters to Lee McBride
White, by H. P. Lovecraft (ed. S. T. Joshi and David E. Schultz); The
Negative Mystics of the Mechanistic Sublime: Walter Benjamin and
Lovecraft's Cosmicism, by Jeff Lacy and Steven J. Zani; Unity in Di-
versity: Fungi from Yuggoth as a Unified Setting, by Phillip A. Ellis;

"They Have Conquered Dream": A. Merritt's "The Face in the Abyss" and H. P. Lovecraft's "The Mound," by Peter Levi; The Master's Eyes Shining with Secrets: H. P. Lovecraft's Influence on Thomas Ligotti, by Matt Cardin; Thomas Ligotti's Metafictional Mapping: The Allegory of "The Last Feast of Harlequin," by John Langan; Reviews; Briefly Noted.

Notes. Cover illustration by Allen Koszowski (uniform, aside from color, in all subsequent issues). The first issue of Hippocampus's scholarly journal devoted to Lovecraft, intended as a replacement of the defunct *Lovecraft Studies* (1979–2005), published by Necronomicon Press.

45. *Dead Reckonings* No. 2 (Fall 2007). EDITED BY S. T. JOSHI AND JACK M. HARINGA. 117 pp.

Contents. The World Down Under, by Sherry Austin [Ekaterina Sedia, *The Secret History of Moscow*]; A Cannibal's Boyhood, by June Pulliam [Thomas Harris, *Hannibal Rising*]; Poe, Poe, and More Poe, by Ben Fisher [Christopher Conlon, *Poe's Lighthouse*; James Robert Smith and Stephen Mark Rainey, ed., *Evermore*]; Green Glows and Trickster Gods, by Tony Fonseca [Thomas Tessier, *Wicked Things*; Philip Haldeman, *Shadow Coast*]; The Ultimate Clark Ashton Smith, by Hubert Van Calenbergh [Clark Ashton Smith, *Collected Fantasies*, Vols. 1 and 2]; Decadence in Verse and Prose, by Steven J. Mariconda [Clark Ashton Smith, *Complete Poems and Translations*, Vol. 3]; Tact and the Ghost Story, by Reggie Oliver [S. T. Joshi and Rosemary Pardoe, ed., *Warnings to the Curious*]; An Anatomist of Technoscience, by Rob Latham [Thomas Pynchon, *Against the Day*]; Ghosts and Scholars, by Brian Showers [Margaret Oliphant, *The Library Window*; Cheiro, *A Study of Destiny*]; Domination of Black, by John Langan [Laird Barron, *The Imago Sequence*]; Ligotti Redivivus?, by S. T. Joshi [Michael Cisco, *Secret Hours*; *The Traitor*]; Some Manifestations of Fantasy, by Ben P. Indick [Sean Wallace and Paul Tremblay, ed., *Fantasy*; Scriptus Innominatus, *Zencore!*]; Ramsey Campbell, Probably; Devouring Yet More Flesh, by Darrell Schweitzer [Kim Paffenroth, *Dying to Live*]; Ambrose Bierce's Moral Art, by Donald R. Burleson [*The Short Fiction of Ambrose Bierce: A Comprehensive Edition*]; Hardboiled and Haunted, by Jack M. Haringa; Tom Piccirilli, *The Midnight Road*]; The Yellow House on Benefit Street, by Scott Connors [Caitlin R. Kiernan, *Daughter of Hounds*]; Good, Bad, and Ugly, by Tony Fonseca [Peter Crowther, ed., *PostScripts 10*; Robert Morrish, ed., *Thrillers Two (II, 2)*]; Danger and Loss, by Paula Guran [Elizabeth Hand, *Illyria*; *Generation Loss*]; Memoirs, Essays, and Frivolities, by Richard Bleiler [Peter Straub,

Sides]; Confronting the Unknowable, by Jim Rockhill [Lucius Shepard, *Dagger Key and Other Stories; Softspoken*]; Thrillers That Don't Thrill, by Michael Marano [Michael Marshall Smith, *The Servants; The Intruder*]; The Dark Delights of Gnostic Nightmares, by Matt Cardin [Richard Gavin, *Omens*]; Breathing Life into Old Plots, by Hank Wagner [Mary SanGiovanni, *The Hollower*; Sarah Langan, *The Missing*]; Unfinished Business, by Van Viator [John Farris, *You Don't Scare Me*; Lee Thomas, *The Dust of Wonderland*]; Open Mouths, Ready to Feed, by John Langan [Conrad Williams, *The Unblemished*]; Dudsville, by Alan Warren [Jeffrey Thomas, *Deadstock*; with Scott Thomas, *The Sea of Flesh and Ash*]; Enough Ghost Sex, Already, by Sherry Austin [Steve Berman, *Vintage: A Ghost Story*]; In the Garden of Yidden, by Ben P. Indick [Michael Chabon, *The Yiddish Policeman's Union*]; The Sounds of Violence, by Jack M. Haringa [Michael Arnzen, *Audiovile*; Elizabeth Monteleone, ed., *Dark Voices, Vols. 1, 2, 4, & 5*; Gruesome, *Johnny Gruesome*]; A Lasting Object of Contemplation, by Darrell Schweitzer [*Pan's Labyrinth* (film)]; The Darkling Plain, by Stefan Dziemianowicz; Capsule Reviews.

46. LELAND HALL. *Sinister House*. FRANCIS BRETT YOUNG. *Cold Harbour*. 2008. 108 + 161 pp.

Notes. Cover and interior illustrations by Haydon Jones (from the original edition of *Sinister House*) and by the anonymous artist of the first American edition of *Cold Harbour*. Part of the Lovecraft's Library series. A reprint of two splendid novels discussed by Lovecraft in "Supernatural Horror in Literature." Neither *Sinister House* (1919) nor *Cold Harbour* (1924) appear to have had any direct influence on Lovecraft's stories, but further investigation may reveal subtle influences here and there. S. T. Joshi has written separate introductions to each novel.

47. EDITH MINITER. *Dead Houses and Other Works*. Edited by Kenneth W. Faig, Jr., and Sean Donnelly. 2008. xiii, 369 pp.

Contents. Introducing Edith Miniter, by Kenneth W. Faig & Sean Donnelly; ABOUT EDITH MINITER: Edith Miniter: A Life, by Kenneth W. Faig, Jr.; Mrs. Miniter—Estimates and Recollections, by H. P. Lovecraft; Edith Miniter, by Edward H. Cole; My Recollections, by William R. Murphy; Memories and Impressions, by Ernest A. Edkins; As I Knew Her, by Arthur H. Goodenough; Some Thoughts of Edith Miniter, by James P. Morton; My Friend Edith Miniter, by Nelson Glazier Morton; My Association with Edith May Miniter, by Truman J. Spencer; Edith Miniter, by H. P. Lovecraft; AMATEUR JOURNALISM:

Salutatory; Editorial; Definitions Definitely Defined; Some Benefits of Amateur Journalism: A Hallowe'en Invitation; Hallowe'en Happenings; The Aftermath; Epgephi Musings; Falco Ossifracus; My Mother as She Seemed to Me; The Aftermath; The February Meeting; The Big Event; FICTION: To Thine Own Heart Be True; A Tragedy of the Hills; A Shadow on the Water; The Homecoming of Cleora; He That Will Not When He May: A Tale of Christmas Time; Wonted Fires; The Root of Age; The Emancipation of Elivra; Utilizing a By-Product; A Bunch of Crocuses; Aunt Ann's Bed; Cinderella Soapman; Nobody Home; Tartar Sauce; Thumbs; Dead Houses; About the Editors; About the Book.

Notes. Cover design by Sean Donnelly. A generous selection of Miniter's writings, including both fiction and amateur journalism. Miniter was a leading figure in the amateur journalism movement of the late 19th and early 20th centuries, and her fiction also appeared professionally. The book contains a lengthy biographical introduction by Faig and memoirs of Miniter by friends and colleagues, including Lovecraft.

48. DONALD WANDREI. *Sanctity and Sin: The Collected Poems and Prose Poems of Donald Wandrei.* Edited by S. T. Joshi. 2008. 195 pp.

Contents. Introduction, by S. T. Joshi; ECSTASY AND OTHER POEMS: The Voice of Beauty; Song of Autumn; Ecstasy; Let Us Love Tonight; Vain Warning; On Some Drawings; Sanctity and Sin; To Myrrhiline; Song of Oblivion; In Mandrikor; The Woodland Pool; Death and the Poet: A Fragment; Satiation; In Memoriam: George Sterling; Bacchanalia; Awakening; Red; Hermaphroditus; Aphrodite; Amphitrite; Philomela; A Drinking Song; At the Bacchic Revel; The Challenger; The Greatest Regret; Futility; From the Shadowlands of Memory; The Poet's Language; Nightmare; Valerian; DARK ODYSSEY: Largo; Aubade; Fata Morgana; Borealis; In Memoriam: No Name; Dark Odyssey; Look Homeward, Angel; Under the Grass; You Will Come Back; After Bacchus, Eros; To Lucasta on Her Birthday; Villanelle à la Mode; For the Perishing Aphrodite; Morning Song; The Whispering Knoll; The Five Lords (Black; Green; Red; Purple; Chorus; White); Lost Atlantis; The Night Wind; The Voyagers' Return to Tyre; The Plague Ship; Chaos Resolved; Epithalamium; Epilude; POEMS FOR MIDNIGHT: Phantom; The Corpse Speaks; The Woman at the Window; Shadowy Night; The Worm-King; Water Sprite; Incubus; The Prehistoric Huntsman; Witches' Sabbath; Forest Shapes; The Dream That Dies; The Sleeper; The Moon-Glen Altar; The Morning of a Nymph; Death and the Traveler: A Fragment; King of the Shadowland; Ishmael; *Sonnets of the Midnight Hours* (After Sleep; Purple; The Old Companions; The Head; In the Attic; The Cocoon; The Metal God; The Little Creature; The Pool; The Prey; The Torturers; The Statues; The Hungry Flowers; The Eye; The Rack; Escape; Capture; In the Pit; The Unknown Color; Monstrous Form; Nightmare in Green; What Followed Me?; Fantastic Sculpture; The Tree; The Bell; The Ultimate Vision); Somewhere Past Ispahan; UNCOLLECTED POEMS: The Poet's Lament; There Was a Smell of Dandelions; The Classicist; Pedagogues; Street Scene . . .; Chant to the Dead; The School of Seduction; *Poems from Broken Mirrors* (Fling Wide the Roses; Drink!; The Dead Mistress; My Lady Hath Two Lovely Lips; Aftermath; Credo; In Mandrikor); *Sonnets of the Midnight Hours* (Dream-Horror; The Grip of Evil Dreams; The Creatures; The Red Specter; Doom); *Moon Magic* (The Glow; The Song; The Overtone; The Dream); *Dead Fruit of the Fugitive Years* (The Dream Changes; Surrender; Though All My Days; The Second Beauty; Twice Excellent Perfection; This Larger Room; The Woman Answers; The Deadly Calm; Corroding Acids; With Cat-like Tread); *Lyrics of Doubt* (A Testament of Desertion; To the God of My Fathers. Marmora; The Cypress-Bog; The Monster Gods; A Queen in Other Skies; Epitaph to a Lady; Portrait of a Lady During a Half Hour Wait While She Finished Dressing; The Little Gods Wait); [Poems from *Invisible Sun*]; [Limerick]; Elegy; September Hill; I Am Man; Golden Poppy; Solitary; Lines; POEMS IN PROSE: The One Who Died; The Messengers; The Pursuers; Paphos; The Woman at the Window; Ebony and Silver; The Death of the Flowers; The Purple Land; The Lost Moon; Dreaming Away My Life; The Black Flame; The Shrieking House; The Kingdom of Dreams; Unforgotten Night; Santon Merlin; A Legend of Yesterday; From "The Tower of Sound"; An Epitaph on Jupiter; Commentary; Index of Titles; Index of First Lines.

Notes. Cover and interior illustrations by Howard Wandrei. Originally designed for a 6 × 9 inch format, although copies were printed at a smaller trim size, resulting in very tight margins. This was corrected in 2011. An exhaustive revision of Joshi's edition of Wandrei's *Collected Poems* (Necronomicon Press, 1988), augmented by several new poems and a sheaf of Wandrei's prose poems.

49. CLARK ASHTON SMITH. *The Hashish-Eater*. Edited by Donald Sidney-Fryer. 2008. 59 pp.

Contents. A Wind from the Unknown, by Ron Hilger; About Clark Ashton Smith and *The Hashish-Eater*; The Crystals, by Clark Ashton Smith; Argument of *The Hashish-Eater*, by Clark Ashton Smith; The

Face from Infinity, by Clark Ashton Smith; Excerpt from a letter by Smith, summer 1950; The Hashish-Eater; or, The Apocalypse of Evil, by Clark Ashton Smith; Commentary; The Final Image; Suggested Interpretation; Conclusion.

Notes. Cover illustration by Clark Ashton Smith. Expanded from the editor's privately printed booklet (1990). Offered free with purchase of Smith's *Complete Poetry and Translations*; eventually made available for separate purchase. Audio CD contains hidden tracks of Sidney-Fryer reading a selection of other poems by Smith.

A thoroughly annotated edition of Smith's longest poem (581 lines) by the leading authority on Smith. The text of the poem comprises the original appearance in *Ebony and Crystal* (1922) and Smith's revised version (dating to the 1940s) from his *Selected Poems* (1971) on facing pages.

50. CLARK ASHTON SMITH. *The Complete Poetry and Translations.* Edited by S. T. Joshi and David E. Schultz, 2008 (rpt. 2012 [paper]). 2 vols. (xxxix, 846 pp., numbered consecutively).

Contents. VOLUME 1 (*THE ABYSS TRIUMPHANT*): Introduction; THE VOICE OF SILENCE (1910–1911): Cloudland; The Fountain of Youth; The Road of Pain; Reincarnation; Lethe; A White Rose; Death; Companionship; Illusion; The Call of the Wind; The Expanding Ideal; Imagination; The Sunrise; Night; To a Yellow Pine; A Sierran Sunrise; The Sierras; The Wind and the Moon; Moonlight; The Altars of Sunset; To George Sterling; The Voice of Silence; Weavings; The West Wind; Before Sunrise; At Nadir; The Besieging Billows; The Butterfly; The Meaning; To the Nightshade; The Garden of Dreams; Ode to Matter; Ode to Poetry; The Pageant of Music; Autumn Dew; The Eclipse; The Falling Leaves; The Freedom of the Hills; The Hosts of Heaven; Ode on the Future of Song; The Suns and the Void; To George Sterling; Moods of the Sea; Sonnets of the Seasons; Spring; Summer; The Wizardry of Winter; The Storm; To the Morning Star; The Flower of the Night; A Sunset; War; Wings of Perfume; The Island of a Dream; Autumn's Pall; The Music of the Gods; The Night of Despair; Somnus; At Midnight; The Fanes of Dawn; The Summer Hills; To George Sterling; The Wind-Threnody; The Voice in the Pines; Black Enchantment; The Burden of the Suns; The Castle of Dreams; A Dream of Oblivion; A Dream of Darkness; The Revelation; The Dream-God's Realm; Ephemera; The Eternal Gleam; Evening; The Harbour of the Past; In Extremis; Lost Beauty; Nature's Orchestra; The Past; The Present; The Future; Time the Wonder; The Palace of Jewels; The Past; The Potion of Dreams; The Power of Eld; Romance; The Song of the Worlds; Sonnet on Music;

Sonnet on Oblivion; Sonnet to the Sphinx; Sphinx and Medusa; The Sphinx of the Infinite; The Tartarus of the Suns; The Temple of Night; The Throne of Winter; Time; To a Cloud; To a Mariposa Lily; To a Snowdrop; To Ambition; To the Crescent Moon; To the Morning Star; To Thomas Paine; To Thomas Paine; Twilight; The Twilight Woods; The Vampire Night; The Waning Moon; THE ABYSS TRIUMPHANT (1911–1912): Antony to Cleopatra; Poetry; The Last Night; The Eternal Snows; The Moonlight Desert; Nocturne; Ode to Music; The Dream-Weaver; Ode to the Abyss; Medusa; The Messengers; Chant to Sirius; The Horizon; A Dream of Beauty; A Live-Oak Leaf; Wind-Ripples; A Song from Hell; The Palace of Jewels; The Star-Treader; To George Sterling; The Dream-Bridge; The Nemesis of Suns; Retrospect and Forecast; The Song of a Comet; Said the Dreamer; Saturn; The Shadow of the Unattained; The Pursuer; Echo of Memnon; Nero; The Mad Wind; Finis; Ode to Light; In the Desert; The Return of Hyperion; To the Daemon Sublimity; Atlantis; Averted Malefice; The Balance; The Cherry-Snows; Copan; A Dead City; The Eldritch Dark; Epitaph for the Earth; Fairy Lanterns; The Fugitives; Lament of the Stars; Lethe; The Masque of Forsaken Gods; The Maze of Sleep; The Medusa of the Skies; The Night Forest; Nirvana; Ode on Imagination; Pine Needles; The Price; The Retribution; Shadow of Nightmare; The Snow-Blossoms; A Song of Dreams; The Song of the Stars; Song to Oblivion; The Soul of the Sea; The Summer Moon; To the Darkness; To the Sun; The Unremembered; White Death; The Winds; The Morning Pool; The Abyss Triumphant; The Last Goddess; Satan Unrepentant; The Titans in Tartarus; The Cloud-Islands; Remembered Light; The Sorrow of the Winds; Luna Aeternalis; [In the Ultimate Valleys]; The Nereid; A PHANTASY AT TWILIGHT (1913–1917): The Ghoul; The Land of Evil Stars; The Clouds; The Doom of America; Nightmare; The City of the Titans; Desire of Vastness; The Medusa of Despair; The Refuge of Beauty; The Years Restored; The Witch in the Graveyard; The Sea-Gods; The Ministers of Law; Decadence; Somnus; To Beauty; The City of Destruction; The Orchid of Beauty; A Phantasy of Twilight; Beauty Implacable; The Nameless Wraith; The Ancient Quest; Aspect of Iron; Beyond the Door; The Harlot of the World; Psalm to the Desert; Inheritance; Memnon at Midnight; The City in the Desert; The Blindness of Orion; The Mirrors of Beauty; The Flight of Azrael; Duality; Love Malevolent; Exotique; Alien Memory; Fire of Snow; In the Wind; Lunar Mystery; Moon-Dawn; The Mummy; Morning on an Eastern Sea; Reclamation; Afterglow; Nocturne; The Crucifixion of Eros; Suggestion; Arabesque; Belated Love; November Twilight; Desolation; Coldness; The Kingdom of Shadows; Give Me Your Lips;

geddon; JUVENILIA: [Untitled]; [Fragment 1]; [Fragment 2]; [Fragment 3]; [Fragment 4]; [Fragment 5]; [Fragment 6]; Benares; The Prayer Rug; The Rubaiyat of Seyyid; Sunrise; The Skull; The Orient; Time; To an Eastern City; Fortune; The Ocean; Allah; Arab Song; Arabian Love-Song; Bedouin Song; The City of the Djinn; The Desert; A Dream of Vathek; A Dream of Zanoni; Eblis Repentant; From the Persian; From the Persian; From the Persian; Haroun Al-Raschid; The Inscription; Jewel of the Orient; Jewel of the Orient; Kismet; Mohammed; The Muezzin; Ode from the Persian; Odes of Alnaschar; Omar's Philosophy; The Palace of the Jinn; The Prayer Rug; The Prince and the Peri; Quatrain; Quatrains; Quatrains; The Snare; Song; Quatrains on Jewels; The Diamond; The Pearl; The Turquoise; The Ruby; The Opal; Rubaiyat; Rubaiyat; Rubaiyat of Saiyed; The Seekers; Some Maxims from the Persian; Stamboul; Suleyman Jan ben Jan; The Temple; The World; Youth and Age; Zuleika; Asia; Aurungzeb's Mosque; The Burning Ghauts; The Burning-Ghauts at Benares; Dawn; Delhi; A Dream of India; The Ganges; Alchemy; The Book of Years; Courage; The Days of Time; The Departed City; A Dream; Fear; The Fear of Death; The Feast; Hate and Love; Hope; The Land o' Dreams; The Leveler; Love; The Lure of Gold; Mercy; The Moon; Perseverance; Poem [?]; Resignation; The River; The River of Life; Sea-Lure; The Sea-Shell; Silence; Solitude; Summer Idleness; To the Best Beloved; The World; [Fragment 7].

VOLUME 2 (THE WINE OF SUMMER): SPECTRAL LIFE (1927–1929): Les Violons; Au Bord du Léthé; The Nevermore-to-Be; Fantaisie d'antan; Canticle; A Fable; De Consolation; De Consolation; Simile; Trope; Venus; One Evening; Tristan to Iseult; Souvenance; To Antares; Song; Amor Autumnalis; Warning; Temporality; Chansonette; Chansonette; Credo; The Autumn Lake; Le Lac d'automne; On a Chinese Vase; November; Chanson de Novembre; Chanson de Novembre; Exorcism; Winter Moonlight; Connaissance; Harmony; Moon-Sight; Sonnet; Similitudes; Calendar; February; Variations; Sufficiency; Lichens; Vaticinations; Nyctalops; The Hill-Top; L'Amour suprême; L'Amour suprême; Alexandrins; Absence; Une Vie spectrale; Spectral Life; Seins; Les Marées; Paysage païen; Le Souvenir; Rêvasserie; La Mare; Le Miroir des blanches fleurs; Le Miroir des blanches fleurs; The Dragon-Fly; September; Shadows; Evanescence; Fellowship; Ougabalys; Ineffability; The Nightmare Tarn; Cumuli; Refuge; SOME OLDER BOURN (1930–1938): Answer; Song at Evenfall; Jungle Twilight; Madrigal of Evanescence; Solicitation; An Old Theme; Psalm; The Pool; Revenant; A Dream of the Abyss; In Slumber; Necromancy; Outlanders; Dominion; In Thessaly; The Phoenix; The Outer Land; Day-Dream; Contra Mortem; The Cycle; Kin; Sanctuary; Simile; Le Refuge; Le Refuge; La Forteresse; The Fortress; Sonnet; Ennui; Adjuration; Song of the Necromancer; Rêves printaniers; Rêves printaniers; Amour bizarre; L'Ensorcellement; Le Fabliau d'un dieu; Orgueil; Sea-Memory; Farewell to Eros; Indian Summer; Mystery; Touch; To Howard Phillips Lovecraft; The Prophet Speaks; Desert Dweller; Requiescat; Wizard's Love; THE LAST AND UTMOST LAND (1939–1947): From Arcady; Ode; Sestet; Bacchante; Resurrection; Witch-Dance; Song of the Bacchic Bards; Anteros; Lamia; Interim; Sonnet; To One Absent; Silent Hour; Grecian Yesterday; But Grant, O Venus; Bond; Madrigal of Memory; "That Last Infirmity"; The Thralls of Circe Climb Parnassus; Dialogue; The Mime of Sleep; The Old Water-Wheel; Fragment; Yerba Buena; Consummation; Humors of Love; Town Lights; The Sorcerer to His Love; To George Sterling; L'Espoir du néant; Amor Hesternalis; "All Is Dross That Is Not Helena"; Future Pastoral; Wine of Summer; In Another August; Nocturne: Grant Avenue; Classic Epigram; Twilight Song; Supplication; Erato; Anodyne of Autumn; The Hill of Dionysus; Before Dawn; Amor; Interval; Postlude; Strange Girl; De Profundis; Midnight Beach; Illumination; Omniety; Even in Slumber; Moly; Cambion; The Knoll; For an Antique Lyre; On Trying to Read *Four Quartets*; Greek Epigram; Lines on a Picture; Alternative; Hymn; The Sorcerer Departs; Surréalist Sonnet; Paean; Do You Forget, Enchantress?; The Horologe; Parnassus à la Mode; Sea Cycle; Dancer; Nevermore; Reverie in August; Tin Can on the Mountain-Top; Some Blind Eidolon; The Pursuer; To Bacchante; Calenture; Copyist; Love and Death; Quintrains; Essence; Epitaph for an Astronomer; The Heron; Bird of Long Ago; Late November Evening; Mithridates; Mummy of the Flower; Nightmare of the Lilliputian; Passing of an Elder God; Poets in Hades; Quiddity; Someone; Dying Prospector; EXPERIMENTS IN HAIKU (1947): Strange Miniatures; Unicorn; Untold Arabian Fable; A Hunter Meets the Martichoras; The Limniad; The Sciapod; The Monacle; Feast of St. Anthony; Paphnutius; Philtre; Borderland; Lethe; Empusa Waylays a Traveller; Perseus and Medusa; Odysseus in Eternity; The Ghost of Theseus; Distillations; Fence and Wall; Growth of Lichen; Cats in Winter Sunlight; Abandoned Plum-Orchard; Harvest Evening; Willow-Cutting in Autumn; Declining Moon; Late Pear-Pruner; Nocturnal Pines; Phallus Impudica; Stormy Afterglow; Geese in the Spring Night; Foggy Night; Reigning Empress; The Sparrow's Nest; The Last Apricot; Mushroom-Gatherers; Spring Nunnery; Nuns Walking in the Orchard; Improbable Dream; Crows in Spring; High Mountain Juniper; Storm's End; Pool at Lobos; Poet in a Barroom; Fallen Grape-Leaf; Gopher-Hole in Orchard; Basin in Boulder; Indian Acorn-Mortar; Old Limestone Kiln; Love in

Dreams; Night of Miletus; Tryst at Lobos; Mountain Trail; Future Meeting; Classic Reminiscence; Goats and Manzanita-Boughs; Bed of Mint; Chainless Captive; California Winter; January Willow; Snowfall on Acacia; Flight of the Yellow-Hammer; Sunset over Farm-Land; Flora; Windows at Lamplighting Time; Old Hydraulic Diggings; Hearth on Old Cabin-Site; Builder of Deserted Hearth; Aftermath of Mining Days; River-Canyon; Childhood; School-Room Pastime; Boys Telling Bawdy Tales; Fight on the Play-Ground; Water-Fight; Boys Rob a Yellow-Hammer's Nest; Nest of the Screech-Owl; Grammar-School Vixen; Girl of Six; Mortal Essences; Snake, Owl, Cat or Hawk; Slaughter-House in Spring; Cattle Salute the Psychopomp; Slaughter-House Pasture; Field Behind the Abatoir; Plague from the Abatoir; La Mort des amants; Vultures Come to the Ambarvalia; For the Dance of Death; Berries of the Deadly Nightshade; Water-Hemlock; Felo-de-se of the Parasite; Pagans Old and New; Initiate of Dionysus; Bacchic Orgy; Abstainer; Picture by Piero di Cosimo; Bacchants and Bacchante; Garden of Priapus; Morning Star of the Mountains; Bygone Interlude; Prisoner in Vain; Epitaphs; Braggart; Slaughtered Cattle; The Earth; Miscellaneous Haiku; Illuminatus; Limestone Cavern; Maternal Prostitute; Ocean Twilight; Radio; Tule-Mists; IF WINTER REMAIN (1948–1950): Hellenic Sequel; No Stranger Dream; On the Mount of Stone; Only to One Returned; Sonnet for the Psychoanalysts; Avowal; Tolometh; If Winter Remain; Almost Anything; "That Motley Drama"; Pour Chercher du nouveau; Dans l'univers lointain; In a Distant Universe; High Surf: Monterey Bay; Isaac Newton; La Muse moderne; The Mystical Number; Pantheistic Dream; Rêve panthéistique; Poèmes d'amour; Sandalwood and Onions; The Dark Chateau; Don Quixote on Market Street; The Isle of Saturn; "O Golden-Tongued Romance"; Averoigne; Zothique; Le poéte parle avec ses biographes; The Poet Talks with the Biographers; Beauty; La Hermosura; Las Poetas del optimismo; The Poets of Optimism; El Cantar de los seres libres; Song of the Free Beings; ¿Donde duermes, Eldorado?; Where Sleepest Thou, O Eldorado?; Los Dueños; Dominium in Excelsis; Parnaso; Parnassus; Las Alquerías perdidas; Lost Farmsteads; Cantar; Song; Eros in the Desert; Dice el soñador; Says the Dreamer; Memoria roja; Red Memory; Dos Mitos y una fábula; Two Myths and a Fable; La Nereida; La Isla de Circe; The Isle of Circe; Lo Ignoto; The Unknown; Leteo; [Lethe]; Añoranza; Melancholia; El Vendaval; El Vendaval; Farmyard Fugue; Didus Ineptus; Amithaine; Malediction; Shapes in the Sunset; Sinbad, It Was Not Well to Brag; El Eros de ébano; Eros of Ebony; THE DEAD WILL CUCKOLD YOU (1950); THE SORCERER DEPARTS (1951–1961): The Stylite; Two on a Pillar; Not Theirs the Cypress-Arch; Alpine Climber; Hesperian Fall; "Not Altogether Sleep"; Seeker; Soliloquy in a Ebon Tower; The Twilight of the Gods; Qu'Importe?; ¿Qué sueñas, Musa?; What Dreamest Thou, Muse?; Que songes-tu, Muse?; Ye Shall Return; Lives of the Saints; Secret Worship; The Song of Songs; STYES WITH SPIRES; In Time of Absence; Nada; Seer of the Cycles; I Shall Not Greatly Grieve; Geometries; Alchemy; Sacraments; Delay; Verity; La Isla del náufrago; Isle of the Shipwrecked; Thebaid; Saturnian Cinema; Dedication: To Carol; The Centaur; Lawn-Mower; Tired Gardener; High Surf; H. P. L.; Cycles; FRAGMENTS AND UNTITLED POEMS: Al borde del Leteo; Ballad of a Lost Soul; The Brook; Demogorgon; Despondency; The Flight of the Seraphim; For Iris; Haunting; The Milky Way; Night; The Night Wind; No-Man's-Land; Ode on Matter; The Regained Past; The Saturnienne; Sonnets of the Desert; The Temptation; To a Comet; To Iris; To Iris; To the Sun; The Vampire Night; [miscellaneous fragments]; Broceliande; [miscellaneous fragments]; Twilight Pilgrimage; [miscellaneous fragments]; Limericks; Ripe Mulberries; From "Ode to Antares"; From "The Song of Xeethra"; From "Song of the Galley Slaves"; From "Song of King Hoaraph's Bowmen"; From "Ludar's Litany to Thasaidon"; From "Ludar's Litany to Thasaidon"; APPENDIX: *Prospective Tables of Contents:* The Jasmine Girdle; The Jasmine Girdle and Other Poems; Incantations; The Abalone Song; *Translations:* The Desire of Loving [a translation of "Le Désir d'Aimer" by Hélène Picard; [Sandalwood]; Voices; Notes; Index of Titles; Index of First Lines.

Notes. Cover photo by Jack Newton (vol. 1) and Anastasia Damianakos (vol. 2). 250 hardcover copies per volume, printed by Covington Group. The first complete edition of Smith's original poetry, completing the set that began with the publication of vol. 3 (Smith's translations) in 2007 (see item 37). The edition was the product of decades of work by Schultz; Joshi contributed editorial guidance only at a late stage of compilation. The edition was based upon the manuscripts of Smith's poetry that form part of the Clark Ashton Smith Papers at the John Hay Library of Brown University; nearly 300 unpublished poems appear here for the first time. The texts have been extensively annotated and arranged in chronological order by date of composition, so far as that can be established. For the paperback edition, see item 113.

51. PHILLIP A. ELLIS. *A Concordance to the Poetry of Donald Wandrei.* 2008. 462 pp.

Notes. Published in hardcover without dust jacket. A concordance to Wandrei's poetry, based on the texts established in *Sanctity and Sin* (item 48). Surely one of the scarcest Hippocampus Press titles, based on number of copies printed; an electronic version of this title was made available as a free download.

52. *Dead Reckonings* No. 3 (Spring 2008). EDITED BY S. T. JOSHI AND JACK M. HARINGA. 94 pp.

Contents. A Swift River of Allusion, by Jim Rockhill [Emma Frances Dawson, *An Itinerant House and Other Ghost Stories*]; The Novel as Tumor, by Michael Marano [Stephen King, *Duma Key*]; Exploring the Breadth of Weird Fiction, by June Pulliam [Ann and Jeff VanderMeer, ed., *The New Weird*; Ellen Datlow, ed., *Inferno*]; Die Laughing, by Stefan Dziemianowicz [Ramsey Campbell, *The Grin of the Dark*]; The Self, the Landscape, by John Langan [Conrad Williams, *The Scalding Rooms*; Conrad Williams, *Rain*]; An Opportunity Lost, by Mike Ashley [Ian Alexander Martin, ed., *The First Humdrumming Book of Horror Stories*]; Kitchen-Sink Naturalism, by Rob Latham [Christopher Barzak, *One for Sorrow*]; In, Between, and Around the Genres, by Bernadette Bosky [Peter Straub, *5 Stories*]; More (of the Same) Can Sometimes Be Less, by Tony Fonseca [John Everson, ed., *Sins of the Sirens*; Hank Schwaeble and Gary Braunbeck, ed., *Five Strokes to Midnight*]; Cthulhuism and Yog-Sothothery, by Steven J. Mariconda [H. P. Lovecraft, *Essential Solitude: Letters to August Derleth*; *O Fortunate Floridian: H. P. Lovecraft's Letters to R. H. Barlow*]; Lives and Deaths at the Edge of Noir, by Jack M. Haringa [Brian Hodge, *Mad Dogs*; John Connolly, *The Unquiet*]; Stormy Weather, by Ben Indick [Nicholas Royle, *The Appetite*]; Ramsey Campbell, Probably; Creeping Nihilism, by Alan Warren [Adam-Try Castro, *The Shallow End of the Pool*; Tim Lebbon and Lindy Moore, *Children of the New Disorder*]; The Sublime and the Ridiculous, by S. T. Joshi [Dennis Etchison, *Got to Kill Them All*; Ray Garton, *Slivers of Bone*]; Liebestod in Lower Manhattan, by John Langan [John Marks, *Fangland*]; Dystopia Now, by Matt Cardin [Thomas Ligotti, *Teatro Grottesco*; Paulo Bacigalupi, *Pump Six and Other Stories*]; Burn This Book, by Hank Wagner [Clive Barker, *The Painter, the Creature, and the Father of Lies*; Clive Barker, *Mister B. Gone*]; It's All in the Telling, by Gary William Crawford [Brian Showers, *The Bleeding Horse and Other Stories*; Reggie Oliver, *Masques of Satan*]; They Know Their South, by Sherry Austin [Beth Massie, *Homeplace*; Will Clarke, *The Worthy: A Ghost's Story*]; Dross in Translation, by Jack M. Haringa [Asa Nonami, *Now You're One of Us*]; Nice Mice, by Ben Indick [Susan Palwick, *The Fate of Mice*]; Heirs to the King?, by Kevin Dole [Brian Keene, *Dark Hollow*; Richard Dansky, *Firefly Rain*]; Two Centuries of American Ghosts, by

Richard Bleiler [S. T. Joshi, ed., *American Supernatural Tales*];
Winning the Resurrection Lottery, by Scott Connors [Stephen Mark
Rainey, *Blue Devil Island*; Greg Lamberson, *Johnny Gruesome*]; Capsule
Reviews.

53. DONALD SIDNEY-FRYER. *The Atlantis Fragments: The Trilogy of
Songs and Sonnets Atlantean.* 2008 (paper edition 2009). 549 pp.

Contents. The Atlantis Fragments: An Introduction, by Brian Stableford; SONGS AND SONNETS ATLANTEAN: THE FIRST SERIES: Introduc-
tion, by Dr. Ibid M. Andor; Avalonessys; The Crown and Trident
Imperial; Atlantis; The Rose and the Thorn; Rose Escarlate; "O Eb-
on-Colored Rose"; Your Mouth of Pomegranate; As Buds and Blos-
soms in the Month of May the Rose; To Clark Ashton Smith; Pavane;
When We Were Prince and Princess; The Crown and Trident; Song;
"Thy Spirit Walks the Sea"; Recompense; To a Youth; Spenserian
Stanza-Sonnet Empourpré; A Symbol for All Splendor Lost; The
Ashes in the Rose Garden; To Edmund Spenser (1552?–1599); Rose
Verdastre; Ave Atque Vale; Thaïs and Alexander in Persepolis; A
Fragment; O Fair Dark Eyes, O Glances Turned Aside; The Cydnus;
Golden Mycenae; Lullaby; *Minor Chronicles of Atlantis* (Proem, by
Michel de Labretagne; The Hippokamp; The Alpha Huge; The River
Called Amphus; The Amphus Delta; The Imperial Crown Jewels of
Atlantis; The Atlantean Obelisk; The Garden of Jealous Roses; The
Tale of an Olden Love; The Shepherd and the Shepherdess; Reci-
procity; The Iffinnix; A Vision of Strange Splendor); Kilcolman Cas-
tle: 20 August 1965; Aubade; The Lilac Hedge at Cassell Prairie: 27
May 1967; Black Poppy and Black Lotus; The House of Roses; "The
Musical Note of Swans . . . Before Their Death"; Green Sleeves; O
Beautiful Dark-Amber Eyes of Old; The Forsaken Palace; For the
Shapes of Clay of Ambrose Bierce; Connaissance Fatale; For the *Black
Beetles in Amber* of Ambrose Bierce; Offrande Exotique; *Sonnets on an
Empire of Many Waters:* Legend; I. Here, where the fountains of the
deep-sea flow; II. Atlantis; III. Gades; IV. Atlantigades; V. Atkantha-
ria; VI. Iffrikonn-Yssthia; VII. Atalantessys; VIII. Atlantillia; IX. Ata-
temthessys; X. At-Thulonn; XI. Avalonessys; XII. Poseidonis; XIII.
The Merchant-Princes; XIV. An Argosy of Trade; XV. Memories of
the Astazhan; XVI. A Letter from Valoth; XVII. No, not until the final age of Earth; *Commendatory and Dedicatory Poems:* To an Atlantean Poet, by Margo Skinner; Inspiration, by Ian M. M. Law; Secretest,
by Fritz Leiber; To Gloria Kathleen; For Master Edmund Spenser: His
Great Song; Preliminary Note, by Brian Stableford; Notes, by Dr. Ibid
M. Andor; SONGS AND SONNETS ATLANTEAN: THE SECOND SERIES:
Preface; An Enchantress out of Time; A Summoning of Shadows;

Valediction; In an Atlantean Bath; Lo Primordial; Strength of Dreams; Copán; Quo Vadis, California?; Our Lady of the Unicorn; Rêverie Gothique; The *Monodon monoceros*; Beyond Ultima Thule; Midnight Visitant; An Invocation; A Miracle in Miniature; Bialowieza; Farewell to Zita; *From the French of José-Maria de Heredia* (Oblivion; Pan; The Goatherd; The Shepherds; Hortorum Deus; On a Ruined Bust of Marble); Return of the Conquistadors; Enigma; Pale Fragile Unicorns; Fantaisie Médiévale; Illumination; Renewal; Epiphany; A Vision of a Castle Deep in Averonne; *Some Further Fragments from Atlantis* (Pharanos Descending; My Mind to Me an Empire Is; Likewise My Mind to Me a Cosmos Is; Re-ascension; Pharanos at Sunset; Oneiromancy; At the Outhanox); Beauty; Notes; SONGS AND SONNETS ATLANTEAN: THE THIRD SERIES: Foreword, by Terence McVicker; To a Dead City; Memorial; The Herdsman; Tropicality; Totem; Abandonment; Amaranth; Rapa-Nui; Pendant; A Game of Chess; The Chest from Otherwhere; Another Species of Epiphany; A Ballade of Prospero; The Reef of Coral; Discovery; The Bitch with Tits of Bronze; Codicil of Contradiction; *As One Jaguär to Another* (Or So You Say; The Warrior and the Jaguär; Well Met by Midnight; The Jaguär and the Astrologer; The Apprentice and the Jaguär; Quoctezu Bids Farewell; The Passing of an Astrologer; Epilogue); Cephalopod in Residence; Colossal Chambered Nautilus; Hippokampoi; *As One Seahorse to Another* (The Little Horses of the Ocean Sea; An Oldster Gives Advice; A Mating Dance by Sunlight; Labor and Deliverance; A Proper Mode of Life; A Ghostly Dance by Starlight; Dominium atque Apotheosis); Hadrian and Antinous; Pan and Priapus; A Ship Sails Out to Sea; Barcarolle; On Reading Edmund Spenser Once Again; Nine Happy Goldfish; An Archaeologist Uncovers the Past; Macabre Arabesque; The Scallop Shell; Triolets du Jour; A Villanelle Not à la Mode; Item: Ariel Sings; Ancestral Memory Revived; The Scroll; To a Conch; Of Some Eternal Realm; Past, Present, Future; Demeure Exotique; The Fugitives; The Music of the Spheres; To Rinaldo for Clark Ashton Smith; Forevermore the Rose; Tableau Sous-Marin; Predicament; Remonstration; Enlightenment; A Rendezvous with Pierrefonds; Rondeau of Winter; Rondeau of Summer; Pierrefonds, Poème en Pierre; A Ballade of Duality; Conundrum; Rondel of Time; Rondel of Space; The Ghost of a Dream; A Fanfare from Atlantis; Appendix; Index of Titles; Register of Subscribers.

Notes. Dust jacket illustration by Gordon R. Barnett. Interior illustrations by William Boddy and Lance Alexander. Paperback edition omits frontispiece of Elizabeth I and endpaper map illustrations by William Boddy. A combined edition of the three volumes of the author's *Songs and Sonnets Atlantean* (1971, 2003, 2005), a scintillating series of poems and prose poems influenced in part by Clark Ashton Smith (whom Sidney-Fryer knew during the latter stages of Smith's life), Edmund Spenser, and others, but also reflecting Sidney-Fryer's vigorously original poetic work. Originally published in a limited hardcover edition by subscription (300 copies, printed by Covington Group) and subsequently issued in paperback.

54. H. P. LOVECRAFT AND AUGUST DERLETH. *Essential Solitude: The Letters of H. P. Lovecraft and August Derleth: 1926–1931* (vol. 1) and *1932–1937* (vol. 2). Edited by David E. Schultz and S. T. Joshi. 2008 (rpt. 2013 [paper]). 880 pp. (numbered consecutively).

Contents. Volume 1: Introduction; A Note on This Edition; Abbreviations; Letters: Volume 2: Letters; APPENDIX : One for the Black Bag, by H. P. Lovecraft; The Weird Tale in English Since 1890 [excerpt], by August Derleth; A Master of the Macabre, by August Derleth; H. P. Lovecraft, Outsider, by August Derleth; H. P. L.—Two Decades After, by August Derleth. Glossary of Frequently Mentioned Names; Bibliography; Index.

Notes. Cover illustrations (different ones for the two volumes) by David C. Verba. 250 hardcover copies, printed by Covington Group. The first complete publication of Lovecraft's letters to Derleth, including 50 or so extant letters by Derleth to Lovecraft. Exhaustively annotated, with an immense bibliography of the hundreds of literary works (including their own) discussed by the authors. The edition constituted, informally, the commencement of Hippocampus Press's ambitious plan to issue the complete Lovecraft letters in book form. For the paperback edition, see item 121.

55. H. P. LOVECRAFT. *Collected Essays* (CD-ROM). 2008.

Notes. An electronic edition of the five volumes of *Collected Essays* (see items 18, 19, 29, 30, 36). It includes both text and digital images of all 13 issues Lovecraft's *Conservative*.

56. *Lovecraft Annual* No. 2 (2008). EDITED BY S. T. JOSHI. 215 pp.

Contents. Dispatches from the Providence Observatory: Astronomical Motifs and Sources in the Writings of H. P. Lovecraft, by T. R. Livesey; The Sickness unto Death in H. P. Lovecraft's "The Hound," by James Goho; Queer Tales? Sexuality, Race, and Architecture in "The Thing on the Doorstep," by Joel Pace; "Clever Lines": Some Thoughts on Lovecraft's "Ad Criticos," by Phillip A. Ellis; "The Rats in the Walls," the Rats in the Trenches, by Robert H. Waugh; Knowledge in the Void: Anomaly, Observation, and the Incomplete Paradigm Shift in H. P. Lovecraft's Fiction, by Kálmán Matolcsy; H. P. Lovecraft and the Archaeology of "Roman" Arizona, by Marc A. Beherec; Reviews; Briefly Noted.

Notes. Of particular note is Livesey's immense and penetrating study of Lovecraft's knowledge of astronomy.

57. JONATHAN THOMAS. *Midnight Call and Other Stories.* 2008. 258 pp.

Contents. Foreword, by S. T. Joshi; Eben's Portrait; The Weird Old Hole; The Returns of Johnny Mapleseed; Fingers of Stone; Conjurings and Celtic Holidays (A Thematic Set) (The May Day Melée, Explained; Doctor Farrell's Goddesses; Some Days Before Shadow Damsel; In the Wake of Bridget; Midnight Call); Damn the Wheelwright; The Road to Schwärmerei; McEveety among the Leisure Elect; The Judgment Birds; An Office Nymph; Another Psychic on Comp; Towbear to Hell; The Christmas Clones; Awakening of No Return; A Vampire Heart; Subway of the Dead; Graveside Friday Night; Dappled Ass; An Alternate History of Annette; Tendrils in Formaldehyde; Ariadne's Hair.

Notes. Cover illustration by David C. Verba. A substantial and well-received collection of stories by a writer who met S. T. Joshi when the latter was giving a lecture at Brown University. Joshi at once recognized Thomas's talent and encouraged him to assemble a collection. A few stories had appeared in Thomas's rare collection, *Stories from the Big Black House* (1992), but these were extensively revised; the other stories are previously unpublished.

58. RAMSEY CAMPBELL. *Inconsequential Tales.* [Edited by S. T. Joshi.] 2008. 249 pp.

Contents. Truth or Consequences; The Childish Fear; The Offering to the Dead; The Reshaping of Rossiter; The Void; The Other House; Broadcast; The Urge; The Sunshine Club; Writer's Curse; Property of the Ring; The Shadows in the Barn; Night Beat; The Precognitive Trip; Murders; Point of View; The Grip of Peace; Only the Wind; Morning Call; Pet; Hain's Island; Bait; Snakes and Ladders; The Burning; A Play for the Jaded.

Notes. Cover and interior illustrations by Jason C. Eckhardt. A volume Joshi had been encouraging Campbell for years to compile. When Joshi assisted Campbell in publishing a bibliography of his writings,

The Core of Ramsey Campbell (1995), he noticed that many of Campbell's stories remained uncollected, and Joshi at last prevailed upon Campbell to gather them for this volume. Two stories were previously unpublished. The self-deprecating title—modeled, perhaps, on T. E. D. Klein's *Reassuring Tales* (2007)—is Campbell's.

59. *Dead Reckonings* No. 4 (Fall 2008). EDITED BY S. T. JOSHI AND JACK M. HARINGA. 97 pp.

Contents. A Grab-Bag of Perverse Delight, by Donald R. Burleson [Thomas M. Disch, *The Word of God*]; Edge-of-Your-Seat Suspense, by Hank Wagner [Joe R. Lansdale, *Leather Maiden*]; An Epic and Long-Awaited Publication, by Donald Sidney-Fryer [Clark Ashton Smith. *The Complete Poetry and Translations, Volumes 1 and 2.*]; Dissecting Thomas Harris, by Bev Vincent [Benjamin Szumskyj, ed. *Dissecting Hannibal Lecter: Essays on the Novels of Thomas Harris.*]; A Slow-Moving Tsunami, by S. T. Joshi [Caitlín R. Kiernan, *Tales of Pain and Wonder*]; Horror on the Ice, by Rob Latham [Dan Simmons, *The Terror*]; "The Weird Old Hole" and Much More, by Sherry Austin [Jonathan Thomas, *Midnight Call and Other Stories*]; The Nightmares That Cling to Us, by John Langan [Ramsey Campbell, *Thieving Fear* and *Inconsequential Tales*]; Sometimes You Just Have to Gush, by Matt Cardin [Stephen Mark Rainey. *Other Gods;* Michael Shea. *The Autopsy and Other Tales*]; Ramsey Campbell, Probably; A Shadow Across the Heart, by Jack M. Haringa [Jack Ketchum, *Old Flames* and *Book of Souls*]; Faster Than You Can Read Them, by Ben P. Indick [Brian Keene. *Kill Whitey* and *Ghost Walk*]; Torture, Cannibalism, and Necrophilia, by Tony Fonseca [Bill Breedlove, ed. *Like a Chinese Tattoo;* Nick Mamatas and Sean Wallace, ed. *Realms: The First Year of Clarkesworld Magazine*]; Everyday Horrors, by Javier A. Martínez [Bentley Little, *The Vanishing* and *The Academy*]; Nightmares and Dreamscapes, by Robert Butterfield [Patrick McGrath, *Trauma;* Greg F. Gifune. *Dominion*]; Confessionals, by John Langan [Christopher Conlon, *Midnight on Mourn Street;* Graham Joyce, *How to Make Friends with Demons*]; Vampires Doing Good, by June Pulliam [Tananarive Due, *Blood Colony;* Jewell Parker Rhodes, *Yellow Moon*]; Only an Abundance of Horror, by Tony Fonseca [Weston Ochse, *Scarecrow Gods*]; Erotic Fantasies and Necromantic Mysteries, by Hank Wagner [Polly Frost, *Deep Inside;* Sarah Monette, *The Bone Key*]; The Departure of "Enigma," by Kevin Dole [Nicholas Royle, *The Enigma of Departure*]; Ambitious Reading and Ambitious Feeling, by Michael Marano [Steve Rasnic Tem and Melanie Tem, *The Man on the Ceiling*]; Put-Downable, But Pick-Upable Again, by Darrell Schweitzer [Alexandra Sokoloff, *The Price*]; A Gothic Landscape, by Jim Rockhill

[James Doig, ed. *Australian Gothic: An Anthology of Australian Supernatural Fiction, 1867–1939*]; Retrospective Reviews: The Line of Terror, by Arthur Machen [Walter de la Mare, *On the Edge*]; The Weird Scholar, by S. T. Joshi; Capsule Reviews; Correspondence.

60. KENNETH W. FAIG, JR. *The Unknown Lovecraft*. 2009. 253 pp.

Contents. Lovecraft: Artist or Poseur?; Quae Amamus Tuemur: Ancestors in Lovecraft's Life and Fiction; Whipple V. Phillips and the Owyhee Land and Irrigation Company; Lovecraft's Parental Heritage; The Friendship of Louise Imogen Guiney and Sarah Susan Phillips; The Unknown Lovecraft I: Political Operative; The Unknown Lovecraft II: Reluctant Laureate; Lovecraft's "He"; "The Silver Key" and Lovecraft's Childhood; The Dream-Quest of Unknown Kadath; Lovecraft's Unknown Friend: Dudley Charles Newton; R. H. Barlow; Robert H. Barlow as H. P. Lovecraft's Literary Executor: An Appreciation; Some Final Thoughts for Readers of This Collection; Sources.

Notes. Cover design (incorporating a photograph of Lovecraft) by Barbara Briggs Silbert. The date of the Lovecraft photo was given as 1936, based on a notation on the back of the photo, though it seems to be the one Lovecraft describes in a letter to R. H. Barlow [January 15, 1935]: "Has Talman sent you any of the surprise snaps he took at the gang meeting? I've just got a partial set—& I fared worst of all! The young rascal caught me as I was looking upward & saying something which put my mouth in an utterly comic position . . . as if I were going to whistle or expectorate!" A small number of copies were printed lacking the "Sources" section, and a few made it into circulation before the error was corrected. A rich collection of Faig's biographical essays on Lovecraft, including his landmark monograph on Barlow, which had never been published in its entirety aside from a limited edition.

61. S. T. JOSHI. *Classics and Contemporaries: Some Notes on Horror Fiction*. 2009. 291 pp.

Contents. Preface; I. SOME OVERVIEWS: Arkham House and Its Legacy; The Haunted House; Professionals and Amateurs; Some Thoughts on Weird Poetry; Bram and Bela and Mary and Boris; What the Hell Is Dark Suspense?; The Small Press. II. CLASSICS: Algernon Blackwood: The Starlight Man; Arthur Machen: A Minor Classic; William Hope Hodgson: Writer on the Borderland; E. F. Benson: Spooks and More Spooks; A. M. Burrage: The Ghost Man; Herbert S. Gorman: Where Is the Place Called Dagon?; Andrew Caldecott: The Well-Crafted Ghost; Rescuing Shirley Jackson. III. CONTEMPORARIES: Les

Daniels: The Sardonic Vampire; Dennis Etchison and His Masters; Thomas Tryon: The Return of the Posthumous Collaboration; Stephen King and God; Peter Straub and the Blue Pencil; Ramsey Campbell: Alone with a Master; Clive Barker: Weird Fiction as Subversion; David J. Schow: Zombies, Tapeworms, and Kamikaze Butterflies; Donald R. Burleson: Enmeshed in the Bizarre; Norman Partridge: Here to Stay; Thomas Harris: Lecter as Albatross; Thomas Ligotti: The Long and the Short of It; Michael Cisco: Ligotti Redivivus?; Sherry Austin: The Southern Ghost Story; Shades of Edgar and Ambrose. IV. SCHOLARSHIP: The Charting of Horror Literature; Classics and Contemporaries. V. H. P. LOVECRAFT: Some Lovecraft Editions; The Cthulhu Mythos; Lovecraft as a Character in Fiction; Some Lovecraft Scholarship (Barton L. St Armand; Donald R. Burleson; Peter Cannon; Robert M. Price; Kenneth W. Faig, Jr; Edward W. O'Brien, Jr; Robert H. Waugh); Index; Acknowledgements.

Notes. Cover illustration by Allen Koszowski, a playful homage to Virgil Finlay's famous drawing of Lovecraft in periwig and smallclothes (see item 18), with Joshi as the Old Gent. An extensive selection of Joshi's book reviews, chiefly from *Necrofile* but also from *Lovecraft Studies, Studies in Weird Fiction, Weird Tales,* and other periodicals. Although written over a span of more than two decades, the volume forms a kind of foretaste of Joshi's forthcoming comprehensive history of supernatural fiction.

62. ADAM NISWANDER. *The Hound Hunters.* 2009. 302 pp.

Notes. Cover illustration by Armand Cabrerra. (There are no interior illustrations, despite what the copyright page says.) An original Cthulhu Mythos novel by Niswander, and a loose sequel to *The Charm* (1993) and *The Serpent Slayers* (1994), published by Integra. *The Hound Hunters* had been scheduled for publication by Integra in 1995, and bound galleys had been issued, but the publisher collapsed before the book could be published. Niswander had outlined a thirteen-volume series of novels adapting the Cthulhu Mythos to a southwestern locale; for the next volume in the series, see item 69.

63. R. E. SPENCER. *The Lady Who Came to Stay.* ARTHUR RANSOME. *The Elixir of Life.* 2009. 153 + 180 pp.

Notes. Cover illustration of *The Lady Who Came to Stay* reprinted from the Knopf edition of 1933; cover illustration of *The Elixir of Life* is a detail from *The Alchemist* by Sir William Fettes Douglas. Part of the Lovecraft's Library series. A reprint of two novels that Lovecraft read and may have been influenced by: Ransome's fabulously rare *The Elix-*

ir of Life (1915) and Spencer's *The Lady Who Came to Stay* (1931). Joshi has written separate introductions to each work.

64. *Dead Reckonings* No. 5 (Spring 2009). EDITED BY S. T. JOSHI AND JACK M. HARINGA. 93 pp.

Contents. The Vampire as Action-Adventure Anti-Hero, by June Pulliam [Rio Youers, *Everdead*]; A Mask Made of Exposition, by Michael Marano [Gene Wolfe, *An Evil Guest*]; The Pathetic and the Mundane, by Kevin Dole [Quentin Crisp, *Shrike*]; Mythos and More Mythos, by Martin Andersson [Richard L. Tierney, *The Drums of Chaos*; Asamatsu Ken, *Queen of K'n-Yan*]; Forget-Me-Nots?, by Tony Fonseca [Ronald Damien Malfi, *Passenger*; Peter Atkins, *Moontown*]; A New Jungle Book, by Hank Wagner [Neil Gaiman, *The Graveyard Book*]; Abandon All Preconceptions, Ye Who Enter Here, by Sherry Austin [Ellen Datlow, ed., *Poe*]; Williams One, Clark Zero, by Robert Morrish [Simon Clark, *Vengeance Child*; Conrad Williams, *One*]; Mini-collections from Major Talent, by Matt Cardin [Douglas Smith, *Impossibilia*; Mark Samuels, *Glyphotech and Other Macabre Processes*]; Ramsey Campbell, Probably; Listing Towards Horror Paralyzed by Discomfort, by Jack M. Haringa [*British Invasion*, ed. Christopher Golden, Tim Lebbon, and James A. Moore]; Passing the Baton, by Ben P. Indick [*New Dark Voices II*, ed. Brian Keene; Jeremy C. Shipp, *Sheep and Wolves*]; Genius Loci, by John Langan [Cherie Priest, *Fathom*]; Enter Ghost, by Bev Vincent [Stieg Larsson, *The Girl with the Dragon Tattoo*; David Wroblewski, *The Story of Edgar Sawtelle*]; The Lovecraft Cult, by S. T. Joshi [Kenneth Hite, *Tour de Lovecraft: The Tales*; Robert M. Price, *Blasphemies & Revelations*]; Two Unique Visions of Horror, by Robert Butterfield [Scott Nicholson, *Scattered Ashes*; Tony Richards, *Shadows and Other Tales*]; Living on a Powder Keg, by Bev Vincent [Joe Hill, *Gunpowder*]; Can You Murder a Dream?, by John Edgar Browning [Jeffrey Ford, *The Drowned Life*]; Doing Your Homework, by Hank Wagner [F. Paul Wilson, *By the Sword*]; Waking to Nightmares, by Jack M. Haringa [Paul Tremblay, *The Little Sleep*]; The Supernatural in Prose and Verse, by Donald R. Burleson [S. T. Joshi, *Emperors of Dreams: Some Notes on Weird Poetry*; S. T. Joshi, *The Rise and Fall of the Cthulhu Mythos*; S. T. Joshi, *Classics and Contemporaries: Some Notes on Horror Fiction*]; The Perfect Museum Edition, by Darrell Schweitzer [Henry S. Whitehead, *Passing of a God and Other Stories*]; The Weird Scholar, by S. T. Joshi; Capsule Reviews.

65. *Lovecraft Annual* No. 3 (2009). EDITED BY S. T. JOSHI. 206 pp.

Contents. Lovecraft and the Ray-Gun, by T. R. Livesey; What Is "the Unnamable"? H. P. Lovecraft and the Problem of Evil, by James Goho; Some Notes on the Topographical Poetry of H. P. Lovecraft, by Phillip A. Ellis; The Theme of Distance in the Tales of H. P. Lovecraft, by Lorenzo Mastropierro; Lovecraft's Avatars: Azathoth, Nyarlathotep, Dagon, and Lovecraftian Utopias, by Brandon Reynolds; Self, Other, and the Evolution of Lovecraft's Treatment of Outsideness, by Massimo Berruti; Some Notes on Lovecraft's "The Transition of Juan Romero," by Leigh Blackmore; "The Shadow out of Time" and Time-Defiance, by Will Murray; Poems Not in *The Ancient Track*, by H. P. Lovecraft (ed. S. T. Joshi); Lovecraft and the Polar Myth, by John M. Navroth; Reviews; Briefly Noted.

66. H. L. MENCKEN. *Collected Poems*. Edited by S. T. Joshi. 2009. 145 pp.

Contents. Introduction, by S. T. Joshi; To R. K.; The Four-Foot Filipino: A Ballad of the Trenches; The Tin-Clads; Joe and Bobs; Auroral; One Man Band; A Frivolous Rondeau; A Few Lines; The Roorback and the Canard; Chrysanthemum; Canzonette; [Untitled]; An Ante-Christmas Rondeau; The Dawn of Love; [Untitled]; Fidelis ad Urnum; [Untitled]; A Ballad of Impecuniosity; A War Song; A Madrigal; A Song for Autumn; Nocturne; An Ode to a "Stein"; The Filipino Maiden; A Rondeau of Two Hours; When the Pipe Goes Out; Thanksgiving Day; Adlai; A Dirge; A Bacteriologal Romance; To O. P. K.; And Now Comes Congress; The Man That Guards the Grub; A Ballad of Looking; Well Buried; The Orf'cer Boy; A Paradox; Madrigal; The Song of the Slapstick; An Old, Old Story; Love and the Rose; The Coming of Winter; Outside, Old Year!; To Isaackhanmofakhammeddovlet; The Boy and the Man; The Donation Party; To Kruger; A Rondeau of Statesmanship; In Eating Soup; Serenade; Im Hinterland; The Snow; A Ballad of Fierce Fighters; The Pantoum of Congress; To Mrs. Nation; In Vaudeville; A Slug of Pessimism; An Ode to Nelson A.; To G. W.; A Sonnet to a Wienerwurst; The Ballade of the Rank and File; To Wu Ting Fang, Envoy Extraordinary and Minister Plenipotentiary; On Phyllis at the Play; Theatrical Alphabet; April; Dawn; A Villanelle; The Transport Gen'ral Ferguson; Faith; The Spanish Main; The Rondeau of Riches; A Ballade of Protest; Preliminary Rebuke; The Song of the Olden Time; The Ballad of Ships in Harbor; The Violet; September; Arabesque; The Rhymes of Mistress Dorothy; Roundel; Within the City Gates; Il Penseroso; Finis; War; On Passing the Island of San Salvador; Starting for the Play; Good-By, Divine Sarah!; The Old Trails; The Ballade of Cockaigne; Song; Invocation; The Voices; APPENDIX: A Kruger, by Edmond Rostand; Notes; Index of Titles; Index of First Lines.

Notes. Cover design (incorporating a photograph of Mencken) by Barbara Briggs Silbert. Perhaps an odd publication for Hippocampus Press, as both the author and the work are well outside the realms of horror or fantasy fiction; but the press has always sought to issue collected editions of poetry, and Mencken's poetry contains substantial merits. Mencken himself issued only 33 of his poems in his first published book, *Ventures into Verse* (1903). The others (most of them published in various columns in the *Baltimore Herald*) are uncollected.

67. JOSEPH S. PULVER, SR. *Blood Will Have Its Season.* 2009. 284 pp.

Contents. Foreword, by S. T. Joshi; Choosing; Carl Lee & Cassilda; A Line of Questions; PITCH nothing . . .; I, Like the Coyote; Blood Will Have Its Season; mr wind sits; The Prisoner; An American Tango Ending in Madness; Orchard Fruit; The Songs Cassilda Shall Sing, Where Flap the Tatters of the King; The Night Music of Oakdeene; Dogs Begin to Bark All Over My Neighborhood; Chasing Shadows; But the Day Is a Tomb of Claws; In This Desert Even the Air Burns; And She Walks into the Room . . .; a certain Mr. Hopfrog, Esq., Nightwalker; The Black Litany of Nug and Yeb; Erendira; An Engagement of Hearts; An Event Without Knives or Rope; One Side's Ice, One's Fire; A Spider in the Distance; PAIN; A Night of Moon and Blood, Then Holstenwall; Under the Mask Another Mask; W a t e r l l i e s; Yvrain's Black Dancers; No Exit Sign; Lovecraft's Sentence; Midnight on a Dead End Street in Noir City; The Master and Margeritha; Hello Is a Yellow Kiss; The Faces of She; Good Night and Good Luck; Patti Smith, Lovecraft, & I; The Collector and the Hand Puppet; The Only Thing We Have to Fear . . .; The Corridor; Stone Cold Fever.

Notes. Cover illustration by Thomas S. Brown. A scintillating collection of weird and fantasy tales by Pulver, previously known to the public as the author of the Lovecraftian novel *Nightmare's Disciple* (Chaosium, 1999).

68. H. P. LOVECRAFT AND ROBERT E. HOWARD. *A Means to Freedom: The Letters of H. P. Lovecraft and Robert E. Howard: 1930–1932* (vol. 1) and *1933–1937* (vol. 2). Edited by S. T. Joshi, David E. Schultz, and Rusty Burke. 2009 (rpt. 2011 [paper]). 1004 pp. (numbered consecutively).

Contents. Volume 1: Introduction; A Note on This Edition; Abbreviations; Letters; Volume 2: Letters; APPENDIX: With a Set of Rattlesnake Rattles; The Beast from the Abyss; Dr. I. M. Howard: Letters to H. P. Lovecraft; Glossary of Frequently Mentioned Names; Bibliography; Index.

Notes. Cover illustrations (different for the two volumes) by David C. Verba. Limited edition of 345 hardcover copies, printed by Covington Group. A project long in the works—the collected correspondence of Lovecraft and Howard over an intense six-year period. The wordage of Howard's letters exceeds that of Lovecraft's, in part because some of Lovecraft's letters do not survive. Many logistical and legal issues had to be resolved before the edition could be published. For the paperback edition, see item 91.

69. ADAM NISWANDER. *The War of the Whisperers.* 2009. 341 pp.

Notes. Cover illustration by Ron Leming. The fourth novel in Niswander's series of thirteen southwestern Cthulhu Mythos novels, and the second to be published by Hippocampus Press (see item 62).

70. DAN CLORE. *Weird Words: A Lovecraftian Lexicon.* 2009. 568 pp.

Notes. Cover illustration by Howard Wandrei. An immense dictionary of words used by Lovecraft and other writers of horror and fantasy fiction, with examples and citations extending back to the Tudor era. A monument of scholarship—a kind of *Oxford English Dictionary* for weird fiction.

71. MICHAEL ARONOVITZ. *Seven Deadly Pleasures.* 2009. 247 pp.

Contents. Foreword, by S. T. Joshi; How Bria Died; The Clever Mask; Quest for Sadness; The Legend of the Slither-Shifter; The Exterminator; Passive Passenger; Toll Booth.

Notes. Cover and interior art by Thomas S. Brown. The debut collection of short stories by a dynamic new writer, who had submitted his work to Joshi a year or so before.

72. NORA MAY FRENCH. *The Outer Gate: The Collected Poems of Nora May French*. Edited by Donald Sidney-Fryer and Alan Gullette. 2009. 254 pp.

Contents. Acknowledgments; Nora May French: One Still, Small Voice out of Time and Space; Sources; THE OUTER GATE: THE COLLECTED POEMS OF NORA MAY FRENCH: The Outer Gate; Rain; Best-Loved; The Rose; Between Two Rains; The Message; By the Hospital; "Oh, Dryad Thoughts"; My Maid of Dreams; Music in the Pavilion; Rebuke; In Camp; The Nymph; Vivisection; The Stranger; The Constant Ones; Instinct; The Lost Chimneys; San Francisco, New Year's, 1907; The Panther Woman; The Poppy Field; Poppies; You; Just a Dog; Mirage; Dusk; THE SPANISH GIRL; PART I: I. The Vine; II. The Chapel; III. The Garden; IV; V; VI; VII; PART II; I; II; III; IV; V; VI; VII; PART III: I; II; III; IV; V; VI; VII; VIII; The Garden of Dolores; Answered; Indifference; After-Knowledge; Be Silent, Love; Two Spendthrift Kings; Growth; Change; Wistaria; How Ends the Day?; My Nook; When Plaintively and Near the Cricket Sings; The Little Memories; Pass By; In Empty Courts; Down the Trail; "Bells from Over the Hills Sound Sweet"; In Town; Moods; A Misty Morning; Two Songs; Noon; Your Beautiful Passing; By Moonlight; A Dream-Love; One Day; The Mission Graves; Along the Track; A Place of Dreams; Think Not, O Lilias?; The Suicide; "To Rosy Buds . . . .": Yesterday; The Mourner; Ave atque Vale; At the End; Notes; NOTICES: General Note; San Francisco *Bulletin*, Friday evening, 15 November 1907; San Francisco *Call*, Friday, 15 November 1907; San Francisco *Chronicle*, Friday, 15 November 1907; San Francisco *Chronicle*, Friday, 15 November 1907, notes; San Francisco *Examiner*, Friday, November 15, 1907; Los Angeles *Times*, Friday, November 15, 1907; Los Angeles *Times*, Sunday, November 17, 1907; Los Angeles *Times*, Monday, 18 November 1907; *Town Talk*, Saturday, 23 November 1907; *Current Literature*, June 1908; San Francisco *Call*, Sunday, June 12, 1910; *The New Age, A Weekly Review of Politics, Literature and Art*, Thursday, 14 July 1910; *Current Literature*, September 1910; *Die Nieuwe Gids* [*The New Guidebook*], November 1910; Poems by Nora May French, *The California Literary Pamphlets*, Number 2; Helen (Augusta) French Hunt (1883–1973): A Little Memoir (A Friendship, 1968–1973); TRIBUTES: General Note; Sources; Untitled, by Henry Anderson Lafler; Sonnet, by Henry Anderson Lafler; Sonnet, by Henry Anderson Lafler; The Pearl, by Henry Anderson Lafler; Nora May French, by George Sterling; The Ashes in the Sea, by George Sterling; Nora May French, In Memoriam, by Louise Gebhard Cann; To Nora May French, by Clark Ashton Smith; "Thy Spirit Walks the Sea," by Donald Sidney-Fryer; [Nora May French], by Dorothy Jesse Beagle; For Nora May in Paradise, by Mary Rudge; Nora May, by Alan Gullette; For Nora May French, by Val Beatts; Quicksilver, by Do Gentry; November, by Do Gentry; The Poet Replies, by Do Gentry; Dear Critic, Dear Abstraction, by Do Gentry; The Poet with Us: Nora May French, by Marvin R. Hiemstra; Index of Titles; Index of First Lines.

Notes. Cover photograph of Nora May French by Arnold Genthe, cover design by Barbara Briggs Silbert. A landmark of scholarship: the editors not only unearthed numerous poems by French (1881–1907) not included in her lone posthumous volume, *Poems* (1910), but also included a generous sampling of reviews of that book along with other interesting matter. French was a beautiful and talented poet in George Sterling's literary circle who committed suicide at the age of 26. Her delicate and sensitive poetry retains a following to this day.

73. *Dead Reckonings* No. 6 (Fall 2009). EDITED BY S. T. JOSHI AND JACK M. HARINGA. 94 pp.

Contents. Crooked House, by Bev Vincent [Sarah Langan, *Audrey's Door*]; From the Sensuous to the Sophomoric, by Zachary Z. E. Bennett [David Niall Wilson, *Ennui and Other Stories of Madness*]; Ending the World: Do's and Don'ts, by Kevin Dole [Lavie Tidhar and Nir Yaniv, *The Tel Aviv Dossier*; Tim Lebbon, *Bar None*]; For Aficionados Only, by Robert Butterfield [Simon Stranzas, *Cold to the Touch*; Alan M. Clark and Elizabeth Massie, *D. D. Murphry, Secret Policeman*]; Destined for the Remainder Shelves, by Scott David Briggs [Brian Knight, *Reservoir Gods*; Seamus Cooper, *The Mall of Cthulhu*]; The Way of Escape, by Sherry Austin [Barbara Roden, *Northwest Passages*; Kealan Patrick Burke, *The 121 to Pennsylvania and Others*]; More Than Just Tentacles, by Martin Andersson [Henrik Harksen, ed., *Eldritch Horrors*; Ellen Datlow, ed., *Lovecraft Unbound*]; Apocalypse Nowadays, by John Edgar Browning [Greg F. Gifune, *Children of Chaos*; Greg F. Gifune, *Blood in Electric Blue*]; Gold, Silver, and Bronze, by Hank Wagner [Stephen Jones, ed. *The Mammoth Book of Best New Horror 20*; Charles Black, ed. *The Fourth Black Book of Horror*; Richard Chizmar, ed. *Shivers V.*]; Ramsey Campbell, Probably: The Edited Version; Impalements at Piccadilly Circus, by John Edgar Browning [Dacre Stoker and Ian Holt, *Dracula the Un-Dead*]; Horror as an Afterthought, by Tony Fonseca [John Harwood, *The Séance*; Gemma Mawdsley, *The Paupers' Graveyard*]; Of Fishmen and Lovecraftian Place-Names, by John M. Navroth [James A. Moore, *Deeper*]; A Modern "Heart of Darkness," by S. T. Joshi [Caitlín R. Kiernan, *The Red Tree*]; The Banality of Evil, by June Pulliam [Bentley Little, *His Father's Son*]; Two (or More) Tales of Dark Religion, by Matt Cardin [Leopoldo Gout, *Ghost Radio*; Brian Evenson, *Last Days*]; Robert Bloch: *Psycho* and Beyond, by Henrik Sandbeck Harksen [Benjamin Szumskyj, ed., *The Man Who Collected Psychos: Critical Essays on Robert Bloch*]; Tradition Viewed through Different Lenses, by Jim Rockhill [Scott Thomas, *The Garden of Ghosts*; John Langan, *Mr. Gaunt and Other Uneasy Encounters*]; Formula and Geography, by Richard Bleiler [Graham Masterton, *Basilisk*; Danel Olson, ed., *Exotic Gothic 2: New Tales of Taboo*]; A Window onto the Real Poe, by Benjamin F. Fisher [John Ward Ostrom, ed., *The Collected Letters of Edgar Allan Poe*]; Vampires, the Holocaust, and 9/11, by Michael Marano [Guillermo del Toro and Chuck Hogan, *The Strain*]; The Weird Tradition in Poetry, by Darrell Schweitzer [Donald Wandrei, *Sanctity and Sin*; Rain Graves, *Barfodder*]; The Perfect Length for Horror, by Hank Wagner [Sarah Pinborough. *The Language of Dying*; Terry Lamsley. *R.I.P.*; Joel Lane. *The Witnesses Are Gone*]; The Weird Scholar, by S. T. Joshi.

Notes. The last issue with Haringa as coeditor.

74. DONALD R. BURLESON. *Wait for the Thunder: Stories for a Stormy Night.* 2010. 300 pp.

Contents. Tumbleweeds; One-Night Strand; Hopscotch; Jigsaw; Country Living; Sheep-Eye; Tummerwunky; A Student of Geometry; Fwoo; Down in the Mouth; Crayons; The Weeping Woman of White Crow; Spider Willie; Jack O'Lantern Jack; The Watcher at the Window; Desert Dreams; Grampa Pus; Gramma Grunt; Sheets; Up and About; Blessed Event; The Cryptogram; Leaves; Pump Jack; Lujan's Trunk; Wait for the Thunder; Papa Loaty.

Notes. Cover illustration by Thomas S. Brown. A substantial collection of stories by Burleson, who has established himself both as a leading literary scholar (especially of H. P. Lovecraft) and a short story writer and novelist. The volume includes stories published since the issuance of his previous collection, *Beyond the Lamplight* (Jack o' Lantern Press, 1996).

75. H. B. DRAKE. *The Shadowy Thing.* 2010. 245 pp.

Notes. Cover illustration taken from the 1928 A. L. Burt reprint of *The Shadowy Thing*. Part of the Lovecraft's Library series. A reprint of the novel first published in the UK as *The Remedy* (1925) and in the US as *The Shadowy Thing* (1928). Lovecraft read it not long after publication, and it manifestly influenced "The Thing on the Doorstep" (1933). Contains an introduction by S. T. Joshi.

76. ROBERT M. PRICE, EDITOR. *The Tindalos Cycle*. 2010. 365 pp.

Contents: Chock Full o' Mutts (introduction), by Robert M. Price; The Maker of Moons, by Robert W. Chambers; The Death of Halpin Frayser, by Ambrose Bierce; The Space-Eaters, by Frank Belknap Long; The Hounds of Tindalos, by Frank Belknap Long; The Letters of Halpin Chalmers, by Peter Cannon; The Death of Halpin Chalmers, by Perry M. Grayson; The Madness out of Time, by Lin Carter; The Hound of the Partridgevilles, by Peter Cannon; Through Outrageous Angles, by David C. Kopaska-Merkel and Ronald McDowell; Firebrands of Torment, by Michael Cisco; The Shore of Madness, by Ann K. Schwader; Gateway to Forever, by Frank Belknap Long; The Gift of Lycanthropy, by Frank Belknap Long; The War Among the Gods, by Adrian Cole; The Ways of Chaos, by Ramsey Campbell; Juggernaut, by C. J. Henderson; Scarlet Obeisance, by Joseph S. Pulver, Sr.; The Horror from the Hills, by Frank Belknap Long; Pompelo's Doom, by Ann K. Schwader; Confession of the White Acolyte, by Ann K. Schwader; When Chaugnar Wakes, by Frank Belknap Long; The Elephant God of Leng, by Robert M. Price; Death Is an Elephant, by Robert Bloch; The Dweller in the Pot by Frank Chimesleep Short, by Robert M. Price; But It's A Long Dark Road, by Joseph S. Pulver, Sr.; Nyarlatophis: A Fable of Ancient Egypt, by Stanley C. Sargent; Mind-Pilot, by William Laughlin.

Notes. Cover illustration by Thomas S. Brown. A rich collection of stories (some of them parodies) playing off of the Hounds of Tindalos, as created in the story of that title by Frank Belknap Long.

77. THOMAS LIGOTTI. *The Conspiracy against the Human Race.* 2010 (rpt. 2011 [paper]). 219 pp.

Notes. Cover design and photograph of the author by Jennifer Gariepy; cover production by Barbara Briggs Silbert. Limited hardcover edition of 1150 copies, printed by Covington Group. For the first time, we also issued roughly 100 uncorrected proof copies in paperback, in advance of publication of the hardcover. A remarkable philosophical treatise by Ligotti, best known as one of the most dynamic and innovative writers of supernatural literature to emerge in recent years. The volume (which includes its share of literary criticism, including discussions of Lovecraft and other weird writers) is a searching examination of the fundamental wretchedness of the human race.

78. JONATHAN THOMAS. *Tempting Providence*. 2010. 261 pp.

Contents: Foreword, by Sherry Austin; Dead Men's Shoes; Into Your Tenement I'll Creep; Tempting Providence; A Different Kind of Heartworm; Gumball Man; The Silence in the Copse; The Lord of the Animals; The Salvage Saints; Passenger Bastion; Power of Midnight; The Men at the Mound; Three Ounces over Advent.

Notes. Cover illustration by Thomas S. Brown. The second collection of Thomas's short fiction featuring a number of richly evocative novelettes, following the well-received *Midnight Call* (see item 57). Most of the stories were previously unpublished.

79. *Dead Reckonings* No. 7 (Spring 2010). EDITED BY S. T. JOSHI AND TONY FONSECA. 120 pp.

Contents. Realms of Perilous Delight, by Jim Rockhill [Richard Gavin, *The Darkly Splendid Realm*; Matt Cardin, *Dark Awakenings*]; The Red and the Blue, by Scott Connors [H. P. Lovecraft and Robert E. Howard, *A Means to Freedom*; Robert E. Howard, *The Horror Stories of Robert E. Howard* and *Heroes in the Wind: From Kull to Kane*]; A Macabre Display, by Javier A. Martínez [Jeffrey Thomas, *Thirteen Specimens: A Collection of the Bizarre*]; The Evil That Lurks Inside Us, by Jonathan Johnson [Michael Aronovitz, *Seven Deadly Pleasures*]; The Eldritch and the Cosmic, by Martin Andersson [S. T. Joshi, ed., *Black Wings: New Tales of Lovecraftian Horror*]; Rain, Rain, Everywhere, by S. T. Joshi [Ramsey Campbell, *Creatures of the Pool* and *Just Behind You*]; My Dear Watson, It's a Zombie Raccoon!, by Tony Fonseca [Martin H. Greenberg and Kerrie Hughes, ed., *Zombie Raccoons and Killer Bunnies*; John Joseph Adams, ed., *The Improbable Adventures of Sherlock Holmes*]; Where's the Plot?, by Andy K. Trevathan [L. A. Banks, *Undead on Arrival* and "Ev'ry Shut Eye Ain't Asleep"]; Living in a Topolganger, by Rob Latham [China Miéville, *The City & ytiC ehT*]; B-Grade and Z-Grade, by Matt Cardin [Richard Laymon, *Flesh* and *Dark Mountain*]; Lesser Straub, But Still Worth Reading, by Richard Bleiler [Peter Straub, *A Dark Matter*]; Ramsey Campbell, Probably: Restyling for Our Time; Bloodbath and Mayhem, by Lisa Nunn [Graham Masterton, *Death Mask* and *Blind Panic*]; Road Dogs and Iron Dead, by S. T. Joshi [Norman Partridge, *Lesser Demons*]; Horrors Down Under, by Leigh Blackmore [Felicity Dowker, *Phantasy Made Grotesk*; Robert Hood, *Creeping in Reptile Flesh*]; The Dead Return and They Have Bite, by Van Viator [Edward Lee, *The Golem*; Ray Garton, *Bestial*]; Less Artful Than Enthusiastic, by Robert Butterfield [Gord Rollo, *Crimson* and *Strange Magic*]; All That Glitters . . ., by Kevin Dole [Ellen Datlow, ed., *The Best Horror of the Year*,

Volume One; William F. Nolan and Jason V Brock, ed., *The Bleeding Edge*]; Post-Columbine and the Gothic, by John Edgar Browning [Gary A. Braunbeck, *Far Dark Fields*]; Cautionary Tales, by Antoinette Winstead [Dean R. Koontz, *Dean Koontz's Frankenstein: Dead and Alive;* Conrad Williams, *Decay Inevitable*]; A Matheson Sampler, by Darrell Schweitzer [Richard Matheson, *The Box*]; The Permeability of Flesh, by Vicky Gilpin [Brian Keene, *Castaways* and *Urban Gothic*]; Lycanthropes and Rotters, by Kendra Kuss Ditto [Laurell K. Hamilton, *Skin Trade;* Cherie Priest, *Boneshaker*]; Scarifyingly Assured, by Matt Cardin [John Langan, *House of Windows*]; Weaponized Affluence, by Michael Marano [Suzanne Collins, *The Hunger Games* and *Catching Fire*]; Skipping the Light Fandango, by Melissa Ursula Dawn Goldsmith [Michael Long, *Beautiful Monsters: Imagining the Classic in Musical Media*]; Cthulhu in San Francisco, by Scott David Briggs [Michael Shea, *Copping Squid and Other Mythos Tales*]; Capsule Reviews.

Notes. The first issue with Fonseca as coeditor.

80. S. T. JOSHI. *I Am Providence: The Life and Times of H. P. Lovecraft.* 2010 (rpt. 2013 [paper]). 2 vols. x, 1151 pp. (numbered consecutively).

   Notes. Cover illustrations consist of photographs of H. P. Lovecraft (different for each volume). Unabridged and updated version of Joshi's *H. P. Lovecraft: A Life* (Necronomicon Press, 1996), with more than 150,000 words restored to the text and much of it brought up to date to take account of recent discoveries in Lovecraft's life and work. Published in a limited hardcover edition (1000 copies) by subscription. For the paperback edition, see item 114.

81. *Lovecraft Annual* No. 4 (2010). EDITED BY S. T. JOSHI. 206 pp.

   Contents. Lovecraft's "The Bride of the Sea" and the Uses of Bathos, by Manuel Pérez-Campos; Following "The Ancient Track," by Jonathan Adams (includes musical composition, "The Ancient Track," by Adams); Letters to Carl Ferdinand Strauch, by H. P. Lovecraft; Appendix: A Library Goes Regionalist, by Carl F. Strauch; The Construction of Race in the Early Poetry of H. P. Lovecraft, by Phillip A. Ellis; The Ecstasies of "The Thing on the Doorstep," "Medusa's Coil," and Other Erotic Studies by Robert H. Waugh; Notes on a Nonentity, by H. P. Lovecraft; In Memoriam: Dr. Harry K. Brobst (1909–2010), by Christopher M. O'Brien; Time, Space, and Natural Law: Science and Pseudo-Science in Lovecraft, by S. T. Joshi; Reviews; Briefly Noted.

Notes. Of note are the lengthy and penetrating discussion of Lovecraft's poetry by Pérez-Campos and the musical setting of "The Ancient Track" by Adams, a professional composer.

82. *Dead Reckonings* No. 8 (Fall 2010). EDITED BY S. T. JOSHI AND TONY FONSECA. 114 pp.

Contents. His Best in Years: King in Fine Form, by Hank Wagner [Stephen King, *Just After Sunset*; Stephen King, *Under the Dome*]; A Sheaf of Horrific Delights, by Leigh Blackmore [Richard L. Tierney, *Savage Menace and Other Poems*]; Motels, Arachnids, and High Heels, by Scott David Briggs [Donald R. Burleson, *Wait for the Thunder*]; Custer's Last Stand, by Bev Vincent [Dan Simmons, *Black Hills*]; Is the Soul Changeless?, by Kendra Ditto [Michael Schiefelbein, *Vampire Maker*; Gail Carriger, *Changeless*]; Doubly Disappointing, by Tony Fonseca [Robert R. McCammon, *Mystery Walk*; Jeffrey Thomas, *Thought Forms*]; Horrors Cosmic and Personal, by Javier A. Martínez [Brian Keene, *Darkness on the Edge of Town*; Ray Garton, *Scissors*]; On the Rack, by Michael Marano [Michael Marshall Smith, *What Happens When You Wake Up in the Night*; Tom Fletcher, *The Safe Children*; Joel Lane, *Black Country*; Alison Moore, *When the Door Closed, It Was Dark*]; A Portrait of the Artist, by Steven J. Mariconda [S. T. Joshi, *I Am Providence: The Life and Times of H. P. Lovecraft*]; The Men Behind the Curtain, by Matt Cardin [Thomas Ligotti, *The Conspiracy against the Human Race*; H. P. Lovecraft, *Against Religion*]; Ramsey Campbell, Probably: The Missing Bits; What If Cthulhu Won?, by Martin Andersson [Darrell Schweitzer, ed., *Cthulhu's Reign*]; Shock or Schlock?, by Hank Wagner [Joe R. Lansdale, *Sanctified and Chicken-Fried*; John Skipp and Cody Goodfellow, *Jake's Wake*]; Horror and Fantasy for the Impecunious, by S. T. Joshi [Michael Kelahan, ed., *The Screaming Skull*; Michael Kelahan, ed., *The End of the World*; Sir Arthur Conan Doyle, *The Horror of the Heights*; Washington Irving, *The Legend of Sleepy Hollow*; Bram Stoker, *Dracula's Guest*; Oscar Wilde, *The Picture of Dorian Gray*]; A Werewolf Story with (Sharp) Teeth, by Robert Butterfield [Tom Fletcher, *The Leaping*]; Writing Above the Zombie Line, by Vicky Gilpin [Darrell Schweitzer and Martin H. Greenberg, ed., *Full Moon City*; Scott Edelman, *What Will Come After*]; Nutrition for the Dead, by Leigh Blackmore [Chris Lane, *Zombies: A Record of the Year of Infection*]; The United States of the Undead, by John Edgar Browning [Robin Becker, *Brains: A Zombie Memoir*]; Two Anthologies, 45 Stories, by Richard Bleiler [Ellen Datlow, ed., *Darkness: Two Decades of Modern Horror*; Stephen Jones, ed., *The Mammoth Book of the Best of Best New Horror*]; A Broad Range of Strange, by Jonathan Johnson

[Jonathan Thomas, *Tempting Providence*]; Darkness with Depth, by Robert Butterfield [Maurice Broaddus and Jerry Gordon, ed., *Dark Faith*]; What Lurks in the Dark, by Van P. Viator [Alyson Hagy, *Ghosts of Wyoming*; Daniel McGachey, *They That Dwell in Dark Places*]; New Writers, New Horror, by John Edgar Browning [Jeani Rector, ed., *And Now the Nightmare Begins: The Horror Zine*]; Dante of the Dead, by Matt Cardin [Kim Paffenroth. *Valley of the Dead: The Truth Behind Dante's Inferno*]; Sympathy for Ig, by John Langan [Joe Hill, *Horns*]; Living in London Is Overrated, by Andy Trevathan [Tim Lebbon, *30 Days of Night: Fear of the Dark*]; A Ghost Melodrama, by June Pulliam [Simon Clark, *Ghost Monster*]; What If?, by Antoinette Winstead [Tananarive Due, *Blood Colony*]; Murder Most Macabre, by Tony Fonseca [Joe R. Lansdale, *The Bottoms*]; The Weird Scholar, by S. T. Joshi; Capsule Reviews.

83. JOSEPH S. PULVER, SR. *Sin & Ashes*. 2010. 325 pp.

Contents. Death's Head Blues, by Laird Barron; Love Her Madly; She's Waiting . . .; *First There Is a Mountain . . . Then*; In This Desert Even the Air Burns; Even Night; Crow in Trick Town; When the Deal Goes Down; Devil's Got the Walkin' Blues; Dead 'Round Here Tonight; The Delirium of a Worm-Wizard; As the Sun Still Burns Away; Caligari, Again; Long-Stemmed Ghost Words; When the Moon Comes to Call; After Reading Michaux's "In the Land of Magic"; The Walking Man Walks; Silent No Longer; The Maiden of the Pines; Last Year in Carcosa; Scarlet Obeisance; Rendezvous Under Shadow Bridge; in front of an empty house in dead city; Ain't No Love on the Street; Perfect Grace; Kynothrabian Dirge; The Exorcism of Iagsat; Lonesome Separate Ways; Just Another Desert Night with Blood; After Death; I Often Dream of Words; Forever Changes; In the White Walls of Silence; Mother Stands for Comfort; Blow Wind Blow; 8's & Aces; A One-Way Fare; Don't Look Back; Long is the way and hard . . .; huddled in rags in a Kingsport alley . . .; Dead Ends and Empties; Sharp Fangs + Blood = Murder; Saint Nicholas Hall; Funeral in a Hate Field; An Orange Tick-Tick-Tick- Tick-Tick; Engravings; The Last Few Nights in a Life of Frost; Epilogue for Two Voices; To Live and Die in Arkham; The Last Twenty Miles of Wandering Again; Acknowledgments.

Notes: Cover illustration by J. Karl Bogartte. A second collection of horrific, fantastic, and surrealistic fiction by Pulver, following on his well-received first collection (item 67).

84. FRED PHILLIPS. *From the Cauldron*. 2010. 132 pp.

Contents. THE FAIR FOLK: The Fair Folk; Metamorphosis; Giliniel; Sleep; De la Marche; One More; The Little Stone; Fleeting Hours; Frederick of Holland; On the Heath; Madrigal to Dian Alene; A Winter Night's Sleep; The Old Tavern; Ode to Asbjorn Gustavsson Haarfagr; Final Quest; Bane of Aeacus; The Gathering of Clan Creachain; The Formula; The Tale of the Scribe; Burleycon 1973; Chanson de Guerre; The Printed Grail; The Inn at the Side of the Road; The Mask; Yesudai; The Honour of Princes; Moira; They Also Rule, Who Only Stand and Baste; The Ballad of the Four Sons; Aisling for Mary Radich; Sonnet LIII. R.E.H. Style #3; Quest; Stand or Fall; The Price of Blood; Tiresias; WEIGHED IN THE SCALES: Origin; Ephemera; Chagrin; Sortilege; A Fragrance; Apathy; Futility; Damozel Alayne; Epitaph on an Unknown Howe in the Foothills of Wales; The Poet to His Bed; Angelique Perdue; Rendezvous; Toilette d'Angelique; Meistersang; At the Inn; Samhain; A Peek at Dürer; Discovery; Wrapped in Fabrics Red; Weighed in the Scales; To Clark Ashton Smith; Conundrum; Anomaly; Raw, New Things; PHANTASMS: The Pathways of the Dead; The Lost Legend of Ingoldsby; A Lovecraftian's Eye-View of Kipling; The Elder Ones; The Lost City; The Book; Janandra; Predecessors; Buried Truths; Caveat; The Presence; The Codex; Outpost; Somnambulist; Witness; A Lovecraftian Reads Caesar Midnight on Hallowe'en; Silent Watchers; The Shop; The Steeple; Recompense; Chiaroscuro; Impasse; Volte-Face; The Sword; Pale Visitor; The House; The Street; Wyckham; Phantasm; Erato; The Wanderer; The Donjon; Rubaiyat of Rub al-Khali; The Journey; Off the Beaten Track; The Pit; The Keep; The Travelers.

Notes. Cover illustration by Howard Wandrei. A distinctive collection of weird and fantastic poetry by Phillips, an elder statesman in the world of Lovecraftian and fantasy fandom.

85. S. T. JOSHI, EDITOR. *A Weird Writer in Our Midst: Early Criticism of H. P. Lovecraft.* 2010. 264 pp.

Contents. Introduction, by S. T. Joshi; I. RECOLLECTIONS OF LOVE-CRAFT: Howard P. Lovecraft [1890–1937], by Walter J. Coates; Amateur Affairs, by Hyman Bradofsky; [Letter to the Editor], by Robert Bloch; Interlude with Lovecraft, by Stuart M. Boland; Howard Phillips Lovecraft, by Muriel E. Eddy; I Met Lovecraft, by Paul Livingston Keil; The Man Who Came at Midnight, by Ruth M. Eddy; II. CRITICISM IN LOVECRAFT'S LIFETIME: A Note on Howard P. Lovecraft's Verse, by Rheinhart Kleiner; Howard P. Lovecraft's Fiction, by

W. Paul Cook; The Vivisector, by Zoilus [Alfred Galpin]; Preface to
The Shunned House, by Frank Belknap Long, Jr.; A Weird Writer Is in
Our Midst, by Vrest Orton; The Sideshow, by B. K. Hart; What
Makes a Story Click?, by J. Randle Luten; III. COMMENTS FROM
READERS; IV. CRITICISM FROM THE FAN WORLD: H. P. Lovecraft,
Outsider, by August Derleth; A Master of the Macabre, by August
Derleth; Disbelievers Ever, by R. W. Sherman; The Last of H. P.
Lovecraft, by J. B. Michel; What of H. P. Lovecraft? or, A Commen-
tary upon J. B. Michel, by Autolycus; H. P. Lovecraft: Strange Weav-
er, by J. Chapman Miske; Lovecraft and Benefit Street, by Dorothy
Walter; [Letters to the Editor], by Thomas Ollive Mabbott; A Plea for
Lovecraft, by W. Paul Cook; Let's All Jump on H.P.L., by P. Schuyler
Miller; Howard Phillips Lovecraft, by Michael Harrison; The Love-
craft Cult, by Arthur F. Hillman; Lovecraft Is 86, by Francis T. Laney;
Rusty Chains, by John Brunner; Some Notes on HPL, by Sam Mos-
kowitz, Fritz Leiber, Edward Wood, and John Brunner; V. NOTICES
FROM THE LITERARY COMMUNITY: Mystery and Adventure, by Will
Cuppy; Horror Story Author Published by Fellow Writers, by Anony-
mous; [Review of *The Outsider and Others*], by T. O. Mabbott; Such
Pulp as Dreams Are Made On, by Robert Allerton Parker; Macabre,
Lyrical and Weird, by Peter De Vries; Mystery and Adventure, by
Will Cuppy; Nightmare in Cthulu, by William Poster; Books Alive, by
Vincent Starrett; Bookman's Holiday, by Charles Collins; Mystery and
Adventure, by Will Cuppy; Poesque Doodles, by Marjorie Farber;
Books Alive, by Vincent Starrett; The Phoenix Nest, by William Rose
Benét; [Review of *Supernatural Horror in Literature*], by Fred Lewis
Pattee; Pilgrims through Space and Time, by J. O. Bailey; Imagination
Runs Wild, by Richard B. Gehman; Books Alive, by Vincent Starrett;
A Bookman's Notebook, by Joseph Henry Jackson; Sabbat-Night
Reading, by E. O. D. Keown; Of Good and Evil, by [Anthony Powell];
The Genius Who Lived Backwards, by Vincent H. Gaddis; APPENDIX:
Some Vignettes; Notes; Index.

Notes. Cover illustration by Jason C. Eckhardt. An extensive collection of criticism of Lovecraft—early articles in the amateur and fan
press, readers' comments from *Weird Tales* and *Astounding Stories*, and
reviews in magazines and newspapers—charting Lovecraft's emergence from a pulp writer to an established literary figure.

86. DERRICK HUSSEY, S. T. JOSHI, AND DAVID E. SCHULTZ. *Ten Years of Hippocampus Press: 2000–2010.* 2010. 80 pp.

Contents. Foreword, by Derrick Hussey; My Years with Hippocampus Press, by S. T. Joshi; Publications of Hippocampus Press: 2000–2010; Index of Authors, Editors, and Artists.

Notes. Cover design by Barbara Briggs Silbert, featuring the distinctive spiderweb logo designed by Anastasia Damianakos. In the grand tradition of August Derleth and Arkham House, the leading figures behind Hippocampus Press provide a history and bibliography of the firm's publications during its first ten years of existence.

87. *Dead Reckonings* No. 9 (Spring 2011). EDITED BY S. T. JOSHI AND TONY FONSECA. 85 pp.

Contents. Sculptures in Prose, by S. T. Joshi [Caitlín R. Kiernan, *The Ammonite Violin*]; They Grow Up So Fast, The Little Monsters, by June Pulliam [M. T. Anderson, *Thirsty*; Patrick McCabe, *Emerald Germs of Ireland*]; Imagination as Arbiter, by Jim Rockhill [Laird Barron, *Occultation*]; Attack of the Subgenre Anthologies: Female Vampires and Southern Shamblers, by Vicky Gilpin [Ty Schwamberger and Jessy Marie Roberts, ed., *Fem-Fangs*; Jessy Marie Roberts, ed., *Gone with the Dirt: Undead Dixie*]; Not Your Average Minas, by Tony Fonseca [Charity Becker, *Presence: Wolf Moon*; Karen Essex, *Dracula in Love*]; E'ch-Pi-El and Two-Gun Bob, by Leigh Blackmore [S. T. Joshi, ed., *A Weird Writer in Our Midst: Early Criticism of H. P. Lovecraft*; Darrell Schweitzer, ed., The Robert E. Howard Reader]; Weird Japan, by Darrell Schweitzer [Higashi Masao, ed., *Kaiki: Uncanny Tales from Japan*]; Killed by a Big Ol' Book, by Andy Trevathan [Paula Guran, ed., *The Year's Best Dark Fantasy and Horror 2010*]; Savoring the Tragic, by Richard Bleiler [Steve Duffy, *Tragic Life Stories*; Frances Oliver, *The Ghosts of Summer*]; Bring Out Your Undead, by June Pulliam [Paula Guran, ed., *Zombies: The Recent Dead*]; Down Dark and Lonesome Highways, by Richard Gavin [Joseph S. Pulver, Sr., *Sin & Ashes*]; Ramsey Campbell, Probably: The Poetry of Shadows; The Shadow Theatre of One's Memory, by John Edgar Browning [Otto Penzler, ed., *Coffins: The Vampire Archives, Volume 3*; Peter Crowther and Nick Gevers, ed., *The Company He Keeps*]; Two Authors with Their Own Voice, by Robert Butterfield [Brian James Freeman, *The Painted Darkness*; Mark Howard Jones, *Songs from Spider Street*]; The Dawning of the Age of Bradbury, by Matt Cardin [Ray Bradbury, *The Collected Stories of Ray Bradbury: A Critical Edition*]; Unhappily Ever After, by Hank Wagner [Stephen King, *Full Dark, No Stars*]; Jack the Ripper Goes Graphic, by Van

Viator [Robert Bloch, Joe R. Lansdale, John L. Lansdale, and Kevin Colden, *Robert Bloch's Yours Truly, Jack the Ripper*]; Bricks and Marble, by Jim Rockhill [Andrew Smith, *The Ghost Story, 1840–1920: A Cultural History*; Helen Conrad O'Briain and Julie Anne Stevens, ed., *The Ghost Story from the Middle Ages to the Twentieth Century*]; A Cornucopia of the Weird, by Leigh Blackmore [S. T. Joshi, ed., *Weird Fiction Review No. 1*]; Cheesy Demons and Whiny Vampires, by Tony Fonseca [Michael Laimo. *The Demonologist*; Jemiah Jefferson. *Fiend. Vampire Quartet Series.*]; Retrospective Reviews: Tales of a Mystic, by Joseph Wood Krutch [Arthur Machen, *The House of Souls*; Arthur Machen, *The Secret Glory*; Arthur Machen, *The Terror*]; The Weird Scholar, by S. T. Joshi; Capsule Reviews.

88. MASSIMO BERRUTI. *Dim-Remembered Stories: A Critical Study of R. H. Barlow.* 2011. 400 pp.

Contents. Foreword, by S. T. Joshi; Abbreviations; 1. Some Notes on an Entity; 2. Dunsanianism; 3. Vagueness; 4. Cosmicism; 5. Time; 6. Nature; 7. Irony; 8. Forbidden/Furtive Search; 9. Poetry; Conclusion. Bibliography.

Notes. Cover illustration by Pete Von Sholly. A penetrating semiotic analysis of Barlow's fiction and poetry by Berruti, an Italian literary critic who has written several substantial articles on Lovecraft.

89. DAVID E. SCHULTZ AND S. T. JOSHI, EDITORS. *An Epicure in the Terrible: A Centennial Anthology of Essays in Honor of H. P. Lovecraft.* 2010. 380 pp.

Contents: Preface; Introduction, by S. T. Joshi; I. BIOGRAPHICAL: The Parents of Howard Phillips Lovecraft, by Kenneth W. Faig, Jr.; The Cosmic Yankee, by Jason C. Eckhardt; H. P. Lovecraft and the Pulp Magazine Tradition, by Will Murray; II. THEMATIC STUDIES: On Lovecraft's Themes: Touching the Glass, by Donald R. Burleson; Letters, Diaries, and Manuscripts: The Handwritten Word in Lovecraft, by Peter Cannon; Outsiders and Aliens: The Uses of Isolation in Lovecraft's Fiction, by Stefan Dziemianowicz; Lovecraft's Cosmic Imagery, by Steven J. Mariconda; From Microcosm to Macrocosm: The Growth of Lovecraft's Cosmic Vision, by David E. Schultz; Landscapes, Selves, and Others in Lovecraft, by Robert H. Waugh; III. COMPARATIVE AND GENRE STUDIES: Lovecraft's "Artificial Mythology," by Robert M. Price; Lovecraft and the Tradition of the Gentleman Narrator, by R. Boerem; The Artist as Antaeus: Lovecraft and Modernism, by Norman R. Gayford;

Synchronistic Worlds: Lovecraft and Borges, by Barton Levi St. Armand; Bibliography.

Notes. Cover illustration by Virgil Finlay. A reprint of the volume first published by Fairleigh Dickinson University Press (1991). A substantial collection of original essays by leading Lovecraft scholars, written to commemorate the centennial of Lovecraft's birth. The original edition, published only in hardcover, was widely purchased by libraries but not easily affordable to individuals.

90. BARRY PAIN. *The Undying Thing and Others.* Edited by S. T. Joshi. 2011. 373 pp.

Contents: Introduction by S. T. Joshi; "Bill"; The Glass of Supreme Moments; Exchange; The Diary of a God; This Is All; The Moon-Slave; The Green Light; The Magnet; The Case of Vincent Pyrwhit; The Bottom of the Gulf; The End of a Show; The Undying Thing; The Gray Cat; The Four-Fingered Hand; The Tower; The Unfinished Game; The Unseen Power; The Widower; Smeath; Linda; Celia and the Ghost; The Tree of Death; Not on the Passenger-List; The Reaction; The Missing Years; The Shadow of the Unseen (with James Blyth).

Notes. Cover illustration by Allen Koszowski. Extensive selection of Pain's short fiction, including the complete contents of the early collection *Stories in the Dark* (1901); also the first reprint of the scarce novel *The Shadow of the Unseen* (1907), cowritten with James Blyth.

91. H. P. LOVECRAFT AND ROBERT E. HOWARD. *A Means to Freedom: The Letters of H. P. Lovecraft and Robert E. Howard: 1930–1932* (vol. 1) and *1933–1937* (vol. 2). Edited by S. T. Joshi, David E. Schultz, and Rusty Burke. 2011. 1004 pp. (numbered consecutively). ppbk. Published in a limited paperback edition (1000 copies) with sewn signatures and French flaps.

92. *Lovecraft Annual* No. 5 (2011). EDITED BY S. T. JOSHI. 246 pp.

Contents. Locked Dimensions out of Reach: The Lost Stories of H. P. Lovecraft, by J.-M. Rajala; Cosmic Maenads and the Music of Madness: Lovecraft's Borrowings from the Greeks, by John Salonia; Blacks, Boxers, and Lovecraft, by Gavin Callaghan; On H. P. Lovecraft's "The House," by J. D. Worthington; From Bodily Fear to Cosmic Horror (and Back Again): The Tentacle Monster from Primordial Chaos to Hello Cthulhu, by T. S. Miller; Lovecraft and I, by Caitlín R. Kiernan; Lovecraft and the Sublime: A Reinterpretation, by Alex

Houstoun; Lovecraft: A Gentleman without Five Senses, by Roland Hölzing; Endless Bacchanal: Rome, Livy, and Lovecraft's Cthulhu Cult, by Dennis Quinn; "Cool Air," the Apartment Above Us, and Other Stories, by Robert H. Waugh; Lovecraft's "The City," by R. Boerem; Briefly Noted.

93. ROBERT H. WAUGH. *A Monster of Voices: Looking for H. P. Lovecraft.* 2011. 384 pp.

Contents. Introduction; PART I: FIRST PRINCIPLES: Lovecraft's Hands; Documents, Creatures, and History; PART II: SORTIES: "The Picture in the House": Images of Complicity; *At the Mountains of Madness:* The Subway and the Shoggoth; PART III: MEDITATIONS ON "THE OUTSIDER": "The Outsider," the Terminal Climax, and Other Conclusions; Lovecraft and Keats Confront the "Awful Rainbow"; The Outsider, the Autodidact, and Other Professions; PART IV: MATERIALISM, THEOLOGY, AND IMAGINATION: Lovecraft and Leopardi: Sunsets and Moonsets; Lovecraft Born Again: An Essay in Apologetic Criticism; Works Cited; Index.

Notes. Cover illustration by Philip Fuller. A second collection of Waugh's always stimulating papers on Lovecraft, following on *The Monster in the Mirror* (item 31 above).

94. ANN K. SCHWADER. *Twisted in Dream: The Collected Weird Poetry of Ann K. Schwader.* 2011. 206 pp.

Contents. Foreword, by Robert M. Price; Introduction; I. MEMORIES OF THE WORM: The Worms Remember; Out of Corruption; Power Failure; The Ghoul-Queen; Out of Egypt; Abul Al-Hol; Ech-Pi-El's Ægypt; Lord of the Land; Dream-Gates; The Coming of Chaos; The Elder Lords; Out of the Nameless City; Asylum Sestina; Night Hungers; Hydra's Daughters; Asenath: A Cautionary Tale (On the Doorstep); Inheritrix; Mad Star Rising; Fear-Stars; The Burrowers Beyond; The Gate Between the Stars; The Wind Beyond; Night Terrors; Night Terrors II; Moot Question; Night Glyphs; Of Stonehenge & Star-Myths; Barrow-Walkers; The Last Betrayal; Auld Leng Signs; The Companion; Tonight on the Late, Late Show . . .; Night Lives; Life Studies; Moon-Fears; The Gatekeeper; Sarnath Remembered; In Memoriam Arthur Jermyn; A Man of Many Parts; Yule-Thoughts in Kingsport; The Whippoorwills; Lavinia in Springtime; Stargazing Along the Miskatonic; Untimely Observation; Sestina: To the Audient Void; Neighborly Whispers; If We Return; The Darkness Whispers; Wide Enough; Elder Signs; Ancient Echoes; The Ones Who Come; Faint Echoes; Blood Calls; Shunned Things; Jaded; Less Fa-

Thawing of Ghosts; In This Season; Sophie, Dying; Death Envy; Brief Darkness; Nachthexen; Eminence Grise; The Night Priests; Mount Pacho; Spirits of Caral; In a Lost City; After the Show at Karnak; Shadows of Kom Ombo; Where Autumn Brings Us; In the Valley of the Kings; Unkindness of Ravens; The Laughter of Small Bones; On This Last Night of Voices; Maiden & Raven; Six Tailors; Chilled Red; Blood Maidens; Breathless Reunion; Nosferatu Surrenders; Sanguine Taggers; For a Deathless Diva; Of Vanity & the Vein; Her Muse Is a Raven; Diving Xibalba; What Remains; Bones of the God; The Dying Year; Summer of Ravens; Whitechapel Autumn, 1888; Specter Moon; In Webs of Autumn.

Notes. Cover illustration by Loretta Young-Gautier; interior illustrations by Steve Lines. A substantial volume of the collected weird poetry of Schwader, perhaps the leading fantasy poet of our time. Includes the complete contents or extensive selections from such earlier volumes as *The Worms Remember* (2001), *In the Yaddith Time* (2007), and others.

95. *Dead Reckonings.* No. 10 (Fall 2011). EDITED BY S. T. JOSHI AND TONY FONSECA. 98 pp.

Contents. Two Masterful Collections, by Hank Wagner [R. B. Russell, *Literary Remains;* Catherine M. Valente, *Ventriloquism*]; The Discovery of Sarban, by Darrell Schweitzer [Mark Valentine, *Time, a Falconer: A Study of Sarban;* Sarban, *Discovery of Heretics: Unseen Writings*]; Pitch-Perfect Grotesquerie, by Robert Butterfield [Brendan Connell, *Metrophilias;* Brendan Connell, *Unpleasant Tales*]; The Australian Horror Tradition, by Leigh Blackmore [James Doig, ed., *Australian Ghost Stories;* James Doig, ed., *Australian Hauntings: Colonial Supernatural Fiction;* Angela Challis and Dr. Marty Young, ed., *Macabre: A Journey through Australia's Darkest Fears*]; A Biography of the Mind, by S. T. Joshi [Jonathan R. Eller, *Becoming Ray Bradbury*]; From Short Story to Novel, by Tony Fonseca [Gary A. Braunbeck, *Mr. Hands*]; A Kinship with Monsters, by Scott Connors [W. H. Pugmire, *The Tangled Muse*]; Fear and Loathing in Suburbia, by Jim Rockhill [Bernice M. Murphy, *The Suburban Gothic in American Popular Culture*]; Ramsey Campbell, Probably: Ramsey's Rant; Horrific Hallucinations, by Van Viator [Stephen M. Irwin, *The Dead Path;* Simon Clark, *King Blood*]; The Vampires of Our Age, by Vicky Gilpin [Paula Guran, ed., *Vampires: The Recent Undead;* Laurell K. Hamilton, *Hit List*]; Dead on Arrival, by June M. Pulliam [Steven E. Metze, *The Zombie Monologues*]; The Return of Cosmic Horror, by S. T. Joshi [Kevin Ross, ed., *Dead But Dreaming 2*]; Look Out, Ole

Jack Is Back!, by Robert Butterfield [Jack Ketchum, *Off Season*; Jack Ketchum, *Offspring*]; Frankie Goes Down Under, by Andy Trevathan [*Midnight Echo* (The Australian Horror Writers Association), February 2011]; Wondrous Wolves and Quirky Quarks, by Richard Bleiler [Kit Reed, *What Wolves Know*; Elton Elliott and Bruce Taylor, ed., *Like Water for Quarks: Science Fiction Meets Magic Realism*]; Horror Film Collection Hits Discordant Note, by Melissa Goldsmith [Neil Lerner, ed., *Music in the Horror Film: Listening to Fear*]; Weird Verse Over the Ages, by Benjamin F. Fisher [Janie Hofmann, *The Engagement of the Spur*; Ann K. Schwader, *Wild Hunt of the Stars*; Brett Rutherford, ed. *Tales of Wonder*]; Retrospective Reviews: A Novel by Mr. Oscar Wilde, by Walter Pater [Oscar Wilde, *The Picture of Dorian Gray*]; The Weird Scholar, by S. T. Joshi; Capsule Reviews; Index to *Dead Reckonings* 1–10.

Notes. The last issue of *Dead Reckonings* with S. T. Joshi as editor; the cover (in flat black) was intended to reflect mourning at his departure.

96. H. P. LOVECRAFT. *Letters to James Ferdinand Morton*. Edited by David E. Schultz and S. T. Joshi. 2011. 493 pp.

Contents. Introduction; Letters to James Ferdinand Morton; APPENDIX: LOVECRAFT AND MORTON: "Conservatism" Gone Mad; The Isaacsonio-Mortoniad; Save the Old Brick Row; [Christmas Greetings to James F. Morton]; CORRESPONDENCE WITH WILLIAM L. BRYANT; WRITINGS BY JAMES F. MORTON: Fragments of a Mental Autobiography; My Intellectual Evolution; A Few Memories; WRITINGS ABOUT JAMES F. MORTON; [James F. Morton in *Who's Who*]; Memorial of James F. Morton, by O. Ivan Lee; James Ferdinand Morton, Jr., by Edward H. Cole; Mortonius, by E. Hoffmann Price; Comments on Mr. Price's Article, by Pearl K. Morton; Jim Morton, by W. Paul Cook; James Morton, by Rheinhart Kleiner; Glossary of Frequently Mentioned Names; Bibliography; Index.

Notes. Cover design by Anastasia Damianakos (uniform with item 13). The first unabridged publication of Lovecraft's surviving letters to Morton, who was in many ways the most intellectually distinguished of Lovecraft's correspondents. The letters are thoroughly annotated by the editors. The volume is part of the *Collected Letters* series.

97. GARY WILLIAM CRAWFORD, JIM ROCKHILL, AND BRIAN J.
SHOWERS, EDITORS. *Reflections in a Glass Darkly: Essays on
J. Sheridan Le Fanu.* 2011.473 pp.

Contents. Foreword, by W. J. Mc Cormack; Introduction, by Gary
William Crawford, Jim Rockhill, and Brian J. Showers; I. SOME NOTES
ON BIOGRAPHY: A Memoir of Joseph Sheridan Le Fanu, by Alfred
Perceval Graves; Anecdotes from Seventy Years of Irish Life, by W. R.
Le Fanu; Extracts from *Wilkie Collins, Le Fanu and Others,* by S. M.
Ellis; Portraits of Joseph Sheridan Le Fanu, by Jim Rockhill, Brian J.
Showers, and Douglas A. Anderson; A Void Which Cannot Be Filled
Up: Obituaries of J. S. Le Fanu, by Brian J. Showers; II. GENERAL
STUDIES: M. R. James on J. S. Le Fanu, by M. R. James; A Forgotten
Creator of Ghosts—Joseph Sheridan Le Fanu, Possible Inspirer of the
Brontës, by Edna Kenton; Sheridan Le Fanu, by E. F. Benson; From
The Supernatural in Fiction, by Peter Penzoldt; An Irish Ghost, by V. S.
Pritchett; Excerpts from the "Prologue" and "Epilogue" to *Madam
Crowl's Ghost,* by M. R. James; Doubles, Shadows, Sedan-Chairs, and
the Past: The "Ghost Stories" of J. S. Le Fanu, by Patricia Coughlan;
III. SOME SPECIAL TOPICS: Making Light in the Shadow Box: The
Artistry of Le Fanu, by Kel Roop; Le Fanu's House by the
Marketplace, by Wayne Hall; Sheridan Le Fanu and the Spirit of
1798, by Albert Power; H. P. Lovecraft's Response to the Work of
Joseph Sheridan Le Fanu, by Jim Rockhill; "A Regular Contributor":
Le Fanu's Short Stories, *All The Year Round,* and the Influence of
Dickens, by Simon Cooke; A Shared Vision: Le Fanu's *In A Glass
Darkly* and Carl Theodor Dreyer's *Vampyr,* by Gary William
Crawford; Dreyer, *Vampyr,* and Sheridan Le Fanu, by Mark Le Fanu;
IV. CONTEMPORARY REVIEWS; V. STUDIES OF INDIVIDUAL WORKS:
"Green Tea": The Archetypal Ghost Story, by Jack Sullivan;
Introduction to *The House by the Church-Yard,* by Elizabeth Bowen;
Three Ghost Stories: "The Judge's House," "An Account of Some
Strange Disturbances in an Old House in Aungier Street," and
"Mr. Justice Harbottle," by Carol A. Senf; Introduction to *Uncle Silas,*
by M. R. James; Conversations in a Shadowed Room: The Blank
Spaces in "Green Tea", by John Langan; Introduction to *Uncle Silas,*
by Elizabeth Bowen; "Addicted to the Supernatural": Spiritualism and
Self-Satire in Le Fanu's *All in the Dark,* by Stephen Carver; In the
Name of the Mother: Perverse Maternity in "Carmilla," by Jarlath
Killeen; Crossing Boundaries, Mixing Genres in *The Wyvern Mystery,*
by Sally C. Harris; "I Resolved To Play the Part of a Good Samaritan":
Metafiction in "The Room in the Dragon Volant," by William
Hughes; "The Child That Went with the Fairies": The Folk Tale and
the Ghost Story, by Peter Bell; The "Smashed Looking-Glass":

Fragmentation and Narrative Perversity in *Willing to Die*, by Victor Sage; Bibliography; Sources; Biographical Notes; Index.

Notes. Cover illustration by Jason Van Hollander from a photograph by Laura Anzuoni. Large volume of both original and reprinted criticism of the great Irish fantaisiste, including an extensive selection of early reviews, memoirs by those who knew him, and much other interesting work. A finalist for the 2011 Bram Stoker Award for nonfiction.

98. ADAM NISWANDER. *The Nemesis of Night.* 2011. 344 pp.

Notes. Cover illustration by Ron Leming. Another installment in the author's Shaman Cycle, where Lovecraftian entities manifest themselves in the American Southwest. The last novel completed by the author before his death on August 12, 2012.

99. PETER CANNON. *Forever Azathoth: Parodies and Pastiches.* 2012. 260 pp.

Contents. Introduction; FOREVER AZATHOTH: I. Azathoth in Arkham; II. The Revenge of Azathoth; III. The House of Azathoth; IV. Azathoth in Analysis; V. Bride of Azathoth; VI. Son of Azathoth; SCREAM FOR JEEVES" I. Cats, Rats, and Bertie Wooster; II. Something Foetid; III. The Rummy Affair of Young Charlie; PARODIES AND PASTICHES: Tender Is the Night-Gaunt; The Sound and the Fungi; All Moon-Beasts Amorphous and Mephitic; The Undercliffe Sentences; The Arkham Collector; Old Man; Nautical-Looking Negroes; The Madness out of Space. A Reading Group Guide to *Forever Azathoth*.

Notes. Cover illustration by Jason C. Eckhardt. A generous selection of the Lovecraftian tales of one of the leading scholars on Lovecraft as well as one of the most engaging writers of Lovecraftian humor. This volume is an expansion of a book of the same title published in 1999 by Tartarus Press.

100. W. H. PUGMIRE. *Uncommon Places: A Collection of Exquisites.* 2012. 270 pp.

Contents. An Identity in Dream; Artifice; Cesare; The Host of Haunted Air; Hempen Rope; Cathedral of Death; House of Legend; Inhabitants of Wraithwood; In Memoriam: Oscar Wilde; The Zanies of Sorrow; In Remembrance: Edgar A. Poe; Keepsake; Postcard from Prague; Necronomicon; Sickness of Heart; The Tangled Muse; Chamber of Dreams; Some Distant Baying Sound; Some Buried Memory; Your Ghost on Glass; Letters from an Old Gent; Uncommon Places; Acknowledgments.

Notes. Cover and interior illustrations by Gwabryel. A collection of stories and prose-poems by one of the leading contemporary writers of Lovecraftian fiction.

101. LOVECRAFT, H. P. *The Annotated Supernatural Horror in Literature.* Edited by S. T. Joshi. 2nd ed. 2012. 228 pp.

Contents. Preface; Introduction; Supernatural Horror in Literature, by H. P. Lovecraft; Appendix: The Favourite Weird Stories of H. P. Lovecraft; Notes; Bibliography of Authors and Works; Index.

Notes. Cover illustration by Vrest Orton. Extensive revision of the first Hippocampus Press title, with exhaustive updating of the bibliography and notes and an overhauling of the overall design.

102. Joshi, S. T. *Lovecraft's Library: A Catalogue.* 3rd ed. 2012. 180 pp.

Contents. Introduction; Explanatory Notes; Lovecraft's Library; Weird &c. Items in Library of H. P. Lovecraft; Indices.

Notes. Cover illustration by Jason C. Eckhardt. Revised version of the listing of titles in Lovecraft's library (for the 2nd ed. of 2002, see item 4), with the addition of 24 new titles.

103. *Dead Reckonings* No. 11 (Spring 2012). EDITED BY JUNE M. PULLIAM AND TONY FONSECA. 102 pp.

Contents. Horror's International Voices, by Hank Wagner [Lavie Tidhar, *Osama;* John Aivide Lindqvist, *Harbor*]; Successes, Excesses, and Failures, by Javier A. Martínez [Reza Negarestani, Cyclonopedia: Complicity with Anonymous Materials; Michael Cisco, *The Great Lover*]; An Ordinary Darkness, by John Edgar Browning [Ellen Datlow, ed., The Best Horror of the Year, Volume 3; Peter Crowther and Nick Gevers, ed. The New and Perfect Man]; The Horror of Revelation, by Robert Butterfield [Steven Savile, *London Macabre;* Michael McBride, *Blindspot*]; Old and New Cthulhu, by S. T. Joshi [Ross E. Lockhart, ed., *The Book of Cthulhu;* Paula Guran, ed. *New Cthulhu*]; Lovecraft Fans Rejoice, by Robert Butterfield [Simon Strantzas, *Nightingale Songs;* James Chambers, *The Engines of Sacrifice*]; Mainstreaming the Zombie Narrative, by June M. Pulliam [Colson Whitehead, *Zone One;* Jonathan Maberry, *Dead of Night*]; Fascination with Tragic Horror, by Tony Fonseca [Charlee Jacob, *This Symbiotic Fascination*]; Literary Nostalgia, with Some Great Fun, by Hank Wagner [Kenneth Robeson, *Doc Savage: The Desert Demons;* Tim Champlin, *Tom Sawyer and the Ghosts of Summer*]; Seductive Vampire with a Heart, by Van Viator [Andrea Dean Van Scoyoc, *Dante's Dia-*

ry]; Sacre Bleu! C'est Le Diable (Encore), by Tony Fonseca [J. K. Huysmans, *La-Bas (Down There)*]; Fifty Years of Ramsey Campbell, by S. T. Joshi [Ramsey Campbell, *The Inhabitant of the Lake & Other Unwelcome Tenants*, and *Ghosts Know*]; The Dark Waters of Capitalism, by Vicky Gilpin [Todd Grimson, *Brand New Cherry Flavor*]; "True" Crime, Stranger Than Fiction, by June M. Pulliam [Susan Mustafa and Sue Israel. *Dismembered*; Susan Mustafa, Tony Clayton, and Sue Israel, *Blood Bath*]; Whip Me, Beat Me, Bite Me, PLEASE!, by Andy Trevathan [Jemiah Jefferson, *Wounds*]; Bridging the YA-Mainstream Gap, by June M. Pulliam [Ransom Riggs, *Miss Peregrine's Home for Peculiar Children*]; A Barlow Primer for Attentive Readers, by Scott Connors [Massimo Berruti, *Dim-Remembered Stories: A Critical Study of R. H. Barlow*]; Got Gothic?, by June M. Pulliam [John Sears, *Stephen King's Gothic*]; Something Beyond Comprehension, by Bev Vincent [Joseph Aisenberg, *Carrie*; Danel Olson, ed. *The Exorcist*]; Re-Possessed, by Andy Trevathan [William Peter Blatty, *The Exorcist*; William Friedkin, *The Exorcist*.]; Silent House Tricks and Treats, by June M. Pulliam [Chris Kentis and Laura Lau, dir., *Silent House*]; Hooked on Maniacs and Bloody Hooks, by Tony Fonseca [Bob Harper, Twisted Rhymes]; Female Trouble, by June M. Pulliam [James Watkins, dir., *The Woman in Black*]; Horrors on the Small Screen, by June M. Pulliam [Ryan Murphy and Brad Falchuk, *American Horror Story*; Frank Darabont, *The Walking Dead*]; A Pair of Kings: Two Views of Time Travel, by Robert Butterfield and Hank Wagner [Stephen King, *11/22/63*]; From Bad Dreams May Come Beauty, by Margi Curtis and Kenneth W. Faig, Jr. [Kyla Lee Ward, *The Land of Bad Dreams*]; Tales of Unease, by Matthew McEver and Hank Wagner [Christopher Fowler, *Red Gloves*]; Ramsey Campbell, Probably: Granted by *Granta*; The Weird Scholar, by S. T. Joshi; Notes on Contributors.

104. DONALD SIDNEY-FRYER. *The Atlantis Fragments: The Novel.* 2012. 322 pp.

Notes. Cover illustration by Gordon R. Barnett. Fantasy novel set in the world of DSF's poetry omnibus *The Atlantis Fragments* (item 53). While technically a reprint of an edition issued by the author by Phosphor Lantern Press, very few copies of that state were ever distributed.

105. DONALD SIDNEY-FRYER. *The Golden State Phantasticks—The California Romantics and Related Subjects: Collected Essays and Reviews.* Associate Editors Leo Grin and Alan Gullette. 2012. 428 pp.

Contents. Foreword/Forward in a Phantastick Mode!; The Sorcerer Departs; Clark Ashton Smith, Poet in Prose (1893–1961); George Sterling (1869–1926): Hesperian Laureate; A Garland of Poems by George Sterling; A Memoir of Timeus Gaylord; A Visionary of Doom: Ambrose Bierce, Poet (1842–1914); Clark Ashton Smith: The Last of the Great Romantic Poets; A Statement for Imagination; The Last Lutenist: Christian Gottlieb Scheidler; Francis Marion Crawford: A Neglected But Not a Forgotten Master; F. Marion Crawford: Romantist Nonpareil; Robert E. Howard: Frontiersman of Letters; Robert E. Howard: Epic Poet in Prose; The Alleged Influence of Lord Dunsany on Clark Ashton Smith; Klarkash-Ton and E'ch-Pi-El: On the Alleged Influence of H. P. Lovecraft on Clark Ashton Smith; Nora May French: Somewhere Between Eulalie and Edna St. Vincent Millay; APPENDIX OF LESSER REVIEWS AND MISCELLANEA: Addendum: Another "Smith"; Don Herron: Echoes and Yet Again Echoes; L. Sprague de Camp: The Art of Modern Enchantment; Frank Belknap Long, *In Mayan Splendor*; Celeste Turner Wright, *Seasoned Timber*; William Hope Hodgson, *The Dream of X: A Creative Alternative to The Night Land*; Jesse F. Knight, *The Romantic Revival*; Clark Ashton Smith, *The City of the Singing Flame* (Introduction); Clark Ashton Smith, *The Last Incantation* (Introduction); Clark Ashton Smith, *The Monster of the Prophecy* (Introduction); G. Sutton Breiding, *Autumn Roses* (Introduction); H. P. Lovecraft, *Fungi From Yuggoth*; "Klarkash-Ton" versus "Clark Ashton": A Minor Issue for Controversy; G. Sutton Breiding, *Journal of an Astronaut* (Introduction); *O Amor atque Realitas!* Clark Ashton Smith's First Adult Fiction; Frank Belknap Long, *The Darkling Tide* (Introduction); Keith Allen Daniels, *What Rough Beast, What Rough Book;* In Memoriam: Keith Allen Daniels (1956–2001); Acknowledgments.

Notes. Cover illustration by Alan Gullette. Compendium of Sidney-Fryer's articles on the California poets of the past century and weird poets of various sorts, written over decades. While technically a reprint of an edition issued by the author via Phosphor Lantern Press, very few copies of that state were ever distributed.

106. RICHARD A. LUPOFF. *Dreams.* 2012. 260 pp.

Contents. Introduction: Into the Weird Blue Yonder, by Cody Goodfellow; The Adventure of the Voorish Sign; At the Esquire; Nothing Personal; Tee Shirts; Dingbats; The River of Fog; Cairo, Good-Bye;

Report of the Admissions Committee; Fourth Avenue Interlude; Sergeant Ghost; The Law; The Green Fairy; THE WEBSTER SLOAT STORIES: dreemz.biz; wyshes.com; heaven.god; Afterword.

Notes. Cover illustration by Steven Gilberts. Reprint of a collection (first published by Mythos Books in 2011) of Lupoff's variegated Lovecraftian tales, with the addition of the tale "The Green Fairy", which appeared in print for the first time here.

107. RICHARD A. LUPOFF. *Visions.* 2012. 268 pp.

Contents: Introduction by Peter S. Beagle; The Ben Zaccheus Case Files: Hebrews Have No Horns; There Are Kings; Steps Leading Downward; April Dawn; Ankareh Minu. Mysteries, Horrors, and Adventures: Petroglyphs; Brackish Waters; A Freeway for Draculas; The Peltonville Horror; Simeon Dimsby's Workshop; Villaggio Sogno; Tangaroa's Eye; Snow Ghosts. Afterword.

Notes. Cover illustration by Steven Gilberts. Reprint of another volume of Lupoff's Lovecraftian tales, first published by Mythos Books in 2009, with the addition of the tale "April Dawn", which appeared in print for the first time here.

108. ALLAN GULLETTE. *Intimations of Unreality: Weird Fiction and Poetry.* 2012. 386 pp.

Contents. Gullette's Ritual, by Robert M. Price; INTIMATIONS OF UNREALITY; The Old Man up the Road; The Admiral's Tale; Derrick's Ritual; Knocker-Over; Within the Machinery of Light; The Door in Lheil; The Desolation of Falithra; The Twilight Necropolis; The Shadow from Yith; In the Realm of Ying; House of Morning, House of Dream; The Legend of the Seeker; The Summons of Hastur; The Tomb of Nyarlathotep; Charles Nathan's Pipe; A Visit from Ray Bradbury; The Axe of the Executioner; Phases; THE GREEN TRANSFER; THE MORE, THE MARIGOLD; INTO THE BEYOND: Dusk; Thoughts I; On a Rainy Eve; Poem to Polymnia; Arcanesia; Lunar Liturgy; For Fear; Song of the Old Ones; Hidden Realization; Flight; Lost Refuge; Song to Helios; Carven Faces; The Witness's Account; Cataclysm; The Portal; Oblivion; Awakening; Vision; Revelation of Night; Home in Autumn; Game; Painting: Dreamscape I; The Sorcerer's Lament; Down to the Harbor; Praise to the Sunrise; Sojourn; Solitude; Selene; I Ask the Fortune Teller; On the Mass Destruction of Starlings Near Fort Campbell, Kentucky; Thoughts II; Vidya; She; Requiem; The Mere Weather Sends Transport; The Absolute Sameness of Change; Lizard Life; Alchemy; Vest; Portal II; Burial Instructions; Epitaph; Invocation: On the 100th Mailing of the Esoteric Order of Dagon; The

Face of Death; Seer; The Last Sonnet; The Menace from the Woodwork; Song for the End of Time; To Keith Allen Daniels (1956–2001); Absinthe; The Dead Priest; Into the Beyond; Stripped to the Bone; The Truth of the Ages; Nora May; I Hitched My Wagon to a Shooting Star; A Trip to the Hypnotist; Acknowledgments.

Notes. Cover art and interior illustrations by Denis Tiani. Generous selection of the prose and poetry of Gullette, who has emerged as a leading critic and follower of the San Francisco weird fictionists and poets, notably George Sterling and Clark Ashton Smith.

109. JOSEPH A. PULVER, SR. *Portraits of Ruin.* 2012. 384 pp.

Contents. Introduction, by Matt Cardin; No Healing Prayers; Lena . . . cries; So Into You; (a piece) about angels left out in the rain; Time . . . and Forever, by Joseph S. Pulver, Sr., and Tara Vanflower; Before and After Science; A Hand at the Door; Le Festin de l'araignée; Herding Fire: A Murder Mystery; THE RUSS MEYER TRIPTYCH: The Director's Cut; Skin Flick sans Money Shot; When There's a Riot Goin' On . . .; But Not for Me, by Joseph S. Pulver, Sr., and Laurence Amiotte; kristamas as an exhibition; Small Ocean After Solar; Lonely . . . and a long way from home; Listen to a Country Song; Memories Can Wait; Jolene; 6 . . . 6—; . . . LIES . . . . . . Thunder . . . . . . ashes . . . .; Rune Grammofon poem [U.N/umbered))))); Marks and Scars and Flags; Mrs. Spriggs' Easter Attire, by Joseph S. Pulver, Sr., and Tara Vanflower; Each Night Begins a New Journey That Leads Only to an End with No Between; BACK to—; Catch Tomorrow; When a Sigh Visits Skin; By the Light . . . of; Her Lips Were Wet with Venom; Now (a parade); After Plath's "Goatsucker"; Tark Left Santiago; How I Survived the Cowboy Movie [or When the Barron Opened His Eye]; In Her Forest Garden Dreaming; Icarus Above . . .; My Mirage; And this is where I go down into the darkness; Acknowledgments.

Notes. Cover illustration by J. Karl Bogartte. A third collection of Pulver's weird work, highlighted by a deft use of prose-poetry and a focus on the paradoxical beauties of terror and death. The final, novella-length tale presciently anticipated the eventual mass appeal of Thomas Ligotti's *The Conspiracy against the Human Race* (item 77).

110. *Lovecraft Annual* No. 6 (2012). EDITED BY S. T. JOSHI. 238 pp.

Contents. Race and War in the Lovecraft Mythos: A Philosophical Reflection, by César Guarde Paz; Of Regner Lodbrog, Hugh Blair, and Mistranslations, by Martin Andersson; The Shadow over "The Lurking Fear," by Michael Cisco; The Aboriginal in the Works of H. P. Lovecraft, by James Goho; Envisaging the Cosmos: A Note on "The

Dreams in the Witch House," by Scott Connors; Lovecraft, Absurdity, and the Modernist Grotesque, by Sean Elliot Martin; Sources of Anxiety in Lovecraft's "Polaris," by J. D. Worthington; *Tekeli-li!* Disturbing Language in Edgar Allan Poe and H. P. Lovecraft, by Lynne Jamneck; Lovecraft's 1937 Diary, by Kenneth W. Faig, Jr.; The Case for "How the Enemy Came to Thlunrana" and *The Case of Charles Dexter Ward*, by Peter Levi; Misperceptions of Malignity: Narrative Form and the Threat to America's Modernity in "The Shadow over Innsmouth," by Anna Klein; Elementary, My Dear Lovecraft: H. P. Lovecraft and Sherlock Holmes, by Gavin Callaghan; Review: Steven J. Mariconda [H. P. Lovecraft, *The Annotated Revisions and Collaborations*]; Briefly Noted.

111. RICHARD GAVIN. *At Fear's Altar*. 2012. 256 pp.

Contents. Prologue: A Gate of Nerves; Chapel in the Reeds; The Abject; Faint Baying from Afar; The Unbound; A Pallid Devil, Bearing Cypress; King Him; The Plain; Only Enuma Elish; The Word-Made Flesh; Annexation; Darksome Leaves; The Eldritch Faith; Acknowledgments; About the Author.

Notes. Cover illustration and frontispiece by Harry O. Morris. Substantial collection of weird tales by a leading Canadian author of supernatural and Lovecraftian fiction.

112. *Dead Reckonings* No. 12 (Fall 2012). EDITED BY JUNE M. PULLIAM AND TONY FONSECA. 96 pp.

Contents. Children of Bram and Poesy *du Macabre*, by John Edgar Browning [Stephen Jones, ed., *The Mammoth Book of Dracula*; Michael A. Arnzen, *The Gorelets Omnibus: Collected Poems, 2001–2011*]; Horror Authors Get Religion, by Kendra Kuss Ditto [Stacia Kane, *Sacrificial Magic*; Michele Lang, *Dark Victory*]; Uttering the Unutterable, by Tony Fonseca [S. T. Joshi, *Unutterable Horror: A History of Supernatural Fiction*]; Time and Time Again, by Antoinette Winstead [Dean Koontz, *The Dead Town: A Novel* and *Odd Apocalypse: An Odd Thomas Novel*]; Weird Poetry, Then and Now, by S. T. Joshi [Matthew Gregory Lewis (ed.), *Tales of Wonder*; Brett Rutherford (ed.), *Last Flowers: The Romance and Poetry of Edgar Allan Poe & Sarah Helen Whitman*; Brett Rutherford, *Whippoorwill Road: The Supernatural Poems of Brett Rutherford*]; The Return of the Old-Fashioned Tale of Terror, by Robert Butterfield [Scott Thomas, *Urn and Willow*; William Meikle, *Dark Melodies*]; Sweet Zombie Jesus!, by June Pulliam [Daryl Gregory, *Raising Stony Mayhall*]; Martin's Classic Vampire Still Lives, by Braden Dauzat [George R. R. Martin, *Fevre*

Dream]; Vampire Sluts, Doppelgangers, and Impossible Abodes, by Javier A. Martínez [Blake Butler, *There Is No Year;* Grace Krilanovich, *The Orange Eats Creeps*]; A Shadow of His Best Work, by Tim Lucas [Tim Burton, dir., *Dark Shadows*]; Shelley's Monster Lives, by Matthew McEver [Mary Shelley, *Frankenstein*]; The Heart of Darkness, by Bev Vincent [Peter Straub, *The Ballad of Ballard and Sandrine;* Graham Joyce, *Some Kind of Fairy Tale*]; Ramsey Campbell, Probably: A Can of Heinz; Love(crafty)an Eccentrics, by Darrell Schweitzer [Peter Cannon, *Forever Azathoth: Parodies and Pastiches;* W. H. Pugmire, *Uncommon Places: A Collection of Exquisites*]; Callers from Hell, by Van Viator [Tom Fletcher, *The Leaping* and *The Thing on the Shore*]; A Brilliant Idea Poorly Executed, by Jim Rockhill [John C. Tibbetts, *The Gothic Imagination*]; The Wonderful World of Nihilism, by Antoinette Winstead [Dean Koontz, *77 Shadow Street;* Adam Nevill, *The Ritual*]; Rekindling Interest in Two Novels, by Tony Fonseca [Ramsey Campbell, *The Seven Days of Cain;* Graham Masterton, *Petrified*]; Two Views of Two Classics, by Hank Wagner, with Bev Vincent [Ray Bradbury, *Dandelion Wine and Something Wicked This Way Comes*]; Vampires on Ice, by Hank Wagner [Matt Forbeck, *Carpathia;* Barbara Hambly, *The Magistrates of Hell*]; Lesser Powers?, by Darrell Schweitzer [Tim Powers, *The Bible Repairman and Other Stories*]; Of Mirrors and Lakes, by Tony Fonseca [Eric A. Jackson, *A Blind Eye to the Rearview;* Ronald [Damien] Malfi, *Floating Staircase*]; Werewolf Novel a Real Dog, by June Pulliam [Anne Rice, *The Wolf Gift*]; Giron "Classic" Promises, But Doesn't Deliver, by Andy Trevathan [Sephera Giron, *The Birds and the Bees*]; The Weird Scholar, by S. T. Joshi; Notes on Contributors.

Notes. The first issue of *Dead Reckonings* with editor June M. Pulliam at the helm. Under her editorship, the journal expanded its scope to cover horror in all media.

113. CLARK ASHTON SMITH. *The Complete Poetry and Translations.* Edited by S. T. Joshi and David E. Schultz. Vol. 1 and 2: xxxix, 846 pp., numbered consecutively); Vol. 3. 2013. 442 pp. ppbk.

Notes. This paperback edition includes "The Canyon" and "Dawn," discovered after publication of the hardcover addition, as well as the original French poems "Paysage Elyséen" and "Fin de souper" by Pierre Lièvre. "The Desire of Loving" by Hélène Picard was moved from volume 2 to volume 3 for the paperback edition.

114. S. T. JOSHI. *I Am Providence: The Life and Times of H. P. Love-craft*. 2013. 2 vols. x, 1151 pp. (numbered consecutively). ppbk.

115. WILLIAM F. NOLAN. *Nolan on Bradbury: Sixty Years of Writing about the Master of Science Fiction*. Edited by S. T. Joshi. 2013. 270 pp.

Contents. Preface; Introduction, by Jason V Brock; Editor's Introduction, by S. T. Joshi; About Bill Nolan, by Ray Bradbury; ARTICLES: R. B.: A Biographical Sketch; Portrait of a Writer; The Bradbury Years; Bradbury: Prose Poet in the Age of Space; The Great White Whale; The Best of Ray Bradbury; Ray Bradbury; Leigh Brackett and Ray Bradbury; Ray Bradbury: Space Age Moralist; Bradbury in the Pulps; Introduction to *The Last Circus and The Electrocution*; Afterword to "The Fireman"; Introduction to *Ray Bradbury Review* (1988 edition); A Half-Century of Creativity; Behind the Illustrations: The Real Ray Bradbury; Fifty Years with Bradbury: A Birthday Tribute; Ray Bradbury: Space-Age Legend; Ray, Ray, and Ray; William F. Nolan Interviews Ray Bradbury; A Bradbury Top Ten, Plus Fifty: My Personal Evaluation of; Ray's Finest Stories; STORIES: The Immortal Ones; Mr. B. Goes to Hollywood; The Joy of Living; And Miles to Go Before I Sleep; To Serve the Ship; Dead Call; Fair Trade; The Dandelion Chronicles; TRIBUTES TO RAY BRADBURY: Goodbye, Old Pal; Kneeling at the Dandelion Shrine, by Jason V Brock; Ray Bradbury's Good Companions, by John C. Tibbetts; A Master of Symbol and Metaphor, by S. T. Joshi; Afterword: The Return of Ray B., by Greg Bear; Select Bibliography.

Notes. Cover illustration ("The Pedestrian") by Joesph Mugnaini, an artist long associated with editions of Bradbury's work. Cover design by Jessica Forsythe. Compendium of articles on Bradbury by Nolan, who knew the great fantaisiste for more than sixty years; also a selection of stories by Nolan influenced by Bradbury and genial parodies of Bradbury's work. Winner of the Bram Stoker Award for best nonfiction book of 2013.

116. *Dreams of Fear: Poetry of Terror and the Supernatural*. Edited by S. T. Joshi and Steven J. Mariconda. 2013. 358 pp.

Contents: Introduction; I. THE ANCIENT WORLD: Homer, *From the Odyssey*; Euripides, *From Medea*; Catullus, Attis; Horace, Epode 5; II. FROM THE MIDDLE AGES TO THE EIGHTEENTH CENTURY: Dante Alighieri, *From Inferno*; Christopher Marlowe, *From Dr. Faustus*; William Shakespeare, *From Hamlet*; *From Macbeth*; John Donne,

The Apparition; John Milton, *From* Paradise Lost; John Gay, A True Story of an Apparition; David Mallet, William and Margaret; William Collins, Ode to Fear; III. THE GOTHICS AND ROMANTICS: Johann Wolfgang von Goethe, The Erl-King, The Bride of Corinth, The Dance of Death; Mary Robinson, The Haunted Beach; William Blake, Fair Elenor; Robert Burns, Tam o' Shanter; Friedrich von Schiller, A Funeral Fantasie; Nathan Drake, Ode to Superstition; James Hogg, The Witch of the Gray Thorn; Sir Walter Scott, William and Helen, The Wild Huntsman; Samuel Taylor Coleridge, The Rime of the Ancient Mariner, Kubla Khan; Robert Southey, To Horror; Matthew Gregory Lewis, Alonzo the Brave and Fair Imogene; Thomas Moore, The Lake of the Dismal Swamp; George Gordon, Lord Byron, Darkness; Percy Bysshe Shelley, Sister Rosa: A Ballad; John Clare, The Nightmare; John Keats, La Belle Dame sans Merci: A Ballad; Heinrich Heine, The Lorelei; Thomas Hood, The Demon-Ship; IV. THE LATER NINETEENTH CENTURY: Victor Hugo, The Vanished City; Thomas Lovell Beddoes, The Ghosts' Moonshine, The Boding Dreams, Doomsday; Henry Wadsworth Longfellow, Haunted Houses, The Haunted Chamber; Edgar Allan Poe, The City in the Sea, The Haunted Palace, The Conqueror Worm, Dream-Land, Ulalume; Alfred, Lord Tennyson, The Kraken; Oliver Wendell Holmes, The Broomstick Train; or, The Return of the Witches; Robert Browning, Chillde Roland to the Dark Tower Came; James Russell Lowell, The Ghost-Seer; Charles Baudelaire, The Phantom, The Irremediable; William Allingham, A Dream; George MacDonald, The Homeless Ghost; George Meredith, Phantasy; Thomas Bailey Aldrich, Eidolons, The Lorelei, Apparitions; Algernon Charles Swinburne, The Witch-Mother; Thomas Hardy, The Dead Man Walking; Ambrose Bierce, A Vision of Doom; Julian Hawthorne, Were-Wolf; W. E. Henley, [Untitled]; Guy de Maupassant, Horror; Edwin Markham, Wail of the Wandering Dead, The Wharf of Dreams; Emile Verhaeren, The Miller; A. E. Housman, Hell Gate; Katharine Tynan, The Witch; Madison Cawein, The Forest of Shadows, The Wood Water, The Night-Wind, Hallowmas; W. B. Yeats, The Phantom Ship; Dora Sigerson Shorter, The Skeleton in the Cupboard, The Fetch; Æ (George William Russell), A Vision of Beauty; V. THE TWENTIETH CENTURY: George Sterling, A Dream of Fear, A Wine of Wizardry, The Thirst of Satan; Edwin Arlington Robinson, The Dead Village, The Dark House; Christopher Brennan, [Untitled]; Paul Laurence Dunbar, The Haunted Oak; Walter de la Mare, Fear, The Listeners, Drugged; Robert W. Service, The Cremation of Sam McGee; Robert Frost, Ghost House, The Demiurge's Laugh; William Hope Hodgson, Storm; Park Barnitz, Mad Sonnet, Mankind; Edward

Thomas, Out in the Dark; Herman George Scheffauer, Phantasmago-
ria, Lilith of Eld, The Shadow o'er the City; Lord Dunsany, Songs
from an Evil Wood, The Watchers; Wilfrid Wilson Gibson, The
Whisperers, The Lodging House; John Masefield, The Haunted; John
G. Neihardt, The Voice of Nemesis; Siegfried Sassoon, Haunted,
Goblin Revel; Vincent Starrett, Villon Strolls at Midnight; Georg
Heym, The Demons of the Cities; Rupert Brooke, Dead Men's Love;
Samuel Loveman, Ship of Dreams; Conrad Aiken, La Belle Morte; H.
P. Lovecraft, Despair, To a Dreamer, The Wood, *From* Fungi from
Yuggoth; Harold Vinal, Apparition, Ghostly Reaper; Clark Ashton
Smith, Ode to the Abyss, The Eldritch Dark, The Medusa of Despair,
The Tears of Lilith, A Vision of Lucifer; Robert Graves, The Haunted
House; Frank Belknap Long, The Goblin Tower, The Abominable
Snow Men; Robert E. Howard, Dead Man's Hate, Recompense; Don-
ald Wandrei, Nightmare, *From* Sonnets of the Midnight Hours; Jo-
seph Payne Brennan, The Scythe of Dreams; Stanley McNail, The
House on Maple Hill; Donald Sidney-Fryer, Midnight Visitant; Rich-
ard L. Tierney, The Evil House, To the Hydrogen Bomb; Bruce Bos-
ton, The Nightmare Collector, Ghost Blood; Brett Rutherford, Fête;
G. Sutton Breiding, The Worm of Midnight, Black Leather Vampyre;
W. H. Pugmire, The Outsider's Song; Gary William Crawford, The
Formicary; Keith Allen Daniels, Stonehenge; Leigh Blackmore, Ter-
ror Australis; Ann K. Schwader, The Coming of Chaos; Index of
Poets; Acknowledgments.

Notes. Cover illustration by Charles E. Burchfield ("Tree", (1946).
Comprehensive new historical anthology of weird poetry from classical
antiquity to the present, meant to be an updating of August Derleth's
noteworthy anthology *Dark of the Moon* (1947).

117. GEORGE STERLING: *Complete Poetry, Volume 1: Chords of Fire.*
Edited by S. T. Joshi and David E. Schultz. 2013. 438 pp.

Contents: PREFACE, by Kevin Starr; INTRODUCTION: THE POET OF
THE SKIES; THE TESTIMONY OF THE SUNS AND OTHER POEMS: Dedi-
cation; Memorial Day; Poesy; The City of Music; To One Loved; The
Summer of the Gods; The Lords of Pain; The Fog Siren; To Miss
Constance Crawley in "Everyman"; To Imagination; To a Lily; "With
the Strength of Dreams"; The Testimony of the Suns; Music; A
White Rose; The Soul's Exile; In the Beginning; Memory of the Dead;
To My Wife; The Haunting; War; Nightmare; The Spirit of Beauty;
To Katherine; Mystery; To My Sister; The Poets; The Reincarnation;
On Reading the Poems of Father Tabb; The Parting; Words for
Lange's "Blumenlied"; The Altar-Flame; To One Asking Lighter

Thy Heart; From Two Skies; The Abiding Presence; Love Complete; By the Western Ocean; A Vision; Love Desolate; The Pain of Beauty; A Constancy of Sleep; Dream's Alchemy; Soul of the World; Dreamland; The Shadow of Immortality; Until Thou Comest; Reborn; The Silent Fane; The Lute-Player; The Heritage of the Skies; Love and Sorrow; In Vain; The Hidden Goddess; Love's Mercy; Song's Futility; At Sunset; The Immortal; Blossom or Bird; Longing; The New Goddess; To the Moon; Lost in Light; The Path to Paradise; Appendix; Worship's Acme; Before Dawn; Separation; [Untitled]; POEMS TO VERA: To Vera; Inclusion; The Song-Font; My Songs; To Vera; "I Loved Thee, Atthis, Long Ago!"; To Vera; To Vera; Intimation; At Noon; The Cup-Bearer; Iphigenia; The Face of the Star; Afterward; Confession; To Vera; Absence; Mystery; "Out of the Night"; Star of the Soul; Before Dawn; To Vera at Night; To Vera (Birthday Ode); To Vera (Blank Verse); BEYOND THE BREAKERS AND OTHER POEMS: The Master-Mariner; The Voice of the Dove; Night-Sentries; The Muse of the Incommunicable; The Coming Singer; At the Grand Cañon; Nightfall; Ode on the Centenary of the Birth of Robert Browning; Afterward; "Tidal, King of Nations"; The Last Monster; Christmas Under Arms; War; Ascension; The Thirst of Satan; Scrutiny; Ballad of Two Seas; Ballad of St. John of Nepomuk; The Rack; Willy Pitcher; "Beyond the Sunset"; Respite; Kindred; "That Walk in Darkness"; In the Market-Place; The Palette; The Hunting of Dian; A Winter Dawn; A Winter Sunset; Forenoon by the Pacific; A Legend of the Dove; Said the Wind:; The Mission Swallows; "Omnia Exeunt in Mysterium"; "On a Western Beach"; Then and Now; Menace; The Secret Room; Past the Panes; From the Mountain; Discord; Lineage; To One Self-Slain; Night on the Mountain; The Abandoned Farm; To H. G. Wells; Caeli Enarrant; "You Never Can Tell"; Dawn from a Western Mountain; The Setting; The Sleepers; The Sleep of Birds; Spring in Monterey; The Last Days; Natural History Items; Father Coyote; The Lagoon; Relativity; The Plaint of the Cotton-Tails; A Possibility; YOSEMITE: AN ODE; THE CAGED EAGLE AND OTHER POEMS: The Slaying of the Witch; To Twilight; Henri; Conspiracy; Indian Summer; Ballad of the Fatal Word; On the Sale of the Love-Letters of a Dead Poet; Mediatrix; A Dog Waits His Dead Mistress; Humility in Art; An Autumn Thrush; The Fall of the Year; October; In Autumn; The Caged Eagle; Time and Tears; To an Old Nurse; To the Mummy of the Lady Isis; The Ramparts and the Rose; On a Portrait of Lincoln; The Tryst; A Yellow Rose; Shakespeare; The Shadow of Nirvana; The Return; Moloch; Three Sonnets on Sleep; Man; On a City Street; Illusion; Essential Night; The Gleaner; California; Poems on the Panama-Pacific International Exposition;

99

Ode on the Opening; The Builders; The Evanescent City; Personal Poems; Frank Unger; To Xavier Martinez, Painter; The Light-Giver; To Margaret Anglin; On the Great War; The Song of the Valkyrs; The Dream of Wilhelm II; Earth's Anthem; To Germany; Betrayal; Belgium, August, 1914; England, August, 1914; To the War-Lords; The War-God; The Little Farm; The House of War; "As It Was in the Beginning"; To Belgium; The Two Prayers; Aftermath; The War-Machine; Bombardment; Germany; The Death-Chords; The Feast; War's Music; The Aeroplane; Before Dawn; The Turk; The New Kings; To France; The Night of Man; To the Allied Arms; The Battlefield at Night; Kingship; The Death of Rupert Brooke; The Helots; The Crown-Prince at Verdun; Before Dawn in America; Gun-Practice; To England; Civilization at Bay; The Day of Decision; Broadway, New York, 1916; The "Lusitania"; War: The Past; War: The Present; War: The Future; ADDITIONAL WAR POEMS FROM *The Binding of the Beast and Other Poems:* To Germany [VI]; The Binding of the Beast; To France at Verdun; In a Thousand Years; Germany in Belgium; Germany on the Seas; A Vision of Germania; To the Hun; THE PLAY OF EVERYMAN.

118. GEORGE STERLING. *Complete Poetry, Volume 2: To a Girl Dancing.* Edited by S. T. Joshi and David E. Schultz. 2013. 384 pp.

Contents: ROSAMUND; LILITH; SAILS AND MIRAGE AND OTHER POEMS: The Queen Forgets; Saul; Ocean Sunsets; Sanctuary; Spring in Carmel; The Setting of Antares; The Deserted Nest; Kingship; The First Food; The Wind; A Lost Garden; The Glass of Time; Reason; Sonnets by the Night-Sea; Sails; Mirage; The Skull of Shakespeare; Two Met; The Common Cult; The Lost Nymph; The Wine of Illusion; To Life; The Roman Wall; "His Own Country"; Lost Colors; The Passing of Bierce; Everest; Afternoon; A Compact?; Autumn in Carmel; Poe's Gravestone; The Secret Garden; Norman Boyer; Of One Asleep; To a Girl Dancing; The Far Feet; Hesperian; The Face of the Skies; The Morning Star; The Evening Star; To Charles Rollo Peters; To Ruth Chatterton; The Cool, Grey City of Love; The Princess on the Headland; To the Moon; The Hidden Pool; The Death of Circe; The Pathway; The Last Island; Infidels; Vox Humana; An Elegy; Sonnets on the Sea's Voice; The Dead Captain; Wind in Pines; TRUTH; TRUTH: A GROVE PLAY; STRANGE WATERS; APPENDIX: Light; By Carmel Mission; A Poet Has Risen, by Ambrose Bierce; A Poet and His Poem, by Ambrose Bierce; An Insurrection of the Peasantry, by Ambrose Bierce; Introduction to Lilith, by Theodore Dreiser; Notes; Index of Titles; Index of First Lines.

119. GEORGE STERLING. *Complete Poetry: Volume 3: The Stranger at the Gate*. 2013. Edited by S. T. Joshi and David E. Schultz. 500 pp.

Contents. DATED POEMS: Farewell; The Sea Waif; The Spaniards in Cuba; To ————; The Furies; In Farewell; To Leopold of Belgium; Brotherhood; Feb. 21, '08; To Mrs. J. B. C; Love's Shrine; The Cliff Dwellers; Inauguration Day, 1909; Romance! Romance!; The Pinions; To Artemis Hunting; Song in Family Club Jinks for 1912; The Golden Past; The Abalone Song; The Loosing; The Seasons; The Path of Portola; R. L. S; Hope; The Star of Love; To Stella; "Seasonal to Date"; To Albert Bierce; To the Goddess of Liberty; The Vision of Portola; Heat in the City; August 1st, 1914; The Blind; At Morning; Night Sounds; The Fish Hawk; At the Last; On Fifth Avenue; The Lifted Wings; Stress of Beauty; Ships of a Day; Under the Rainbow; Back to Back against the Mainmast; Ballad of the Bells; The First Snow; The Beach by Winter Twilight; Easter Dawn on Rubidoux; Lilies of Stone; Rendezvous; To the Unknown Goddess; "57"; Transmutation; Art; Joan of Arc; To Jack London; A Brother to Christ; Butterflies; Farmer Haynes' Niece; California to the Artist; Before Dawn; Holy River of Sleep; A Star; To Jack; To Robinson Jeffers; Democracy; The Passing of Buffalo Bill; To Sir Ernest Shackleton; The Revenge; The Friends of Wilhelm; "You Coward!"; To General White and Visiting Officers; The Path of Gold; The Immutable; You Are So Beautiful; The Symboled Spirit; Song of the Swineherds; "The White Logic"; The Flag; Moll; *Songs from* The Twilight of the Kings (1918); A Morning Hymn; The Messenger; Ever of You; We're A-Going; The Dust Hopes; Service; Nov. 11, 1918; The World-Rachel; Lucifer; To Joyce Kilmer; Outward; Visual Beauty; Altars of War; The Modern Muse; Memorial Day, 1919; [The Doughboy's Love Song]; From the Train; Morning in the Pines; To Raphael Weill; To Rachmaninoff; To Science; My Brook; Three Voices; Art and Life; Witch-Fire; Autumnal Love; To One Asleep; To Ned Greenway; To Louis Untermeyer; "Indulge the Genial Hour!"; Incarnation; Good and Evil; The Three Gifts; To Frank Mathieu; Distance; Rainbow's End; The "Bohemian Club"; Beyond the Music; Love and Time; Careless; The Wiser Prophet; Lost Sunsets; Three Sonnets on Beauty; The Parting of the Ways; The Day of Decision; Youth and Time; The Gulls; At Midnight; Flame; Happiest; The Kiss of Consummation; To an Irate Father; Problem; The Twilight of the Grape; Pumas; Ode to Shelley; Beauty Renounced; To Edwin Markham on His Seventieth Birt; The Wild Swan; Warning; The Killdee; The Night Migration; The Voice of the Wheat; The Trapping of Rung; To a Water-Fowl; The Midway Peace; Penitence; The Tracker; A Moth; To Serra of Carmel; The Stranger at the Gate; Ephemera; Shelley at Spezia; Sorcery; Venus Letalis; Song; A Critic;

The Sailor Turns Street-Sweeper; The City by the Sea; Long Island Pebbles; The Wings of Beauty; Waste; The Kiss; To a Stenographer; Gulls at Night; By Another Sea; Mystery; Suppose Nobody Cared; The Fog-Sea; The Housebreaker; Fog-Horns; The Black Hound Bays; The Dog; Return, Romance!; Chivalry; The Stranger; Eidolon; To Carl Sandburg; The Strange Bird; A Sceptic's Fate; After Sunset; A Lumberjack Yearns; The First-Born; The Flight; A Knee Is Bent; The Last of Sunset; Old Partings; The Pirate's Grave; Amber; The Daughters of Disillusion; The Young Witch; The Pony Express; Paradox; Transition; One Poem; Wet Beaches; Three Mysteries; Vigil; What Porridge Had John Keats?; Nepenthe; The Night-Watch; To a Reformer; A Face in the Crowd; High Noon; To Wordsworth; From the Valley; The Voice of the Deep; "The Ice-Age"; To Charles Warren Stoddard; Two Pictures by Dickman; The Little Hills; The Unconditioned; Dear to Me; Old Anchors; The Street; Three That Knew Helen; Solitude; Farm of Fools; A Deserted Farm; Once; Caucasus; The Sailing of Keats; Which Was, and Never Shall Be; The Aëroplane; To Bernice di Pasquali; "The Grizzly Giant"; Hostage; Life, Toil, and Love; Wayfarers; Disillusion; Ballad of the Seeker; Compensation; An Old Pine; To a Monk's Skull; Miocene; The Dreamer; Hope; An Old Road; The Fleet Comes; The Hawk's Nest; The Oldest Book; The Faithful; The Transfusion; The Steelyard; Familiar Beauty; Seismos; Sierran Dawn; Yerba Buena: July 9, 1846; To George Edwards; A Day of Truce; Ballad of the Grapes; Ballad of the Swabs; The Way to the West; The Grey Man; Infusion; The Unborn; The Meteor; Beauty and Truth; The Caravan; Echo; An Old Poem; The Pathfinders; To Friend W. Richardson; The Last Man; Late Tidings; Repartee; The Balance; North Wind; The Quarrel; Peace; Love and Custom; Lost Companion; Implication; On Certain Verses; Grasshopper; Safe; Insincerities; To California; Wings; The Restoration; The Seventh Veil; Coup de Grace; Counsel; Silence; An Old Indian Remembers; Adullam; My Swan Song; Abraham Lincoln; "And on Earth Peace, to Men of Good Wil; At Villa Montalvo; The Ballad of the Ghost-Arrow; Contributor; The Dark Nation; The Dweller in Darkness; The Final Faith; Sacrament; Sorrow; The Sowers; To Pain; To Ray Coyle; UNDATED POEMS: Above the Sea; Above the Stream; After Sunset; Amara; Annus Mirabilis; Answering; Arabian Lullaby; Archer and Arrow; The Ashes of Astarte; At the Club; At the Keyboard; At the Sea's Verge; Autumn; Autumn in California; Autumnal Hope; Before an Ocean; Beyond the Tides; Blue Ranges; Breakers; By the Sea of Time; The Carmel Millionaire; The Castaways; Change; The City and the Night; The Cocktail Song; Cold Altars; The Coming of Helen; Communion; Comparison; Completion; Comradeship;

102

Conclusion; Confiteor; Contrition; Conviction; Coronal; A Couch of Love; A Cry of the Heart; The Cynic; "Dad" Tatlow Advises; Darling!; Dawn; A Day; Deep-Sea Limericks; The Desert; Devotion; Division; A Dream of Arcady; The Dusks of Destiny; Earth-Worms; Endearment; Enigma; Entreaty; Exiles; "A Fair Exchange"; Far and Near; Far Day; The Far Goddess; Far Peace; Farewell and Meeting; Fate's Flower; Flags o' Truce; For E. H. Sothern; Foreshadowed; Forest Music; Forever and Ever; From Dawn to Dusk; From Sun to Star; The Fugitives; Fulfillment; The Futile Song; The Glory of the Globe; The Goal; Goddess-Love; Good-Bye; Haunted; Heart-ache; Her Welcome; Here and Now; The Hidden Garden; The Horse in War; Hotaling's Fancy Farm; A Hymn for Americans; The Immortal Moment; In the Shadow; In the Valley; In the Valley; Inarticulate; Inclusion; Interpeace; Journey's End; June; The Last Mirage; The Last of Beauty; The Last of the Year; The Last Veil; Lilies of Lethe; A Listener; Lonely Beauty; The Lost Empire; Love Adoring; Love and Faith; Love and the Sea; Love at Sunset; Love at Twilight; Love Inexhaustible; Love Song; Love's Consummation; Love's Farewell; Love's Hunger; Love's Silence; The Lutes of Exile; Magdalene; Man and Woman; Martyrdom; Meeting; Melodie in E; Memory and Rain; The Merciful Man; The Messenger; The Mirror; The Moon of Memory; The Music of Memory; Myrrh; Night-Separation; The Night-Wind; Nimrod; November Carol; The Oceans; "The Old Black-a Bull"; "Old Cats o' Carmel"; On His Blindness; On the Late Payment of Rent— Followed b; One Day; Origin; Pain and Joy; The Palace of the Moon; Parted; Parted; Passion's Prayer; Pavement; The Peace of the Hills; A Prayer; Protest; The Quest; The Rain; Recompense; Recompense; The Redwoods; Redwoods by Morning; The Redwoods Wait; Reflections on the Cat; Regret; Relatives; Remembered; Renouncement; "The Return of Faith"; Revealing Music; Revelation; Rosa Mystica; Rosa Mystica; Rose of the Winds; Roses of Sunset; Sarah the Whale; The Sea; Separation; Serenade; Silver Sword; The Sisters; Song; Song; Song; Song; Song; The Song of Henry Maxwell; Song of the Pirates; Song's Lesson; Sonnets of Realization; Sonnets of the True Beauty; The Sphinx; Spontaneity 37; Spontaneity 40; Spontaneity 42; Spontaneity 44; Spontaneity 92; Star and Storm; Starlight; Stars; Surety; The Swimmer; Tears; Testimony; That Which Abides; Thou and I; Through Love's Eyes; Thy Lineage; To a Dusk-Rose; To Anne Bremer; To Antonoë; To Astarte; To Love the God; To Mrs. Phoebe A. Hearst; To One Who Passed; To Stella; To the Bosom of Antonoë, Handmaiden of; To the True Heart; To Wilhelm II; To Ylla; To You; To You; Together; Too Late; Transfiguration; Twilight at Midway Point; Twilight Song; The Two Buzzards; The Unattainable; Until the Dawn; Valerie; A Visitant; A Voice; The Wayfarer; The Wayside Garden; Western Twilight; What It's Like; What Shall Be; Willy Smith at the Ball Game; Wind and Rain; "With Brief Thanksgiving"; Wonderment; The Woof of the Stars; The Word-Shrine; Yearning; Young Love; [Untitled Poems]; [Untitled Fragments]; [Untitled Fragmentary Poetic Drama]; Appendix; Holy River of Sleep; We're A-Going; A Christmas Hymn; [Untitled], by François Coppée; Notes; Index of Titles; Index of First Lines.

Notes. Bound in hardcover (no dust jacket) in an edition of 300 sets by Covington Group, including a slipcased edition of 50 sets which was released by subscription. Facsimile signature of George Sterling stamped in foil on the front cover of each volume. First complete edition of the poetry by the great California poet (1869–1926). Volumes 1 and 2 contain the complete contents of the volumes of poetry published in Sterling's lifetime, from *The Testimony of the Suns* (1903) to *Sails and Mirage* (1921), as well as his verse dramas and individually published poems; Volume 3 contains unpublished or uncollected poems. The edition features commentary on each of the poems and full bibliographical information on their publication during and shortly after Sterling's lifetime.

120. JOHN LANGAN. *The Wide, Carnivorous Sky and Other Monstrous Geographies*. 2013. 324 pp.

Contents. Introduction: Reading Langan, by Jeffrey Ford; Kids; How the Day Runs Down; Technicolor; The Wide, Carnivorous Sky; City of the Dog; The Shallows; The Revel; June, 1987. Hitchhiking. Mr. Norris.; Mother of Stone; Story Notes; Afterword: Note Found in a Glenfiddich Bottle, by Laird Barron; Acknowledgments.

Notes. Cover illustration by Santiago Caruso. The second collection of Langan's short fiction, following on *Mr. Gaunt and Other Uncanny Encounters* (Prime, 2008).

121. H. P. LOVECRAFT AND AUGUST DERLETH. *Essential Solitude: The Letters of H. P. Lovecraft and August Derleth, 1926–1931* (vol. 1) and *1932–1937* (vol. 2). Edited by David E. Schultz and S. T. Joshi. 2013. 880 pp. (numbered consecutively). ppbk.

122. JASON V BROCK. *Simulacrum and Other Possible Realities*. 2013. 248 pp.

Contents. Foreword: Man of Many Talents, by William F. Nolan; Preface; Introduction, by James Robert Smith; What the Dead's Eyes Behold; Pathologist's Roulette; The Central Coast; Passage; One for the Road; Palindrome Syndrome; The Hex Factor; Valve: The Heart as a Metaphor for Postmodern Blight; Valor: A Fable; Dragon; Object Lesson; Dream Poem #00; Where Everything That Is Lost Goes; Godhead: How to Become a God/Goddess in Six Steps; The Underground; Frac/tion; Van Helsing: His True Story; Story of a Blade; P.O.V.; People After Their Murder by the U.S. CIA; "By Any Other Name ...", Fever/Wart; Red-Wat-Shod; Poem from the Future; The History of a Letter; Wind; Black Box; Milton's Children; Simulacrum; Acknowledgments; About the Author.

Notes. Cover design, cover illustration and interior artwork by Jason V Brock. The first short story collection by a dynamic young writer of weird fiction, including stories that range from psychological suspense to Lovecraftian horror to a melding of weirdness and science fiction. Also features examples of Brock's striking free verse.

123. S. T. JOSHI. *The Assaults of Chaos: A Novel about H. P. Lovecraft.* 2013. 246 pp.

Notes. Cover illustration by Pete Von Sholly. Printed in a limited hardcover edition (500 copies, Covington Group). A novel that envisions Lovecraft, in the summer of 1914, encountering Ambrose Bierce and then venturing to England to team up with Arthur Machen, Lord Dunsany, M. R. James, Algernon Blackwood, and William Hope Hodgson to battle a cosmic threat posed by Nyarlathotep. Many of the words uttered by the various characters are taken from their essays, letters, and other writings.

124. S. T. JOSHI. *Suicide in Brooklyn.* 2013. 36 pp.

Notes. Cover illustration by Daniele Serra. A short story included as a bonus to the first 200 purchasers of *The Assaults of Chaos.* A detective story without supernatural elements, but featuring covert references to details of Lovecraft's life and work.

125. DAVID GOUDSWARD. *H. P. Lovecraft in the Merrimack Valley.* 2013. 192 pp.

Contents. Foreword, by Kenneth W. Faig, Jr.; Preface; Acknowledgments; 1. Transformations; 2. First Visits: 1921; 3. Whittierland and Newburyport; 4. Intermezzo: 1924–26; 5. Innsmouth Ascendant: 1927–31; 6. Dreams and Eclipses: 1932–33; 7. Shadows out of Haverhill: 1934–36; 8. Coda; APPENDIXES: A. The Haverhill Convention, by H. P. Lovecraft; B. First Impressions of Newburyport, by H. P.

Lovecraft; C. Tryout's Return to Haverhill; Plaistow, N.H., by C. W. Smith; The Return, by H. P. Lovecraft; D. The Published Works of Myrta Alice Little Davies; E. Howard Prescott Lovecraft, by C. W. Smith; F. The Publications of Charles W. Smith; G. H. P. Lovecraft, "The Dunwich Horror," and Mystery Hill; H. Sites Open to the Public; Notes; Lovecraft: A Sense of Place and High Strangeness, by Chris Perridas; Bibliography; Index.

Notes. Cover photograph by Logan Seale, with copious interior illustrations. Interesting treatise on Lovecraft's travels in Massachusetts and New Hampshire and his encounters with such colleagues as Charles W. Smith and Myrta Alice Little; with a discussion of the influence of these visits on his fiction.

126. STEVEN J. MARICONDA. *H. P. Lovecraft: Art, Artifact, and Reality.* 2013. 306 pp.

Contents. Introduction; I. GENERAL STUDIES: H. P. Lovecraft: Consummate Prose Stylist; Lovecraft's Concept of "Background"; Toward a Reader-Response Approach to the Lovecraft Mythos; Lovecraft's Cosmic Imagery; H. P. Lovecraft: Art, Artifact, and Reality; H. P. Lovecraft: Reluctant American Modernist; "Expect Great Revelations": Lovecraft Criticism in His Centennial Year; II. ESSAYS ON SPECIFIC WORKS: On "Amissa Minerva"; "The Hound"—A Dead Dog?; "Hypnos": Art, Philosophy, and Insanity; *Curious Myths of the Middle Ages* and "The Rats in the Walls"; Lovecraft's "Elizabethtown"; On the Emergence of "Cthulhu"; The Subversion of Sense in "The Colour out of Space"; Tightening the Coil: The Revision of "The Whisperer in Darkness"; Lovecraft's Role in "The Tree on the Hill"; Some Antecedents of the Shining Trapezohedron; III. REVIEWS: The Corrected Texts of Lovecraft's Tales; Lovecraft's Essays, Poems, and Letters; Some Lovecraft Scholars; Anodyne. Amusing Appendix; Afterword; Works Cited; Sources; Index.

Notes. Cover illustration by Charles E. Burchfield ("Afterglow", 1916). Rich collection of the collected essays and reviews of one of the leading Lovecraft scholars over the past thirty years. A radical expansion of Mariconda's earlier essay collection, *On the Emergence of "Cthulhu" and Other Observations* (Necronomicon Press, 1995).

127. KENNETH W. FAIG, JR. *Lovecraft's Pillow and Other Strange Stories.* 2013. 234 pp.

Contents. Preface; TALES OF THE LOVECRAFT COLLECTORS: Introduction; Collector the First—Major Geoffrey Hopkinton-Smith (1857–

1943); Collector the Second—Dean Alan Edgerton Noble (1876–
1959); Collector the Third—Charles Wilson Hodap (1842–1944);
Collectors the Fourth and Fifth—David Parkes Boynton (1897–1956)
and Another Gentleman of the Hope Club; Collectors the Sixth and
Seventh—Miss Susan M. Rounds (1780–1878) and James N. Arnold
(1844–1927). Life and Death; The Squirrel Pond; Innsmouth 1984;
Boy in Summer; The Haunting of Huber's; Lovecraft's Pillow; Leng;
Gothic Studies; Sources.

Notes. Cover illustration by Daniele Serra. A substantial—and perhaps surprising—collection of stories by a writer who has distinguished himself as a leading authority on Lovecraft's life. Faig here
brings that knowledge to bear in many of these stories, especially in an
expanded version of *Tales of the Lovecraft Collectors* (first published by
Necronomicon Press in 1995), as well as in other tales.

128. JONATHAN THOMAS. *Thirteen Conjurations.* 2013. 278 pp.

Contents. In Situ: Excavating the Art of Jonathan Thomas, by Barton
Levi St. Armand; FROM OUT OF THE MYTHOS: Mobymart After Mid-
night; King of Cat Swamp; Pictures of Lily; The Last Jar; FROM ELSE-
WHERE: The Copper God's Treat; Sympathy for the Deadbeats; Way
Up When; The Comeuppance Hour; A Retouch in Camonica; Elec-
tion Roundup; SWEDISH-AMERICAN TRIPTYCH: Missing the Boat
(The Promised Land); Harm Like Water (The Undiscovered Coun-
try); Taking the Plunge (The Old Country).

Notes. Cover illustration by Jason C. Eckhardt. Thomas's third story
collection, containing ingenious elaborations of the Lovecraft Mythos
as well as other tales of terror and strangeness.

129. H. P. LOVECRAFT. *The Ancient Track: The Complete Poetical
Works of H. P. Lovecraft.* Edited by S. T. Joshi. 2013. 604 pp.

Contents: Introduction; I. JUVENILIA: 1897–1905: ; The Poem of Ulys-
ses, or The Odyssey; Ovid's Metamorphoses; H. Lovecraft's Attempt-
ed Journey betwixt Providence & Fall River on the N.Y.N.H. &
H.R.R.; *Poemata Minora, Volume II:* Ode to Selene or Diana; To the
Old Pagan Religion; On the Ruin of Rome; To Pan; On the Vanity of
Human Ambition; C. S. A.: 1861–1865; De Triumpho Naturae; II.
FANTASY AND HORROR: To the Late John H. Fowler, Esq.; The Un-
known; The Poe-et's Nightmare; The Rutted Road; Nemesis; As-
trophobos; Psychopompos: A Tale in Rhyme; The Eidolon; A Cycle of
Verse (Oceanus, Clouds, Mother Earth); Despair; Revelation; The
House; The City; To Edward John Moreton Drax Plunkett, Eight-
eenth Baron Dunsany; Bells; The Nightmare Lake; On Reading Lord

Dunsany's *Book of Wonder*; To a Dreamer; With a Copy of Wilde's Fairy Tales; [On *The Thing in the Woods* by Harper Williams]; The Cats; Primavera; Festival; Hallowe'en in a Suburb; [On Ambrose Bierce]; The Wood; The Outpost; The Ancient Track; The Messenger; *Fungi from Yuggoth:* I. The Book; II. Pursuit; III. The Key; IV. Recognition; V. Homecoming; VI. The Lamp; VII. Zaman's Hill; VIII. The Port; IX. The Courtyard; X. The Pigeon-Flyers; XI. The Well; XII. The Howler; XIII. Hesperia; XIV. Star-Winds; XV. Antarktos; XVI. The Window; XVII. A Memory; XVIII. The Gardens of Yin; XIX. The Bells; XX. Night-Gaunts; XXI. Nyarlathotep; XXII. Azathoth; XXIII. Mirage; XXIV. The Canal; XXV. St. Toad's; XXVI. The Familiars; XXVII. The Elder Pharos; XXVIII. Expectancy; XXIX. Nostalgia; XXX. Background; XXXI. The Dweller; XXXII. Alienation; XXXIII. Harbour Whistles; XXXIV. Recapture; XXXV. Evening Star; XXXVI. Continuity; Bouts Rimés (Beyond Zimbabwe, The White Elephant); In a Sequester'd Providence Churchyard Where Once Poe Walk'd; To Mr. Finlay, upon His Drawing for Mr. Bloch's Tale, "The Faceless God"; To Clark Ashton Smith, Esq., upon His Phantastick Tales, Verses, Pictures, and Sculptures; Nathicana; III. OCCASIONAL VERSE: The Members of the Men's Club of the First Universalist Church of Providence, R.I., to Its President, About to Leave for Florida on Account of His Health; To Mr. Terhune, on His Historical Fiction; To Mr. Munroe, on His Instructive and Entertaining Account of Switzerland; Regner Lodbrog's Epicedium; To an Accomplished Young Gentlewoman on Her Birthday, Decr. 2, 1914; To the Recipient of This Volume; On Receiving a Picture of Swans; To Charlie of the Comics; On the Cowboys of the West; To Samuel Loveman, Esquire, on His Poetry and Drama, Writ in the Elizabethan Style; The Bookstall; Content; The Smile; Inspiration; Respite; Brotherhood; Lines on Graduation from the R.I. Hospital's School of Nurses; Fact and Fancy; Percival Lowell; Prologue to "Fragments from an Hour of Inspiration" by Jonathan E. Hoag; Earth and Sky; To M. W. M.; Lines on the 25th. Anniversary of the *Providence Evening News*, 1892–1917; To the Nurses of the Red Cross; To the Arcadian; Laeta; a Lament; To Mr. Kleiner, on Receiving from Him the Poetical Works of Addison, Gay, and Somerville; A Pastoral Tragedy of Appleton, Wisconsin; Damon and Delia, a Pastoral; To Delia, Avoiding Damon; Hellas; Ambition; To Alfred Galpin, Esq.; To the Eighth of November; Damon: A Monody; Hylas and Myrrha: A Tale; John Oldham: A Defence; Myrrha and Strephon; Wisdom; Birthday Lines to Margfred Galbraham; Tryout's Lament for the Vanished Spider; Cindy: Scrub-Lady in a State Street Skyscraper; The Voice; On a Grecian Colonnade in a Park; The Dream; On Receiving a Portraiture of Mrs. Berke-

109

lips Howard's Profound Poem Entitled "Life's Mystery"; On an Accomplished Young Linguist; "The Poetical Punch" Pushed from His Pedestal; The Road to Ruin; Sors Poetae; V. SEASONAL AND TOPOGRAPHICAL: Quinsnicket Park; New England; March; A Mississippi Autumn; A Rural Summer Eve; Brumalia; On Receiving a Picture of the Marshes at Ipswich; A Garden; April; On Receiving a Picture of yᵉ Towne of Templeton, in the Colonie of Massachusetts-Bay, with Mount Monadnock, in New-Hampshire, Shewn in the Distance; Autumn; Sunset; Old Christmas; A Summer Sunset and Evening; A Winter Wish; Ver Rusticum; A June Afternoon; The Spirit of Summer; August; Spring; April Dawn; January; October; Christmas; [On Marblehead]; [On a Scene in Rural Rhode Island]; Providence; Solstice; October; [On Newport, Rhode Island]; The East India Brick Row; On an Unspoil'd Rural Prospect; Saturnalia; [Christmas Greetings]; VI. AMATEUR AFFAIRS: To the Members of the Pin-Feathers on the Merits of Their Organisation, and of Their New Publication, *The Pinfeather*; To the Rev. James Pyke; To the Members of the United Amateur Press Association from the Providence Amateur Press Club; The Bay-Stater's Policy; To "The Scribblers"; R. Kleiner, Laureatus, in Heliconem; Providence Amateur Press Club (Deceased) to the Athenaeum Club of Journalism; To Mr. Lockhart, on His Poetry; To Jonathan E. Hoag, Esq.; To Arthur Goodenough, Esq.; To the A.H.S.P.C., on Receipt of the Christmas *Pippin*; Greetings (To Arthur Goodenough, Esq.; To W. Paul Cook, Esq.; To E. Sherman Cole; To the *Silver Clarion*); To Jonathan Hoag, Esq.; In Memoriam: J. E. T. D.; To the A.H.S.P.C., on Receipt of the May *Pippin*; Helene Hoffman Cole: 1893–1919; On Collaboration; Ad Scribam; Ex-Poet's Reply; To Two Epgephi; Theobaldian Aestivation; The Prophecy of Capys Secundus; (Wet) Dream Song; To Mr. Hoag; On a Poet's Ninety-first Birthday; To Saml: Loveman, Gent.,; To Mr. Hoag; The Feast; Lines for Poets' Night at the Scribblers' Club; To Mr. Hoag; To Mr. Hoag; To Jonathan Hoag; To Jonathan E. Hoag, Esq.; The Absent Leader; Ave atque Vale; VII. POLITICS AND SOCIETY: New-England Fallen; On the Creation of Niggers; On a New-England Village Seen by Moonlight; To General Villa; The Teuton's Battle-Song; 1914; The Crime of Crimes; An American to Mother England; Temperance Song; The Rose of England; Lines on Gen. Robert Edward Lee; Britannia Victura; Pacifist War Song—1917; Iterum Conjunctae; The Peace Advocate; To Greece, 1917; Ode for July Fourth, 1917; An American to the British Flag; The Volunteer; Ad Britannos—1918; On a Battlefield in Picardy; The Link; To Alan Seeger; Germania—1918; The Conscript; To Maj.-Gen. Omar Bundy, U.S.A.; Theodore Roosevelt; North and South Britons; VIII. *Personal*: [To His Mother on Thanksgiving]; An Elegy on Franklin Chase Clark, M.D.; [The Solace of Georgian Poetry]; [On Phillips Gamwell]; An Elegy on Phillips Gamwell, Esq.; Sonnet on Myself; Phaeton; Monos: An Ode; Oct. 17, 1919; To S. S. L.—October 17, 1920; S. S. L.: Christmas 1920; To Xanthippe, on Her Birthday—March 16, 1925; Εἰς Σφίγγην; [On Cheating the Post Office]; An Epistle to the Rt. Honble Maurice Winter Moe, Esq. of Zythopolis, in the Northwest Territory of HIS MAJESTY'S American Dominions; [Anthem of the Kappa Alpha Tau]; Edith Miniter; [Little Sam Perkins]; IX. ALFREDO; A TRAGEDY; X. FRAGMENTS; Appendix 1: Lovecraft's Revisions of Poetry: A Prayer for Universal Peace, by Robert L. Selle, D.D.; [On the Duke of Leeds], by Unknown; Mors Omnibus Communis, by Sonia H. Greene; Alone, by Jonathan E. Hoag; Unity, by Unknown; The Dweller, by William Lumley; Dreams of Yith, by Duane W. Rimel; [On John Donne], by Lee McBride White; The Wanderer's Return, by Wilson Shepherd; Appendix 2: Poems by Others: Metamorphoses 1.1–88, by Ovid (P. Ovidius Naso); Our Apology to E. M. W., by John Russell; Florida, by John Russell; Regner Lodbrog's Epicedium, by Olaus Wormius, tr. Hugh Blair; A Prayer for Universal Peace, by Robert L. Selle, D.D.; To Mary of the Movies, by Rheinhart Kleiner; A Prayer for Peace and Justice, by Henry F. Thomas; The Modern Business Man to His Love, by Olive G. Owen; His Frank Self-Expression, by Paul Shivell; To a Movie Star, by Rheinhart Kleiner; [On the Duke of Leeds], by Unknown; Ruth, by Rheinhart Kleiner; Only a Volunteer, by Sergt. Hayes P. Miller; John Oldham: 1653–1683, by Rheinhart Kleiner; To Miriam, by Rheinhart Kleiner; Ethel: Cashier in a Broad Street Buffet, by Rheinhart Kleiner; Pastorale, by Hart Crane; Odes 3.9, by Horace (Q. Horatius Flaccus); [On John Donne], by Lee McBride White; Irony, by Wilson Shepherd; Notes; Bibliography; A Chronology of Lovecraft's Poems; Index of Titles; Index of First Lines.

Notes. Cover illustration by Charles E. Burchfield ("The Sphinx and the Milky Way", 1946). A thorough overhauling of Joshi's edition of Lovecraft's collected poetry (first published by Night Shade Books in 2001), containing several new poems and poem fragments and with an exhaustive revision of notes, bibliography, and other matter. The first and to date only Hippocampus Press book to be released in an oversized (7 × 10 in.) trim size.

130. *Lovecraft Annual* No. 7 (2013). EDITED BY S. T. JOSHI. 218 pp.

Contents. New Deal Politics in the Correspondence of H. P. Lovecraft, by Tyler L. Wolanin; Letters between H. P. Lovecraft and Orville L. Leach, edited by Donovan K. Loucks; Lovecraft's Rats and Doyle's

Hound: A Study in Reason and Madness, by Robert H. Waugh; Lovecraft's Travelogues of Foster, Rhode Island, by Kenneth W. Faig, Jr.; Reappraising "The Haunter of the Dark," by John D. Haefele; Department of Public Criticism: July 1918, by H. P. Lovecraft; A Mountain Walked or Stumbled, by Stephen Walker; Excised Passages from "The Thing on the Doorstep," by S. T. Joshi; Additions and Corrections for "Lovecraft's 1937 Diary," by David Haden; Lovecraft, Reality, and the Real: A Žižekian Approach, by Juan Luis Pérez de Luque; Reviews: S. T. Joshi [H. P. Lovecraft, The Classic Horror Stories, ed. Roger Luckhurst]; Scott Connors [Robert H. Waugh, ed., Lovecraft and Influence]; Briefly Noted.

131. Dead Reckonings No. 13 (Spring 2013). EDITED BY JUNE M. PULLIAM AND TONY FONSECA. 106 pp.

Contents. Wagner and Vincent on King, by Hank Wagner and Bev Vincent [Stephen King, Doctor Sleep]; A Dazzling Collection of Weird Fiction Gems, by Robert Butterfield [Peter Bell, Strange Epiphanies]; Ramsey Campbell, Probably: A Ghostly Poll; Rhyme, Rhythm, and Revenants, by Leigh Blackmore [S. T. Joshi and Steven J. Mariconda, ed., Dreams of Fear: Poetry of Terror and the Supernatural]; Don't Play It Again, Sam, by Tony Fonseca [Ed Kurtz, Catch My Killer!]; From Forties Noir to Cheesy Sci-Fi, by Robert Butterfield [Brandon Zuern, The Last Invasion]; Future Zombies and Past Scary-otypes, by June Pulliam [Marc Forster, dir., World War Z; James Wan, dir., The Conjuring]; A Distinctive Talent, by S. T. Joshi [W. H. Pugmire, The Strange Dark One: Tales of Nyarlathotep; Bohemians of Sesqua Valley; W. H. Pugmire and Jeffrey Thomas, Encounters with Enoch Coffin]; Werewolves and the War on Terror, by Matthew McEver [Benjamin Percy, Red Moon]; Subtlety Scares, by Hank Wagner [John Langan, The Wide, Carnivorous Sky and Other Monstrous Geographies; Guy N. Smith, Deadbeat]; Klarkash-Ton Revealed, by Darrell Schweitzer [Steve Behrends, Clark Ashton Smith: A Critical Guide]; Recommended Reading Despite Reservations, by Leigh Blackmore [Danel Olson, ed., Exotic Gothic 4]; Brainless Zombies and Horror with a Heart, by Richard Bleiler [K. Bennett, Pay Me in Flesh; The Year of Eating Dangerously; I Ate the Sheriff; Mark Valentine, Selected Stories]; Retrospective Review: Remarks on Frankenstein, by Sir Walter Scott; The Weird Scholar, by S. T. Joshi; Strange Days and Stranger Nights, by John Edgar Browning [Jeffrey Ford, Crackpot Palace: Stories; Brian J. Showers, Old Albert: An Epilogue]; Body Horror Squared, by June Pulliam [Shane Stadler, Exoskeleton; Paul Kane and Marie O'Regan, ed., The Mammoth Book of Body Horror]; Driven to Madness with Fright, by S. T. Joshi [Simon Strantzas, ed., Shadows Edge; Joseph S. Pulver,

Sr., ed., A *Season in Carcosa*]; Fangs for Fans, but no Braiiins for Scholars, by June Pulliam [Joni Richards Bodart, *They Suck, They Bite, They Eat, They Kill*]; Is This the End of Zombie Shakespeare?, by June Pulliam [Isaac Marion, *Warm Bodies*; Jonathan Levine, dir., *Warm Bodies*]; Horror, Harmony, and Discord, by Tony Fonseca [Philip Hayward, *Terror Tracks: Music, Sound and Horror Cinema*; Neil Lerner, *Music in the Horror Film: Listening to Fear*]; Supernatural Cliché Powers, by June Pulliam [Libba Bray, *The Diviners*]; Blood Lust, by Van Viator [Ed Kurtz, *Bleed*; Chuck Wendig, *Double Dead*; *Bad Blood*]; See a Zombie; Fuck a Zombie; Repeat . . ., by Tony Fonseca [Stacey Turner, ed., *Fifty Shades of Decay: Zombie Erotica*]; Dome and Dumber, by June Pulliam [*Under the Dome*, developed by Stephen King and Brian K. Vaughan]; Don't Touch That Dial!, by June Pulliam [*American Horror Story*, Season 2; *The Walking Dead*, Season 3]; From Heroin to Heroine, by June Pulliam [Fede Alvarez, dir., *Evil Dead*]; Portrait of the Monster as a Young Man, by June Pulliam [Derf Backderf, *My Friend Dahmer*]; Capsule Reviews; Notes on Contributors.

132. EDITH MINITER. *The Village Green and Other Pieces.* Edited by Kenneth W. Faig, Jr. and Sean Donnelly. 2013. xvii, 363 pp.

Contents. Introduction; UNFINISHED NOVELS: *Lydia 'n Gerald; The Village Green; Love Without Wings*; SHORT FICTION: Who Brought the Children Home? 'lizbeth Prue; The Woman Over Way; The Other Elizabeth; When the Fog Lifted; For a Big Roll of Money; Overheard on the Beach; Maggie; An Unknown Mystery; Cindy's Child; Bookends; A Rearward Glance; How to Dress on $40 a Year.

Notes. Cover design by Sean Donnelly incorporating a photograph from *Ex-Presidents of the National Amateur Press Association: Sketches* by Wm. C. Ahlhauser (Athol: W. Paul Cook, 1919). Interesting second assemblage of fiction by a close friend of Lovecraft in the realm of amateur journalism, who also published much work professionally.

133. *Dead Reckonings* No. 14 (Fall 2013). EDITED BY JUNE M. PULLIAM AND TONY FONSECA. 100 pp.

Contents. Wagner and Vincent on Simmons, by Hank Wagner and Bev Vincent [Dan Simmons, *The Abominable*]; Ramsey Campbell, Probably: The Grin Beneath the Flesh; From Horror to Homage, by Richard Bleiler [J. E. Mooney and Bill Fawcett, eds., *Shadows of the New Sun: Stories in Honor of Gene Wolfe*; Joseph S. Pulver, Sr., ed. *The Grimscribe's Puppets*]; Joel Lane: In Memoriam, by Robert Butterfield; Other Realities—Alternate Readings: Two Views on Jason V Brock: Outlier, by

Jonathan Johnson; Brock as Intriguing New Voice, by Darrell Schweitzer [Jason V Brock, *Simulacrum and Other Possible Realities*]; Malignant Mothers, by Richard Bleiler [John Boyne, *This House Is Haunted*; Sophie Hannah, *The Orphan Choir*]; What Happens After?, by Sarah Simms [Ellen Datlow and Terri Windling, ed., *After: Nineteen Stories of Apocalypse and Dystopia*]; 571 Forrester Lane Eats Babies, by Matthew McEver [Sonja Condit, *Starter House*]; Triskaidekaphilia, by Jonathan Johnson [Jonathan Thomas, *Thirteen Conjurations*]; Submitted: My Stamp of Approval, by Tony Fonseca [Reba Wissner, *A Dimension of Sound: The Music of The Twilight Zone*]; Religious Fanaticism Run Amok, by Antoinette F. Winstead [L. Andrew Cooper, *Burning the Middle Ground*]; Fifty Years of Ramsey Campbell, by S. T. Joshi [Ramsey Campbell, *Holes for Faces*; *The Kind Folk*; and *The Last Revelation of Gla'aki*]; Two Veteran Storytellers Demonstrate How It Is Done, by Robert Butterfield [Darrell Schweitzer, *The Emperor of the Ancient Word*; Tony Richards, *The Universal and Other Terrors*]; Zombie Scholarship Earns Respect, by June Pulliam [Jennifer Rutherford, *Zombies*; Aalya Ahmad and Sean Moreland, eds., *Fear and Learning: Essays on the Pedagogy of Horror*]; Sequel Deserves to be a Forgotten Chapter, by Braden Dauzat [James Wan, dir., *Insidious: Chapter 2*]; Haunted from Within and Without, by Richard Bleiler [Ellen Datlow, ed. *Hauntings*]; A Darker Piece of Darkness, by John Edgar Browning [Ellen Datlow, ed., *The Best Horror of the Year, Volume 5* and *Blood and Other Cravings*; Laird Barron, *The Beautiful Thing That Awaits Us All and Other Stories*]; The Lovecraftian Magickal Mystery Tour, by Leigh Blackmore [Peter Levenda, *The Dark Lord: H. P. Lovecraft, Kenneth Grant and the Typhonian Tradition in Magic*]; A Smorgasbord of Weird, by S. T. Joshi [Lois H. Gresh, ed., *Dark Fusions: Where Monsters Lurk!*]; Portrait of the Mythos-Maker as a Young Man, by Tony Fonseca [S. T. Joshi, *The Assaults of Chaos: A Novel about H. P. Lovecraft*]; Second Time's the Charm, by Leigh Blackmore [H. P. Lovecraft, *The Ancient Track: The Complete Poetical Works*]; Covens, Witchcraft, and Murder, Oh My!, by Antoinette Winstead [Debbie Viguie, *The Thirteenth Sacrifice: A Witch Hunt Novel*]; Zombies Are People Too, by June Pulliam [Jonny Campbell, dir., *In the Flesh*]; The Weird Scholar, by S. T. Joshi; Notes on Contributors.

134. H. P. LOVECRAFT. *Letters to Elizabeth Toldridge and Anne Tillery Renshaw*. Edited by David E. Schultz and S. T. Joshi. 2014. 470 pp.

Contents. Introduction; Letters to Elizabeth Toldridge; Letters to Anne Tillery Renshaw; APPENDIX: *Poems by Elizabeth Toldridge*: Expectancy; I Know a Forest Dark and Deep; Locusts and Wild Honey; Poe; H. P. Lovecraft; Mist; Ephemera; Midnight Sky;

Divinity; Toldridge's Poetry Manuscripts at JHL; Contents of *Winnings* (ms., New York Public Library); Letters by Elizabeth Toldridge; Unpublished Parts of *Well-Bred Speech* as written by H. P. Lovecraft; Glossary of Frequently Mentioned Names; Bibliography; Index.

Notes. Cover design by Anastasia Damianakos (uniform with item 13). Meticulously edited volume of Lovecraft's complete surviving letters to two women, the disabled poet Elizabeth Toldridge and the amateur writer Anne Tillery Renshaw, whose elementary treatise *Well Bred Speech* (1936) Lovecraft revised late in life. Several chapters from that treatise that Lovecraft had written for Renshaw, but which were rejected by her, are published here for the first time.

135. SIMON STRANTZAS. *Burnt Black Suns: A Collection of Weird Tales.* 2014. 308 pp.

Contents. Dig My Grave, by Laird Barron; On Ice; Dwelling on the Past; Strong as a Rock; By Invisible Hands; One Last Bloom; Thistle's Find; Beyond the Banks of the River Seine; Emotional Dues; Burnt Black Suns; Acknowledgments.

Notes. Cover illustration by Santiago Caruso. Strong collection of weird stories by one of the leading contemporary figures in the field. A finalist for the 2014 Shirley Jackson Awards.

136. CLINT SMITH. *Ghouljaw and Other Stories.* 2014. 258 pp.

Contains. Introduction, by S. T. Joshi; Benthos; Ghouljaw; Dirt on Vicky; Don't Let the Bedbugs Bite; Retrograde; What About the Little One?; Double Back; The Tell-Tale Offal; Like Father, Like . . .; Corbin's Gore; The Hatchet; The Jellyfish; What Happens in Hell Stays in Hell; The Day of the Earwig.

Notes. Cover design and illustration by Jared Boggess. First collection of weird tales by a dynamic young author whose work is bound to be noticed in the years to come. Notably, a "soundtrack" to the collection was issued on audio CD by Kell of Shadowland.

137. *Dead Reckonings* No. 15 (Spring 2014). EDITED BY JUNE M. PULLIAM AND TONY FONSECA. 100 pp.

Contents. HPL^3: A Multi-Dimensional View of Lovecraft, by Leigh Blackmore [David Goudsward, H. P. Lovecraft in the Merrimack Valley; Kenneth W. Faig, Jr., Lovecraft's Pillow and Other Strange Stories; Steven J. Mariconda. H. P. Lovecraft: Art, Artifact, and Reality]; Ramsey Campbell, Probably: Here Comes the Code; A Weird Fiction Tour de Force, by Robert Butterfield [Simon Strantzas, Burnt Black

Suns]; Carnacki Lives Again!, by S. T. Joshi [Sam Gafford, ed. Carnacki: The New Adventures]; Holding Up the Undead as a Mirror, by June Pulliam [Rob Kuhns, dir., Birth of the Living Dead]; Reading the Impenetrable, by Javier A. Martínez [Luigi Serafini, Codex Seraphinianus]; Instant Rarity, by Darrell Schweitzer [John Shire, Their Hand Is at Your Throats: Stories After Lovecraft]; The Return of Fedogan & Bremer, by Leigh Blackmore [Scott Nicolay, Ana Kai Tangata: Tales of the Outer, the Other, the Damned and the Doomed; S. T. Joshi, ed., Searchers After Horror: New Tales of the Weird and Fantastic.]; Robocraftian Myths, by Martin Andersson [Brian M. Sammons and Glynn Owen Barrass, ed., Eldritch Chrome: Unquiet Tales of a Mythos-Haunted Future]; This Is the Forest Primeval . . ., by Jim Rockhill [Bernice M. Murphy, The Rural Gothic in American Popular Culture: Backwoods Horror and Terror in the Wilderness]; Out of the Distant Dark, by John Edgar Browning [Jeffrey Andrew Weinstock, ed., The Ashgate Encyclopedia of Literary and Cinematic Monsters; Steve Rasnic Tem, Here with the Shadows]; Portrait of the Gothic Fan as a Young Child, by Sarah Simms [Gert Jan Bekenkamp, The World of Wonder: On Children's Lust for Terror]; Spanning the Genres with William F. Nolan, by S. T. Joshi [William F. Nolan. Like a Dead Man Walking and Other Shadow Tales]; The Expanding Fictional Universe of the Small Screen, by June Pulliam [Hannibal, created by Bryan Fuller; Fargo, created by Noah Hawley]; The World Is Beautiful, Dark and Deep, by Richard Bleiler [Bruce Boston, Dark Roads: Selected Long Poems, 1971–2012]; From Japan with Love, by June Pulliam [Gareth Edwards, dir., Godzilla]; Immorality Story Dead on Arrival, by Richard Bleiler [Walter Jarvis, The Fleshing]; Even in Horror, Boys Will Be Boys, by June Pulliam [Andrew Smith, Grasshopper Jungle: A History; Geoffrey Girard, Project Cain and Cain's Blood]; The Blood Is the Life, by John Edgar Browning [Cole Hadden, creator, Dracula]; Zombies as Social (Media) Creatures, by June Pulliam [Murali Balaji, ed. Thinking Dead: What the Zombie Apocalypse Means]; A Thoroughly Engaging Collection of Mythos-Inspired Tales, by Robert Butterfield [Don Webb, Through Dark Angles]; Unedited and Uneven, by June Pulliam [Willy Adkins, et al., The Dead Walk]; No Hollow Praise for The Hollow City, by Van Viator [Ransom Riggs, The Hollow City: The Second Novel of Miss Peregrine's Peculiar Children]; Edgar Allan Poe, by Walter de la Mare; Capsule Reviews; Notes on Contributors.

138. DON WEBB. *Through Dark Angles: Works Inspired by H. P. Lovecraft*, 2014. 250 pp.

Contents. The Mythos and I; The Man Who Scared Lovecraft; The Megalith Plague; Lavinia's Lament; The Gold of the Vulgar; The Doom That Came to Devil's Reef; Wilbur's Song; Pages from a Diary; Sanctuary; Wilbur Whatley's Twin; Platinum Hearts; Plush Cthulhu; Emily's Rose Window; A Ship Afar; Looking Glass; To Mars and Providence; After Alhazred; Lovecraft's Pillow; The Codex; Doc Corman's Haunted Palace One Fourth of July; Slowness; Rats; A Game of Nine Pins; Powers of Air and Darkness; Casting Call; Acknowledgments.

Notes. Cover design and illustration by Fergal Fitzpatrick. A volume of the selected Lovecraftian tales by a veteran writer of weird fiction.

139. *Spectral Realms:* No. 1 (Summer 2014). EDITED BY S. T. JOSHI. 138 pp.

Contents. Editorial, by S. T. Joshi; POETRY: Spectral Province, by Wade German; The Laundrymen, by Ann K. Schwader; Seasonal Affective Disorder, by Richard L. Tierney; Nocturnal Poet, by K. A. Opperman; Old Graveyard in the Woods, by Jonathan Thomas; Carathis, by Ashley Dioses; Night Stalker, by Michael Fantina; A Weird Tale, by Charles Lovecraft; The Star's Prisoner, by D. L. Myers; Emerald-esse, by Leigh Blackmore; Black Wings, by Ian Futter; Fortune Teller, by Carole Abourjeili; The Stomach Only Tries, by Marge Simon; Audience at Sunset, by David Barker and W. H. Pugmire; As Told to My Infant Grandchildren, by Phillip A. Ellis; The Hidden God, by Adam Bolivar; Siren of the Dead, by K. A. Opperman; Climate of Fear, by Ann K. Schwader; The Meromylls of Lake Lurd, by Donald R. Broyles; White Chapel, by Kendall Evans; Horror, by Ashley Dioses; Night Visit, by Charles Lovecraft; Fairy Song, by Darrell Schweitzer; Miranda, by Michael Fantina; States, by Ian Futter; In Splendour All Arrayed, by Leigh Blackmore; Dark Mirage, by Fred Phillips; In Cavernous Depths Yawning, by Randall D. Larson; Sea Princess, by Claire Smith; Necromancy, by Kyla Lee Ward; The Asteroid, by Richard L. Tierney; The Thing on the Mountain, by D. L. Myers; Note of the Executioner, by David Schembri; Ex Nihilo, by Daniel Kolbe Strange; The Den, by Chad Hensley; Awakening, by Carole Abourjeili; The Witches' House, by Margaret Curtis; Museum Piece, by Oliver Smith; Kiss the Stars, by Ashley Dioses; Pursuit, by Ian Futter; Afrasiab Down the Oxus, by Charles Lovecraft; Omens from Afar, by Phillip A. Ellis; Titan, by Michael Fantina; Lines on a Drawing by Hannes Bok, by Leigh Blackmore; Beneath the Ferny Trees, by David Schembri; "The Hound", by W. H. Pugmire; The Angels All Are Corpses in the Sky, by K. A. Opperman; A Carcass, Waiting, by Jason V Brock; The Rim, by Chad Hensley; CLASSIC REPRINTS: The Hidden Pool, by George Sterling; Resurrection Night, by Benjamin De Casseres; The Angels, by Théodore de Banville (tr. Stuart Merrill); Three Prose Poems, by Lord Dunsany; A Night with the Boys, by Bruce Boston; REVIEWS: To the Stars and Beyond, by Donald Sidney-Fryer; Ligotti on Sterling; Petrifying Poesy and Shivers in Verse, by Alan Gullette; Notes on Contributors.

Notes. Cover illustration by Eugenio Lucas ("Death Reading from a Human Lectern, Congregation in Background", c. 1850). The first issue of a journal devoted to weird poetry—a literary mode that has clearly experienced a renaissance in recent years. The journal also contains articles and reviews on weird poetry.

140. S. T. JOSHI. Lovecraft and a World in Transition: Collected Essays on H. P. Lovecraft. 2014. 620 pp.

Contents. Introduction; I. BIOGRAPHICAL STUDIES: Lovecraft and Weird Tales; Further Notes on Lovecraft and Music; Lovecraft's Library; Lovecraft's Revisions: How Much of Them Did He Write?; Lovecraft and His Wife; Lovecraft and the Films of His Day; The Rationale of Lovecraft's Pseudonyms; Lovecraft and the Munsey Magazines; Barbarism vs. Civilization: Robert E. Howard and H. P. Lovecraft in Their Correspondence; II. PHILOSOPHICAL STUDIES; The Political and Economic Thought of H. P. Lovecraft; "Reality" and Knowledge: Some Notes on Lovecraft's Aesthetic; In Defence of Dagon and Lovecraft's Philosophy; Lovecraft's Alien Civilisations: A Political Interpretation; Lovecraft and a World in Transition; Lovecraft and the "Big Issue"; H. P. Lovecraft: The Fiction of Materialism; Lovecraft and Religion; Time, Space, and Natural Law: Science and Pseudo-Science in Lovecraft; III. THEMATIC AND TEXTUAL STUDIES: Autobiography in Lovecraft; Lovecraft's Other Planets; Textual Problems in Lovecraft; The Structure of Lovecraft's Longer Narratives; The Dream World and the Real World in Lovecraft; Topical References in Lovecraft; Humour and Satire in Lovecraft; A Guide to the Lovecraft Fiction Manuscripts at the John Hay Library; IV. STUDIES OF INDIVIDUAL WORKS: Who Wrote "The Mound"?; On "The Book"; On "Polaris"; On "The Tree on the Hill"; Lovecraft and the Regnum Congo; The Sources for "From Beyond"; On "The Descendant"; What Happens in "Arthur Jermyn"; "The Tree" and Ancient History; Lovecraft and Dunsany's Chronicles of Rodriguez; Some Sources for "The Mound" and At the Mountains of Madness; The

Case of Charles Dexter Ward; Excised Passages from "The Thing on the Doorstep"; V. ON LOVECRAFT'S ESSAYS, POETRY, AND LETTERS: "History of the *Necronomicon*"; "Supernatural Horror in Literature"; Two Spurious Lovecraft Poems; A Look at Lovecraft's Letters; Lovecraft's Fantastic Poetry; Lovecraft, Regner Lodbrog, and Olaus Wormius; Lovecraft's Essays; VI. ON LOVECRAFT'S LEGACY AND INFLUENCE: The Development of Lovecraftian Studies: 1971–1982; R. H. Barlow and the Recognition of H. P. Lovecraft; A Literary Tutelage: Robert Bloch and H. P. Lovecraft; Passing the Torch: H. P. Lovecraft and Fritz Leiber; *Lovecraft at Last*; The Cthulhu Mythos; The Recognition of H. P. Lovecraft, 1937–2013. Sources; Index.

Notes. Cover design by Jessica Forsythe, incorporating a seldom seen photograph of HPL. Enormous volume of Joshi's collected essays on Lovecraft, with some dating to as early as 1979 and others written in 2013. Supersedes such earlier volumes as *Selected Papers on Lovecraft* (Necronomicon Press, 1989) and *Primal Sources* (item 16 above). Printed in a signed, limited hardcover edition (1000 copies) by Covington Group; the paperback edition (see item 149) was released almost simultaneously. A finalist for the 2014 Bram Stoker Award for nonfiction.

141. S. T. JOSHI. *200 Books by S. T. Joshi: A Comprehensive Bibliography.* 2014. 200 pp.

Contents. Introduction; I. Books Written; II. Books Edited; III. Editions of Works by H. P. Lovecraft; IV. Books Translated; V. Joshi as Series Editor; VI. Contributions to Books and Periodicals; VII. Journals Edited; VIII. Translations of Works by S. T. Joshi; IX. Forthcoming Books; APPENDIX: Murder; The Writing of *Mystery and Horror Writers of the Twentieth Century*; Books Published by Year.

Notes. Cover illustration by Jason C. Eckhardt. A volume that contains more information than anyone wants to know on Joshi's books, articles, reviews, stories, and other writings. Copies were sent free to advance purchasers of item 140, above; in addition, one hundred complimentary copies were distributed at the 2014 World Fantasy Convention.

142. WADE GERMAN. *Dreams from a Black Nebula.* 2014. 134 pp.

Contents. PHANTASMAGORICAL REALMS: Starry Wisdom; New Lost Worlds; The Black Idol; The Witch of Time; The Black Abbess; The Demon Sea; Astral Hierarchy; In Ultima Thule; December in the Druid Woods; Château Nevreant; Swamp Fantasy; Valley of the Sorcerers; Moonflowers; Hendecasyllabics; Walpurgisnacht; Spectral

Province; HYPNAGOGIC TERRAIN: Beyond the Wall of Tsang; A Voyage to Carcosa; In Carsultyal; The House of Neptune; Restoration; The Night Forest; Shadow and Silence; Prophecy of the Red Death; Lemurian Night Dive; Oneiromancy; Grimoire; The Necromantic Wine; Night Vigil for the Necromancer; Green Wine of Xei Cambael; Dragon; Barbarian; Black Sabbath Sestina; Trans-Neptunian Shores; Lords of Chaos; Hwamgaarl, the City of Screaming Statues; Dead Meadow; IN SPECTRAL PROVINCES: Plutonian; Event Horizon; Solarized; Return at Evening; Nocturne; Ghost Sonata; Eclogue; Nature Unveiled; Dreams in the Lich House; The Barrow in the Highlands; Ghost Mountains; Succubus; Night Winds; *"Curst be he yt moves my bones"*; De Vermis Mysteriis; Inscriptions; Necuratul; SONGS FROM THE NAMELESS HERMITAGE: The Eremite; A Vessel for Black Waters; Brotherhood of the Black Waters; Tombs of the Dead Gods; Procession; Dreams from the Black Nebula; Night Songs; In Term; Astronomy Domine; Black Suns; Apparitions of Astral Night; Revelation in Black; ANOMALIES: The Kin Fetch; Supernatural Refugees; The Propagule; Thing of Spring; Mooncalf; Dunwich Pastoral; The Worm Conjurer; Anadromous; Weavers; Old Growth; Golem Variant; From Tindalos; Brood of the Black Goat; Overheard at a Wharfside Tavern; The Necklace; Gothic Blue Book; The Stains; Classical Revenant; Remembrancer of the Bibliognostic Hippocamp; The Sales Pitch; Chimera Park; The Priest of P'rea; Nightfall in Sesqua; Inquisition on the Dunes; Atlach-Nacha; Monastic Ruins; Divine Invasion; 90482 Orcus; Acknowledgments.

Notes. Cover illustration by Dariusz Zawadzki ("Artefact", 2008). A strong collection of weird poetry by one of the leading contemporary practitioners, a Canadian poet who specializes in finely crafted formalist verse, especially in the sonnet form.

143. BOBBY DERIE. *Sex and the Cthulhu Mythos.* 2014. 314 pp.

Contents. Introduction; A Note on Sources and Citations; 1. SEX AND LOVECRAFT: Lovecraft and Love; Views on Sex; Views on Love and Relationships; Views on Eroticism and Pornography; The Shadow of Syphilis; Views on Gender and Homosexuality; Views on Miscegenation; Mrs. H. P. Lovecraft; 2. SEX AND THE LOVECRAFT MYTHOS: Precursors and Influences; Analyses; Themes and Parallels; The Role of Women; Asexual Aliens; Homosexual Interpretation; 3. SEX AND THE CTHULHU MYTHOS: New Developments; Family Trees of the Gods; Naming the Unnamable; The *Necronomicon* as Pornography; Body Horror; Alien Heats; Parody; Lovecraft as a Sexual Character; Gender, Sexuality, and Mythos Writers; Key Works and Authors (Robert E. Howard; Clark Ashton Smith; Robert Bloch; August Derleth; Ramsey Campbell; Richard A. Lupoff; Peter H. Cannon; Brian McNaughton; Robert M. Price; W. H. Pugmire; Caitlín R. Kiernan; Edward Lee; Alan Moore; *Cthulhu Sex* Magazine; *Eldritch Blue: Love & Sex in the Cthulhu Mythos*; *Cthulhu-rotica*; *Whispers in Darkness: Lovecraftian Erotica*; Other Authors and Works of Note; Sex and Mythos Poetry; Mythos Ebook Erotica); 4. BEYOND CTHULHUROTICA: Sex and the Lovecraftian Occult; Sex and the Mythos in Art; Sex and the Mythos in Comics; Sex and the Mythos in Japanese Manga and Anime; Sex and the Mythos Cinema; The Mythos and Rule 34; Afterword; Works Cited; Suggested Further Reading; Index.

Notes. Cover artwork by Gahan Wilson ("Flasher", c. 1973). Learned and comprehensive treatise on the sexual elements in the work of Lovecraft, his contemporaries, and his disciples, including such issues as Lovecraft's own sexuality, homosexuality, rape, and other matters, all treated with delicacy and scholarly rigor.

144. *Lovecraft Annual* No. 8 (2014). EDITED BY S. T. JOSHI. 222 pp.

Contents. Editorial; Letters to Farnsworth Wright, by H. P. Lovecraft; The Night Ocean, by R. H. Barlow and H. P. Lovecraft; Sanity, Subjectivity, and the Supernatural: Dreams of the Devil in Existentialism and the Weird Tale, by Dustin Geeraert; Terror and Terrain: The Environmental Semantics of Lovecraft County, by James O. Butler; Two Poets and Beauty: H. P. Lovecraft and James Elroy Flecker, by Phillip A. Ellis; Lovecraft's Third Meeting with David V. Bush, by Kenneth W. Faig, Jr.; Echoes of a Warrior Poet: The Influence of Alan Seeger on Lovecraft, by J. D. Worthington; Gothic Mythology: "The Moon-Bog" and the Greek Connection, by Juan Luis Pérez de Luque; Reviews: S. T. Joshi [Jack Koblas, *The Lovecraft Circle and Others as I Remember Them*; H. P. Lovecraft, *The New Annotated H. P. Lovecraft*, ed. Leslie S. Klinger]; Michael J. Abolafia [Gavin Callaghan, *H. P. Lovecraft's Dark Arcadia*].

Notes. The cover in "Pugmire Pink," a color created by Barbara Briggs Silbert, honors our steadfast friend, author W. H. Pugmire.

145. S. T. JOSHI. *Unutterable Horror: A History of Supernatural Fiction.* 2014. 2 vols.

Contents: VOLUME 1 (FROM GILGAMESH TO THE END OF THE NINETEENTH CENTURY): Preface; I. Introduction; II. Anticipations; III. The Gothics; IV. Interregnum; V. Edgar Allan Poe; VI. Mid-Victorian Horrors; VII. The Deluge: British and European Branch; VIII. The

Deluge: American Branch; Epilogue; Bibliographical Essay; Bibliography; VOLUME 2 (THE TWENTIETH AND TWENTY-FIRST CENTURIES): Preface; IX. The Titans; X. Other Early-Twentieth Century Masters; XI. Novelists, Satirists, and Poets; XII. H. P. Lovecraft and His Influence; XIII. American Pulpsmiths; XIV. Horrors at Midcentury; XV. Anticipations of the Boom; XVI. The Boom: The Blockbusters; XVII. The Boom: The Literati; XVIII. The Contemporary Era; Epilogue; Bibliographical Essay; Bibliography; Index.

Notes. Cover illustrations by Harry Clarke (Vol. 1) and S. H. Sime (Vol. 1). A reprint of Joshi's exhaustive history of supernatural fiction over the millennia; slightly corrected from the original edition (PS Publishing, 2012), which won the World Fantasy Award (special award, non-professional) in 2013.

146. MASSIMO BERRUTI, S. T. JOSHI, AND SAM GAFFORD, EDITORS. *William Hope Hodgson: Voices from the Borderland Seven Decades of Criticism on the Master of Cosmic Horror.* Edited by 2014. 326 pp.

Contents. Introduction, by Sam Gafford; I. SOME STUDIES OF HODGSON'S LIFE AND EARLY RECEPTION: Houdini v. Hodgson: The Blackburn Challenge, by Sam Gafford; William Hope Hodgson: In His Own Day, by A. Langley Searles; Pioneering Essays (H. P. Lovecraft, "The Weird Work of William Hope Hodgson"; Clark Ashton Smith, "In Appreciation of William Hope Hodgson"; H. C. Koenig, "William Hope Hodgson: Master of the Weird and Fantastic"; August Derleth, "William Hope Hodgson"; Ellery Queen, "William Hope Hodgson and the Detective Story"; Fritz Leiber, "William Hope Hodgson: Writer of Supernatural Horror"); II. SOME SPECIAL TOPICS: William Hope Hodgson, by Brian Stableford; The Dark Mythos of the Sea: William Hope Hodgson's Transformation of Maritime Legends, by Emily Alder; Things in the Weeds: The Supernatural in Hodgson's Short Stories, by S. T. Joshi; Against the Abyss: Carnacki the Ghost-Finder, Mark Valentine; William Hope Hodgson in the Underworld: Mythic Aspects of the Novels, by Phillip A. Ellis; Decay and Disease in the Fiction of William Hope Hodgson, by Sam Gafford; Hodgson's Women, by Sam Gafford; III. STUDIES OF INDIVIDUAL TALES: Things Invisible: Human and Ab-Human in Two of Hodgson's Carnacki Stories, by Leigh Blackmore; Sexual Symbolism in W. H. Hodgson, Sid Birchby; The "Wonder Unlimited"—The Tales of Captain Gault, Mark Valentine; *The House on the Borderland:* On Humanity and Love, by Henrik Harksen; IV. COMPARATIVE STUDIES; Time Machines Go Both Ways: Past and Future in H. G. Wells and W. H. Hodgson, by Andy Sawyer; The Long Apocalypse: The Experimental

Eschatologies of H. G. Wells and William Hope Hodgson, by Brett Davidson; Shadow out of Hodgson, by John D. Haefele; R. H. Barlow's "A Memory" in William Hope Hodgson's *The Night Land*, Marcos Legaria; WILLIAM HOPE HODGSON: A BIBLIOGRAPHY, by S. T. Joshi and Sam Gafford, with Mike Ashley: I. Works by Hodgson in English: A. Books and Pamphlets; B. Contributions to Books and Periodicals; C. Media Adaptations; II. Hodgson in Translation; III. Works about Hodgson; INDEXES: A. Names; B. Works by Hodgson; C. Periodicals; General Index.

Notes. Cover illustration by Daniele Serra. Comprehensive anthology of essays, both new and reprinted, on the master of sea horror and one of the pioneers of the "psychic detective." Concludes with the first exhaustive bibliography of work by and about Hodgson.

147. RHYS HUGHES. *Bone Idle in the Charnel House: A Collection of Weird Stories.* 2014. 246 pp.

Contents. Introduction; The Swinger; Bitter in Sour; The Old House Under the Snow; Degrees of Separation; The Warlord; Vampiric Gramps; Bone Idle in the Charnel House; What I Fear Most; Rediffusion; Casimir the Converter; Smuggling Old Nick to Newfoundland; Shelling the Toad; The Hydrothermal Reich; The Spoon; Chameleons; Happiness Leasehold; Life and the Plumbline; The Unsubtle Cages; Sigma Octantis; The Century Just Gone; Acknowledgements.

Notes. Cover illustration by Mike Dubisch. Striking collection of weird and fantastic tales by the popular and critically acclaimed Welsh author, whose work draws upon the tradition of Borges and Calvino.

148. DONALD TYSON. *The Lovecraft Coven.* 2014. 218 pp.

Contents. The Lovecraft Coven; Iron Chain.

Notes. Cover illustration by Robert H. Knox. A pair of substantial novellas of Lovecraftian horror.

149. S. T. JOSHI. *H. P. Lovecraft in a World of Transition;* 2014. 620 pp. ppbk.

150. MICHAEL ARONOVITZ. *The Witch of the Wood.* 2014. 234 pp.

Notes. Cover illustration by Lyndsay Harper. A vivid short novel of witchcraft, eroticism, and cosmic terror by a rising star in the realm of weird fiction.

151. *Dead Reckonings* No. 16 (Fall 2014). EDITED BY JUNE M. PUL-
LIAM AND TONY FONSECA. 102 pp.

Contents. Ramsey Campbell, Probably: Four Colour Horror; From
Mythos to Icon, by Martin Andersson [S. T. Joshi, ed., *A Mountain
Walked*]; Recommended by Stephen King, by Hank Wagner and Bev
Vincent [Christopher Golden, *Snowblind; Nick Cutter, The Troop*];
Tales of Two (Word)Smiths, by Robert Butterfield [Clint Smith,
Ghouljaw and Other Stories; James Robert Smith, *A Confederacy of
Horrors*]; Horror Everlasting, by Jonathan Johnson [Michael
Aronovitz, *The Voices in Our Heads; Alice Walks;* and *The Witch of the
Wood*]; Le Fanu at 200: Dublin Celebrates the Bicentenary of Its
"Invisible Prince," by Jim Rockhill; Memories and Ghosts of Ireland,
the *Other* Europe, and Beyond, by John Edgar Browning [John
Howard, *The Silver Voices;* Jim Rockhill and Brian J. Showers, ed.
Dreams of Shadow and Smoke: Stories for J. S. Le Fanu]; Uneven But
Essential for Researchers, by Richard Bleiler [James Goho, *Journeys
into Darkness: Critical Essays on Gothic Horror;* Gary Hoppenstand, ed.
Critical Insights: The American Thriller]; Why We Need Horror Film
Fanzines, by Chris Dallis [John Szpunar, *Xerox Ferox: The Wild World
of the Horror Film Fanzine*]; Obscure But Excellent, by Greg Gbur
[John Blackburn, *Our Lady of Pain*]; Girls Will Be Ghouls, by
Stephanie A. Graves [June Pulliam, *Monstrous Bodies*]; Vampire
Classic Back in Print, by Darrell Schweitzer [Michael Talbot, *The
Delicate Dependency*]; The Tale Remains Untold, by Tony Fonseca
[Robin Spriggs, *The Untold Tales of Ozman Droom*]; Old Ghouls Gone
Wild, by Martin Andersson [Ellen Datlow, ed. *Lovecraft's Monsters*];
Scholar Alert!, by June Pulliam [Alexandra Heller-Nicholas, *Found
Footage Horror Films;* Katarzyna Marak, *Japanese and American Horror;*
Shaka McGlotten and Steve Jones, ed. *Zombies and Sexuality;* William
Schoell. *The Horror Comics—1940s–1980s;* and Jon Towelson,
Subversive Horror Cinema]; Chambers, Lovecraft, and Pastiche, by
S. T. Joshi [Glynn Owen Barrass, ed. *In the Court of the Yellow King*
and Jesse Bullington, ed. *Letters to Lovecraft*]; A Fate Worse Than
Death, by Hank Wagner and Bev Vincent [Stephen King, *Mr.
Mercedes,* and *Revival*]; Idle Minds and Literary Playthings, by Richard
Bleiler [Rhys Hughes, *Bone Idle in the Charnel House*]; A Fine and
Diverse New Horror Anthology, by Robert Butterfield [Ellen Datlow,
ed. *The Best Horror of the Year: Volume Six*]; Doomed to Fail, by Tony
Fonseca [Daryl Gregory, *We Are All Completely Fine*]; Victorian,
Verbose, and Never Picks Up Steam, by Leigh Blackmore [K. W.
Jeter, *Fiendish Schemes*]; Kamog! Kamog!, by S. T. Joshi [David Barker
and W. H. Pugmire, *The Revenant of Rebecca Pascal*]; A Dark Shadow
from the Past, by Darrell Schweitzer [Evangeline Walton, *She Walks in*

Darkness]; The Mystery Man of Weird Fiction, by S. T. Joshi [Matt Cardin, ed. *Born to Fear: Interviews with Thomas Ligotti*; Thomas Ligotti, *The Spectral Link*]; Eeking Out a Passable Adult Novel, or Not, by Richard Bleiler [Greg van Eekhout, *California Bones*]; The *Schauerroman* in Its Proper Context . . ., by Jim Rockhill [Andrew Cusack and Barry Murnane, ed. *Popular Revenants*]; Supernatural Senility, by June Pulliam [*The Taking of Deborah Logan*, dir. Adam Robitel]; Capsule Reviews; Notes on Contributors.

152. JOSH KENT. *The Witch at Sparrow Creek: A Jim Falk Novel.* 2015. 356 pp.

Notes. Cover illustration by Jason C. Eckhardt. A gripping first novel of witchcraft set in rural Appalachia, evoking echoes of Manly Wade Wellman's John the Balladeer novels but with an atmosphere and richly textured characterization that are the author's own. The first of an expected series of novels featuring the central character, Jim Falk.

153. JAMES ROBERT SMITH. *A Confederacy of Horrors.* 2015. 232 pp.

Contents. A CONFEDERACY OF GHOSTS: Listen; Through Becky's Eyes; Of Rodents and Sinking Vessels; Toke Ghost; Tommy; Moving; The Pool; A CONFEDERACY OF VENGEANCE: On the First Day; The Jawbone of an Ass; Dope; Translator; Love & Magick; A CONFEDERACY OF OBSESSION: NUMHED; A Last, Longing Look; Symptom; Wet; One of Those Days; The Call; Just Like Jesus, He Said; A CONFEDERACY OF BLOOD: It's Not a Blessing, She Said; Just a Gigolo; The Old Man's Final Visit; Ice Bounty; The Reliable Vacuum Company; Pure Southern; Afterword, by Stephen Mark Rainey; Acknowledgments.

Notes. Cover illustration by Pete Von Sholly. The first short story collection by a noted and popular horror novelist and editor.

154. *Spectral Realms:* No. 2 (Winter 2015). EDITED BY S. T. JOSHI. 2015. 160 pp.

Contents. POETRY: A Spectral Realm Mystery, by Donald Sidney-Fryer; At the Last of Carcosa, by Ann K. Schwader; The Spire, by Chad Hensley; Fallen: A Lament and Affirmation, by Jason V Brock; The Dark Road from Yorehaven, by D. L. Myers; Mummify Me, by Jonathan Thomas; The Apple, by Claire Smith; Conundrum, by Fred Phillips; The Song of the Unformed, by Gemma Files; Occult Agency, by Wade German; The Promise, by Darrell Schweitzer; Witch's Love, by Ashley Dioses; The Lamp: A Fable, by John C. Tibbetts; When Rose Petals Fall, by John Shirley; Haunted, by William F. Nolan;

Among the Ghouls, by K. A. Opperman; Incantations, by Michael Fantina; Revenant, by F. J. Bergmann; Another Knife-Grey Day, by Michael Kelly; Song for Naughty Children, by David Barker; Rock On, by Marge Simon; The Ballad of Jack Keeper, by Adam Bolivar; The Desolate Kirkyard, by Liam Garriock; The Realm of Angels, by David Schembri; Invocation to Dispel Loneliness on Insomniac Nights, by Dan Clore; The Final Conversation, by Ian Futter; Robert Nelson: An Invitation, by Charles D. O'Connor III; The Sire, by Chad Hensley; Foiled Design, by Fred Phillips; "The Outsider", by W. H. Pugmire; Calving, by Gemma Files; Girls and Their Balloons, by Stephanie M. Wytovich; Barn, by Jonathan Thomas; The Night Is Black and White, by Leigh Blackmore; Harrow, by D. L. Myers; Mother Killer, by Melissa Frederick; Void Music, by Ann K. Schwader; Lavinia Whateley, by Darrell Schweitzer; Lines on Reading A. Merritt, by John C. Tibbetts; The Mood of the Moon, by Wade German; The Keeper of the Innsmouth Light, by M. F. Webb; The Cobbled Trail, by Michael Fantina; The Depths of Enlightenment, by Sean Elliot Martin; A Billion Souls Gaze West, by David Barker; The Bone Bird, by Mike Allen; Furaq, by Carole Abourjeili; The Blood Garden, by K. A. Opperman; Tricks, by Ian Futter; Legacy, by Fred Phillips; Ligeia, by Ashley Dioses; Hungry, the Rain-God Wakens, by Michael Kelly; A Search for Light in Night; A Search for Dark in Day, by John Shirley; Palimpsest, by F. J. Bergmann; Kiosk to Kadath, by Chad Hensley; The Nightmare-Monger, by Dan Clore; A Devil's Nursery Book, by Adam Bolivar; Swampsong, by Oliver Smith; Beauty and Oblivion, by K. A. Opperman and Charles D. O'Connor III; Head Ornaments, by Stephanie M. Wytovich; The Dream Sorceress, by Michael Fantina; My Ashen Heart, by Leigh Blackmore; Oblivion's Daughter, by David Barker; Vexteria, by Ashley Dioses; The Writer, by Ian Futter; Purloined, by Mike Allen; CLASSIC REPRINTS: The Skeleton Sexton, by Francis S. Saltus; The Ballad of Dead Men's Bay, by Algernon Charles Swinburne; The Cathedral of Lost Faces, by Bruce Boston; ARTICLES: "Figures in a Nightmare"—The Poetry of Leah Bodine Drake: Part 1, by Leigh Blackmore; REVIEWS: Some Hits, Some Misses, by Sunni K Brock; Notes on Contributors.

Notes. Cover illustration by Charles E. Burchfield ("Childhood's Garden", 1917).

155. WILLIAM F. NOLAN AND JASON V BROCK, EDITORS. *The Bleeding Edge: Dark Barriers, Dark Frontiers.* 2015. 318 pp.

Contents. Foreword, by S. T. Joshi; Welcome to the Dark Side, by William F. Nolan and Jason V Brock; "Some of My Best Friends Are Martians . . .," by Ray Bradbury; Just a Suggestion, by John Shirley; Love & Magick, by James Robert Smith; MADRI-Gall: A Short Skit for the Stage, by Richard Matheson and Richard Christian Matheson, Hope and the Maiden, by Nancy Kilpatrick; The Death and Life of Caesar LaRue, by Earl Hamner, Jr.; A Certain Disquieting Darkness, by Gary A. Braunbeck; The Boy Who Became Invisible, by Joe R. Lansdale; Getting Along Just Fine, by William F. Nolan; The Grandfather Clock: A Teleplay for *The Twilight Zone*, by George Clayton Johnson; Triptych: Three Bon-Bons, by Christopher Conlon; The Hand That Feeds, by Kurt Newton; The Central Coast, by Jason V Brock; Omnivore: An Illustrated Screenplay Excerpt, by Dan O'Bannon; De Mortuis, by John Tomerlin; I, My Father, and Weird Tales, by Frank M. Robinson; Silk City, by Lisa Morton; Red Light, by Steve Rasnic Tem; How it Feels to Murder: A Teleplay, by Norman Corwin; At the Riding School, by Cody Goodfellow; Notes on Contributors.

Notes. Cover illustration by Kris Kuksi ("Ode to Decadence [detail]", 2009). Interior illustrations by Dan O'Bannon. First paperback edition of an acclaimed anthology of original tales, teleplays, and other matter, first published by Cycatrix Press in 2009.

156. JOSEPH S. PULVER, SR. *A House of Hollow Wounds.* Edited by Jeffrey Thomas. 2015. 316 pp.

Contents. On the Embankment of Tangibility: An Introduction, by Jeffrey Thomas; A Thousand Injuries—; A (~BIG~) Fishy Menu; and the bass keeps thumpin'; (he) Dreams of Lovecraftian Horror . . .; Saturday Night . . . With a Dead Girl in It; Doom . . . & Sigh; into the world; A Night of Moon & Blood,   Then   Holstenwall; she sings. I sob......; The Golem; The Ozymandias Display; under stars with no desire to flee; no one ever talks about there will come a day these days; "c"-O[lLi(S)I;o!N,S   iN tHE word   box or   (i)'s Disintegration; On a Faraway Beach . . .; Down . . . and down we go; The Pencil; Tender. Sins.; Movietime . . . with popcorn and . . .; Caroline No. Bleue; Brick. By . . Brick; A House of Hollow Wounds; Desert Highway Motel; One Window, Two Hearts; The Sommerset Tales; Aubade in a Graveyard; I once possessed a fragile blue vase; Twilight Sonatas; Tears & the stars fall; Certain Sunday Evenings in Summer; A Traveler Came with Gifts; In a Raven's Eye; She Comes in Blood; Words Touching; Under June; I'll simply call her V; Sarah smile; In the spaces in between; The blood of a damsel's breast on the green door of the forest; I once possessed little other than a fragile blue vase; wind. ardent. circular, back on itself as if in dismay.; Being Led by Pictures . . .; The Ground She Sleeps upon Is a Clue . . . and a

Mystery; 8mm . . . soil; a stained translation [in 2 acts]; In a Black Studio No. 76; Vase; A Cold Yellow Moon; Acknowledgments.

Notes. Cover illustration by Daniele Serra. *Pulver's* fourth collection of stories, prose-poems, and vignettes.

157. PARK BARNITZ. *The Book of Jade: A New Critical Edition.* Compiled by David E. Schultz and Michael J. Abolafia. 2015. 324 pp.

Contents. THE BOOK OF JADE: Prelude; PART ONE: Ashtoreth; Parfait Amour; Opium; Sombre Sonnet; Languor; Ennui; Litany; Harvard; Pride; Song of Golden Youth; Mais Moi Je Vis la Vie en Rouge; Louanges d'Elle; Hélas; Sonnet; Sonnet; Rondeau; Autumn Song; Ballad; Changelessness; Madonna; Poppy Song; Consolation; Liebes-Tod; Evening Song; Song of the Stars in Praise of Her; Aubade; Remember; Song; Song; Constancy; Requiem; Autumn Burial; Sonnet of Burial; Nocturne; PART TWO: Mad Sonnet; The House of Youth; De Profundis; Prayer; Sestettes; Sonnet of the Instruments of Death; Truth; Hegel; Monotony; Sepulture; Miserrimus; Scorn; The Grave; Mummy; Sepulchral Life; Corpse; Mankind; The Defilers; The Grotesques; Dead Dialogue; Fragments; Envoi; Postlude; Song of India; Dedication; UNCOLLECTED WRITINGS: After-Life; Danse Macabre; [Letter to Doxey's, 1901]; The Truth about Rudyard Kipling; The Art of the Future; [Review]; Bibliography; PARK BARNITZ: A BIOGRAPHY, by Gavin Callaghan; CRITICISM: Contemporary Reviews; The Promise of Contemporary Art; Two American Poets: A Study in Possibilities, by Floyd Dell; We (Almost) Die for Art, by Floyd Dell; The Poet of Montsalvat, by Carey McWilliams; A Land of Poets, by Carey McWilliams; America's "Yellow Nineties" Poet, by Joseph Payne Brennan; Renaissance, by David E. Schultz; The Perfection of the Corpse: Necrophilia in The Book of Jade by K. A. Opperman; The Grotesques: Sins against the Afterlife, by Ashley Dioses; Barnitz and Pessimism, by Matt Sarraf; "I Am Weary of That Lidless Eye": Gazing into the Hegelian Abyss of Subjectivity in the Mad Sonnets of Park Barnitz, by Chuck Caruso, Ph.D.; Two Dead Men: Park Barnitz and Rudyard Kipling, by Gavin Callaghan; Afterword, by Michael J. Abolafia; Index of Titles and First Lines.

Notes. Cover artist (from original edition) unknown. A reprint of the fabulously rare poetry volume first issued in 1901, with additional uncollected and unpublished material. Barnitz (1878–1901) was rumored to have committed suicide shortly after the book appeared. Thanks in part to the interest of Donald Wandrei and H. P. Lovecraft, the volume has become a choice acquisition for the weird collector. This edition includes a substantial biography of Barnitz by Gavin Callaghan, who has spent years researching the poet's life and work.

158. JONATHAN THOMAS. *Dreams of Ys and Other Invisible Worlds.* 2015. 268 pp.

Contents. Three Dreams of Ys; Down the Hatch; We Are Made of Stars; Pests: A Provisional Translation; A Quirk of the Mistral; Welcome Back; Houdini Fish; Girl on a Swing; Sinister Illuminator; DEAD CITY SUITE: Introduction: Some Homebrew from a Haunted Cellar; Integrity; The Immortality Sequence; A Light in the Wilderness; Watcher of the Invisible World; Acknowledgments.

Notes. Cover illustration by David C. Verba. Thomas's fourth story collection, containing not only several vivid Lovecraftian tales but also some previously unpublished stories written as part of his M.A. thesis at Brown University in the 1980s.

159. *Dead Reckonings* No. 17 (Spring 2015). EDITED BY JUNE M. PULLIAM AND TONY FONSECA. 94 pp.

Contents. Hidden City Deserves Discovery, by Chris Dallis [Robert Butterfield, *The Hidden City: Van Ark I*]; Ramsey Campbell, Probably; Excursions into the Imagination: Report on ICFA 36, by Simone Caroti; The Variegated World of Ray Bradbury, by S. T. Joshi [Jonathan R. Eller, *Ray Bradbury Unbound*]; Elementary, My Dear James, by Bev Vincent [Dan Simmons, *The Fifth Heart*]; The Poetry of Darkness, by Greg Gbur [David E. Cowen, *The Madness of Empty Spaces*]; Darker Than Any Earth-Bound Sea, by Jeremy Cavaterra [Scott Thomas, *The Sea of Ash*]; Terror in a Sentence, by S. T. Joshi [Ramsey Campbell, *Think Yourself Lucky*]; Book of Fiction of the Month!, by Chris Dallis [Michael Loughrey, *The Parallax Groove*]; Of Poetry and Corpses, by Leigh Blackmore [Stephanie M. Wytovich, *Mourning Jewelry*]; The Weird Is Alive and All Too Real, by Chris Dallis [M. A. Katz-Savoy, *The Place Where Nothing Is Real*]; Life in the Urban Gothic: One Big Ghost Rope, by June Pulliam [David Robert Mitchell, dir., *It Follows*]; H. P. Lovecraft and Subtle Realms of Dark Matter, by John Edgar Browning [S. T. Joshi, ed., *Black Wings III: New Tales of Lovecraftian Horror*]; Silence Is Deadly, by Hank Wagner [Tim Lebbon, *The Silence*]; Creepy Stories That Send Shivers, by Beth Younger [Jeani Rector, ed., *Shrieks and Shivers from The Horror Zine*]; For the Vintage Paperback Nostalgia Market, by Darrell Schweitzer [Gregory Luce, ed., *Horror Gems, Vol 7*]; Dig Wide, Dig Deep: The Need for Better Research, by Tony Fonseca [Patrick McAleer and Michael A. Perry, ed. *Stephen King's Modern Macabre: Essays on the Later*

Works]; Keeping the Undead Fascinating, by Chris Dallis [June Michele Pulliam, and Anthony J. Fonseca, *Encyclopedia of the Zombie: The Walking Dead in Popular Culture and Myth*]; Mangling Brothers and Burn'em and Burry: The Circus Is in Town, by Danel Olson [Ellen Datlow, ed. *Nightmare Carnival*]; Burrage: Back in Print, by Greg Gbur [A. M. Burrage, *The Waxwork and Other Stories*]; For Horror Fans, It's a Small, Weird World, by June Pulliam [Jennifer Kent, dir., *The Babadook*; Gerard Johnstone, dir., *Housebound*; Tommy Wirkola, dir., *Dead Snø II: Red vs. Dead*]; Fantasy, or Disneyfied Horror?, by Tony Fonseca [Greg van Eekhout, *Pacific Fire*]; One Mother of a TV Series, by June Pulliam [Carlton Cuse, Kerry Ehrin, and Anthony Cipriano, creators, *Bates Motel*]; All You Ever Wanted to Know about Vampires, by June Pulliam [Margot Adler. *Vampires Are Us: Understand Our Love Affair with the Immortal Dark Side*]; Retrospective Review: The Woods of Weir, by Allan Nevins [Leonard Cline, *The Dark Chamber*]; Notes on Contributors.

160. ANN K. SCHWADER. *Dark Equinox and Other Tales of Lovecraftian Horror.* 2015. 259 pp.

Contents. Dark Equinox; The Sweetness of Your Heart; When the Stars Run Away; Wings of Memory; Her Beloved Son; Custom Order; Desert Mystery! Gas & Go!; Rehab; Scream Saver; The Water Lily Room; The Death Verses of Yian-Ho; Twenty Mile; Experiencing the Other; Paradigm Wash; Night of the Piper; The Wind-Caller; Acknowledgments.

Notes. Cover illustration and frontispiece by Lyndsay Harper. Generous selection of the Lovecraftian tales of one of the leading weird poets and fiction writers of our time, timed for her appearance as Poet Laureate at the NecronomiCon II convention. Many of the tales are set in or around the author's native Wyoming and draw deeply upon her knowledge of the area and of the Native American traditions that linger there.

161. ROBERT H. WAUGH. *The Bloody Tugboat and Other Witcheries.* 2015. 268 pp.

Contents. The Portrait of Miss Constance; Iceboy; In Her Eye; The Hot Tub Horror; The Bloody Tugboat; The Bright Thin Room; Yet Here's a Spot; The Churches on the Hill; The *Narcissus* Anchors in the Caribees; The Puzzle in the Cellar Pantry; The Black Plastic Rag; Alice by the Beautiful Sea; Mr. Hoffmann's Cat; Playing with Fire; Punch Stands Alone; The Broker and His Pet; Down by the Alyscamps, Up on the Hill; The Violinist; Johnny's Tin Toy; Her Crooked Mouth; The Wind of His Passing; Nancy's Dreams; The Infected Land; The Creature from the Zodiacal Crab; Click.

Notes. Cover illustration by Mike Dubisch. Engaging and diverse collection of stories by a leading critic of weird, fantasy, and science fiction.

162. LOIS H. GRESH. *Cult of the Dead and Other Weird and Lovecraftian Tales.* 2015. 238 pp.

Contents. Introduction, by S. T. Joshi; Cult of the Dead; Devil's Bathtub; Dreams of Death; Necrotic Cove; Old Enough to Drink; Death Doll; Willie the Protector; Wee Sweet Girlies; Debutante Ball; Let Me Make You Suffer; Where I Go, Mi-Go; The Lagoon of Insane Plants; Soleman; Snip My Suckers; Psychomildew Love; Digital Pistil; Algorithms and Nasal Structures; Little Whorehouse of Horrors; Showdown at Red Hook; Mandelbrot Moldrot; Acknowledgments.

Notes. Cover illustration by Robert H. Knox. Rich collection of stories by a leading contemporary practitioner of Lovecraftian fiction, timed for her appearance as a Guest of Honor at the NecronomiCon II convention.

163. W. H. PUGMIRE. *Monstrous Aftermath: Stories in the Lovecraftian Tradition.* 2015. 266 pp.

Contents. Within Your Unholy Pit of Shoggoths; Your Weighing of My Heart; The Tomb of Oscar Wilde; These Harpies of Carcosa; An Ecstasy of Fear; Darkness Dancing in Your Eyes; Beyond the Wakeful Senses; Ye Unkempt Thing; Half Lost in Shadow; Circular Bone; Jester of Yellow Day; This Splendor of the Goat; Monstrous Aftermath; An Element of Nightmare; Some Unknown Gulf of Night; *Fungi from Yuggoth,* by H. P. Lovecraft; Acknowledgments.

Notes. Cover illustration and interior illustrations by Matthew Jaffe. New collection of tales by one of our leading contemporary Lovecraftians, gifted with a prose style of unexcelled fluency and poetic lyricism.

164. H. P. LOVECRAFT. *Letters to Robert Bloch and Others.* Edited by David E. Schultz and S. T. Joshi. 2015. 548 pp.

Contents. Introduction; LETTERS: To Robert Bloch; To Natalie H. Wooley; To Robert and Mrs. Elmer Nelson; To William Frederick Anger; To Kenneth Sterling; To Donald A. Wollheim; To Wilson Shepherd; To Willis Conover; APPENDIX: *Robert Bloch:* A Visit with H. P. Lovecraft; Lilies; The Black Lotus; How I Get My Inspiration; [*unsigned*] Milwaukee Youth Writes Horror Tales, Sells 'Em; *Natalie*

H. Wooley: Admonition; Dream Fantasy; Antares; Avatar; The Alien; Flight; A Heavenly Tragedy; Lines to Cleopatra; Coward; Sailor's Child; Western Night; Mountain Trail; End of the Trail; Mountain Pool; Sanctuary; Dream Tryst; The Adventure Story; Is Criticism Necessary?; Have You a Hobby?; "Tillicum"; The Dance; Reminiscense; Spurs of Death; *Robert Nelson:* Night of Unrest; Fragment; The Unremembered Realm; Below the Phosphor; Dream-Stair; Jorgas; Sable Revelry; Under the Tomb; Lost Excerpts; Trilogy of Death; The Weird Tale (A Dialogue); *Fred Anger:* Fantastic Bread & Butter; or, the Mystery of the Missing Authors [and An Answer to Mr. Anger, by Farnsworth Wright; A Writer Comments on the Anger–Wright Controversy, by Anonymous]; An Interview with E. Hoffmann Price, with Louis C. Smith; *Donald A. Wollheim:* Review of THE NECRONOMICON; Allalieor; Umbriel; Pure Fantasy; Howard Phillips Lovecraft; Editor's Preface [to "The Shadow out of Time"]; The Future of Publishing; *Kenneth Sterling:* The Horror Element in Poe; *Wilson Shepherd:* Death; *Willis Conover, Jr.:* Observations and Otherwise; The Lost Chord; The Spirits Mourn; Chronology; Glossary of Frequently Mentioned Names; Bibliography; Index.

Notes. Cover design by Anastasia Damianakos (uniform with item 13). Another volume of the *Collected Letters* project, printing the complete extant letters to Robert Bloch (first published in an edition by Necronomicon Press, 1993) and other related correspondents of the 1930s, with substantial ancillary material and exhaustive annotations by the editors.

165. S. T. JOSHI. *The Rise, Fall, and Rise of the Cthulhu Mythos.* 2015. 412 pp.

Contents. Preface; Introduction; I. Anticipations; II. The Lovecraft Mythos: Emergence; III. The Lovecraft Mythos: Expansion; IV. Contemporaries: Peers; V. Contemporaries: Scions; VI. The Derleth Mythos; VII. Interregnum; VIII. The Scholarly Revolution; IX. Recrudescence; X. Resurgence; Epilogue; Notes; Index.

Notes. Cover illustration by Jason C. Eckhardt. Exhaustively revised edition of a book first published (as *The Rise and Fall of the Cthulhu Mythos*) by Mythos Books in 2008, containing extensive discussion of work written by leading Lovecraftian writers (Caitlín R. Kiernan, Donald Tyson, Jonathan Thomas, W. H. Pugmire, and others) in the years since the book's first appearance.

166. *Spectral Realms:* No. 3 (Summer 2015). EDITED BY S. T. JOSHI. 155 pp.

POETRY: Song of the Rushes, by M. F. Webb; In Fits of Wildest Dreaming, by K. A. Opperman; Inheritance, by Christina Sng; Rune, by Wade German; Preserves, by G. O. Clark; Barley Night, by Jonathan Thomas; Ode to Hecate, by Liam Garriock; A Shuddery Tale, by Charles Lovecraft; Arcane Stars, by DJ Tyrer; Northern Lights, by Mary Krawczak Wilson; Always Look under the Bed, by Mark McLaughlin; The Cave of Ebon Boughs, by D. L. Myers; The Empty Room, by Darrell Schweitzer; Dolls, by Jason V Brock; Painted Ladies, by David Barker; Brownfields, by John Mundy; Even Madness Cannot Hide, by Ashley Dioses; Revelation, by Fred Phillips; Daemon Insectarium, by Chad Hensley; Sorcerers in Love, by Don Webb; Moonrise, by Christina Sng; The Game of Cat and Dragon, by Pat Calhoun; Lovers' Wine, by Stanley Gemmell; Childe Jackson Drake, by Adam Bolivar; Zann, by Ian Futter; The Golden Diadem, by Leigh Blackmore; To See or Not to See?, by Nicole Cushing; The Dark at the Top of the Stairs, by Jonathan Thomas; Butterfly, by Carole Abourjeili; Carcosa in Mind, by DJ Tyrer; The Death of Twilight, by D. L. Myers; Tragic, Trembling Giant, by Linda D. Addison; Witches at the Switches, by David Barker; My Heart's Thin Veil, by Margi Curtis; Clarethea, by K. A. Opperman; Ghoul of the Enamel, by Jason Sturner; A Queen in Hell, by Ashley Dioses; Azathoth, by Charles Lovecraft; Waking, by Ian Futter; Spinal Piano, by Reiss McGuinness; The Thirst of Sekhmet, by Ann K. Schwader; The Shadow within Darkness, by Randall Larson; Guardians of the Seven Gates, by Chad Hensley; Schadenfreude, by John Mundy; Dead Pale Moon, by Leigh Blackmore; To Reach Carcosa, by Mark McLaughlin; Sand Bar, by Jonathan Thomas; Toujours Il Coûte Trop Cher, by Mike Allen and C. S. E. Cooney; Alone in the Desert, by Mary Krawczak Wilson; Mother, by Christina Sng; The Perfect Rose, by Ashley Dioses; End Times, by DJ Tyrer; The Lich's Last Laugh, by Dan Clore; A Garden of Unearthly Delights, by Marge Simon; Masque Macabre, by K. A. Opperman; Gorgoneion, by Oliver Smith; Unexpected Meetings, by Ian Futter; Black Panther, by David Barker; CLASSIC REPRINTS: Old Trinity Churchard, by A. Merritt; Illumination in the Mutant Rain Forest, by Bruce Boston; Three Songs from Nosferatu, by Dana Gioia; ARTICLES: "Figures in a Nightmare"— The Poetry of Leah Bodine Drake: Part 2, by Leigh Blackmore; REVIEWS: Studies of Death, by Michael Dirda; Two from Eldritch, by D. L. Myers; Notes on Contributors. *Notes.* Cover illustration by Rabban.

167. H. P. LOVECRAFT. *Collected Fiction: A Variorum Edition, Volume 1: 1905–1925*. Edited by S. T. Joshi. 2015. 530 pp.

Contents. Introduction; The Beast in the Cave; The Alchemist; The Tomb; Dagon; A Reminiscence of Dr. Samuel Johnson; Polaris; Beyond the Wall of Sleep; Memory; Old Bugs; The Transition of Juan Romero; The White Ship; The Street; The Doom That Came to Sarnath; The Statement of Randolph Carter; The Terrible Old Man; The Tree; The Cats of Ulthar; The Temple; Facts concerning the Late Arthur Jermyn and His Family; Celephaïs; From Beyond; Nyarlathotep; The Picture in the House; Ex Oblivione; Sweet Ermengarde; or, The Heart of a Country Girl; The Nameless City; The Quest of Iranon; The Moon-Bog; The Outsider; The Other Gods; The Music of Erich Zann; Herbert West—Reanimator; Hypnos; What the Moon Brings; Azathoth; The Hound; The Lurking Fear; The Rats in the Walls; The Unnamable; The Festival; Under the Pyramids; The Shunned House; The Horror at Red Hook; He; In the Vault.

168. H. P. LOVECRAFT. *Collected Fiction: A Variorum Edition, Volume 2: 1926–1930*. Edited by S. T. Joshi. 2015. 538 pp.

Contents. Introduction; Cool Air; The Call of Cthulhu; Pickman's Model; The Silver Key; The Strange High House in the Mist; *The Dream-Quest of Unknown Kadath; The Case of Charles Dexter Ward;* The Colour out of Space; The Descendant; History of the "Necronomicon"; Ibid; The Dunwich Horror; The Whisperer in Darkness.

169. H. P. LOVECRAFT. *Collected Fiction: A Variorum Edition, Volume 3: 1931–1936*. Edited by S. T. Joshi. 2015. 520 pp.

Contents. Introduction; *At the Mountains of Madness;* The Shadow over Innsmouth; The Dreams in the Witch House; Through the Gates of the Silver Key; The Thing on the Doorstep; The Book; The Shadow out of Time; The Haunter of the Dark; APPENDIX: Juvenilia (The Little Glass Bottle; The Secret Cave; The Mystery of the Grave-Yard; The Mysteriovs Ship [short version]; The Mysterious Ship [long version]); The Very Old Folk; Discarded Draft of "The Shadow over Innsmouth"; The Evil Clergyman; [Cigarette Characterizations]; Of Evill Sorceries done in New England, of Daemons in No Humane Shape; Bibliography.

Notes. Cover design and illustrations by Fergal Fitzpatrick. The three cover illustrations represent Lovecraft's famous description of his own nature as "tripartite" (in item 25, p. 184). The facsimile signature of Lovecraft stamped in foil on the front cover of each volume was offset from his ownership signature in a book of stories by M. R. James. These three volumes contain roughly 10,300 footnotes.

A new edition of Lovecraft that draws upon decades of research by the editor. It is the first edition that prints textual variants for all relevant publications of Lovecraft's stories from their first publication to recent editions. The stories are printed in chronological order, and Joshi has made slight revisions from his earlier corrected editions based on new information and a refined awareness of Lovecraft's stylistic and punctuational preferences. This should become the definitive text of Lovecraft's fiction for decades to come.

170. K. A. OPPERMAN. *The Crimson Tome.* 2015. 181 pp.

Contents. Preface: Opperman's Opus, by Dr. W. C. Farmer. Introduction: Crimson Pages from the Future Perfect Past, by Donald Sidney-Fryer, THE NIGHTMARE MUSE: *The Land of Darkest Dreams:* I. The Nightmare Muse; II. Yorehaven; III. Tavern Rumors; IV. A Daemon Impulse; V. The Witch-Light; VI. The Trail Between Two Trees; VII. The Pumpkin King; VIII. The Wood of Hissing Shadows; IX. The Cemetery of Dead Dreamers; X. The Muttering Mushroom; XI. The Windows; XII. The Shadow of Yorehaven; XIII. The Bookshop; XIV. Transformation; XV. A Mirror Image; XVI. The Beckoning Hand; XVII. Necromancy; XVIII. Initiation; XIX. The Black Kiss; XX. Dream Decay; UNPLEASANT DREAMS: Nocturnal Poet; The Crimson Tome; The Chimeras of Midnight; Unpleasant Dreams; Halloween; Mandrake; The Fatal Flower; Soul Rot; The Darkness Within; What the Moon Saw; The Treachery of the Stars; Sirius; And They Took Her Away; Corpse Moon; The Crimson Unicorn; The Thirst of Count Aster; A Vampire Fear; The Scarlet Font; Vampiric Roses; Blood; Bathory; Siren of the Dead; My Darling Bride; NOCTURNAL LOVERS PART I: Succubus; Nocturnal Lover; Dark Poetry; Witch's Charms; A Heart Defiled; O Pale Temptress; Ashiel; Ashiel's Gem; Ashiel's Mirror; Ashiel's Prisoner; Ashiel's Diary; Ashiel's Ritual; *Three Poems After* Venus in Furs: Severin's Venus; Wanda von Dunajew; Venus in Furs; Mistress of Torture; Priestess of Pleasure; The Demon and the Vampiress; NOCTURNAL LOVERS PART II: Dark Star of My Desire; Dark Poetess of My Heart; Sorcerer's Lament; A Secret Sorcery; Sorcerous Bond; The Scarlet Seal; Lunar Love; Dark Valentine; Love Atlantean; To an Unknown Enchantress; Beneath the Cold, Cold Stars; The Perishing Rose; Decapitated Kiss; Love Beyond the Grave; Graveyard Promise; THE PALACE OF PHANTASIES; Cemetery of Broken Hearts; The Corpse of Beauty; Moonrise; The Moonward Trail; Possibilities; Faerie Song; The Faerie Moon; Duel with the Dark Double; Nocturnal Flowers;

The Well of Purple Wine; Zeriatis; The Dreamer; Writing Shrine; Oracle of the Black Pool; The Wrath of Xyre; The Wizard; Khayyam's Wine; Lord of Illusion; The Palace of Phantasies; TWILIGHT SORROWS: The Tree; Autumn Hearts; Toadstools; October; All Hallow's Eve; Jack-o'-Lanterns; The Wraith; Thin Grows the Veil; November; Funereal Sun; Winter Crow; Twilight Sorrows; The Angels All Are Corpses in the Sky; The Mascaron; The Gargoyle; Shattered Hopes; Ancientness; In Mortal Dream; The Doom of Words; TRIBUTES: Twisted Trails of Thought, by Ashley Dioses; A Sorcerous Tome, by Ashley Dioses; The Crimson Kist, by D. L. Myers; The Sorcerous Scribe, by D. L. Myers; ACKNOWLEDGMENTS.

Notes. Cover and interior art by Steve Lines. Cover design by Barbara Briggs Silbert. A scintillating book of mostly formalist verse by a young California poet who has drawn deeply from the work of Edgar Allan Poe, George Sterling, Clark Ashton Smith, and other weird poets.

171. *Lovecraft Annual* No. 9 (2015). EDITED BY S. T. JOSHI. 231 pp.

Contents. Letters to Marian F. Bonner, by H. P. Lovecraft; Miscellaneous Impressions of H.P.L., by Marian F. Bonner; Can You Direct Me to Ely Court?: Some Notes on 66 College Street, by Kenneth W. Faig, Jr.; 66 College Street, by David E. Schultz; The Thing (Flung Daily) on the Doorstep: Lovecraft in the Antipodean Press, 1803–2007, by Brendan Whyte; The Search for Joseph Curwen's Town Home, by Donovan K. Loucks; Charles Baxter on Lovecraft, by S. T. Joshi; Six Degrees of Lovecraft: Henry Miller, by Bobby Derie; Cassie Symmes: Inadvertent Lovecraftian, by David Goudsward; Clergymen among Lovecraft's Paternal Ancestors, by Kenneth W. Faig, Jr.; Lovecraft and Houellebecq: Two Against the World, by Todd Spaulding; Donald A. Wollheim's Hoax Review of the Necronomicon, by Donovan K. Loucks; Reviews: Steven J. Mariconda [H. P. Lovecraft, *Collected Fiction: A Variorum Edition*, ed. by S. T. Joshi]; Darrell Schweitzer [Paul Roland, *The Curious Case of H. P. Lovecraft*]; Briefly Noted.

172. *Lovecraftian Proceedings: Papers from NecronomiCon Providence: 2013.* EDITED BY JOHN MICHAEL SEFEL AND NIELS-VIGGO S. HOBBS. 2015. 264 pp.

Contents. Preface, by John Michael Sefel; Introduction, by Niels-Viggo S. Hobbs; Poe, Lovecraft, and "the Uncanny": The Horror of the Self, by Anthony Conrad Chieffalo; "A Stalking Monster": The Influence of Radiation Poisoning on H. P. Lovecraft's "The Colour out of Space", by Andy Troy; Dead Lies Dreaming: H. P. Lovecraft and the

Other Side of Modernity, by Andrew Lenoir; Lovecraftian Milton: Prophetic Certainties, Romantic Rebellions, and Horrific Imaginings in the Weird Worlds of Milton and Lovecraft, by Marcello C. Ricciardi; The Failed Promises of Rationality: Sam J. Lundwall on the Individual Lost in an Uncaring and Soulless World, by Lars G. E. Backstrom; New England's Curator: Colonial Revival in the Travelogue and Fiction of H. P. Lovecraft, by Kenneth W. Lai; Lovecraft, Fear, and the Medieval Body Frame, by Perry Neil Harrison; Attempting to "Untangle" the Mind, Body, and Phallus in Lovecraft's "The Thing on the Doorstep," by Zack Rearick; The Shadow of His Smile: Humor in H. P. Lovecraft's Fiction, by Stephen Walker; Monstrous Modernism: H. P. Lovecraft's Theory of the Aesthetic in Modernity, by Jason Ray Carney; Dagon and Derrida: The Modern and Post-Modern in Dialogue in the Cthulhu Mythos, by Lyle Enright; I and Cthulhu: Using Martin Buber's Ontology of Dialogue to Examine H. P. Lovecraft's Cosmic Dread, by Daniel Holmes; Thinking Ecocritically: A Look at Embodiment and Nature in the Fiction of H. P. Lovecraft, by Cory Willard; Genuine Pagans: A Foray into Lovecraftian Religions, by Dennis P. Quinn; Appendix: Abstracts of Papers Presented at NecronomiCon Providence—2013 Emerging Scholarship Symposium, by John Michael Sefel; Index.

Notes. Cover illustration by Pete Von Sholly. A collection of papers presented at the "Emerging Scholarship Symposium" at NecronomiCon Providence (August 20–23, 2013), containing a variety of subtle and innovative analyses of Lovecraft the man, writer, and thinker.

173. DONALD R. BURLESON. *Lovecraft—An American Allegory: Selected Essays on H. P. Lovecraft.* 2015. 259 pp.

Contents. Abbreviations; Darkness and Light: Lovecraft's Impact on My Life; THEMATIC STUDIES: Zen and the Art of Lovecraft; A Note on Lovecraft, Mathematics, and the Outer Spheres; Lovecraft and Chiasmus, Chiasmus and Lovecraft; Lovecraft and the World as Cryptogram; Lovecraft and the Death of Tragedy; Lovecraft and Romanticism; Lovecraft: An American Allegory; Lovecraft and Adjectivitis: A Deconstructionist View; Lovecraft and Chaos; Lovecraft and Interstitiality; Lovecraft and Gender; H. P. Lovecraft: Textual Keys; SOURCES AND INFLUENCES: H. P. Lovecraft: The Hawthorne Influence; Strange High Houses: Lovecraft and Melville; Ambrose Bierce and H. P. Lovecraft; A Note on Lovecraft and Rupert Brooke; STUDIES OF INDIVIDUAL TALES: Iranon and Kuranes: An Intertextual Gloss; On Lovecraft's Fragment "Azathoth"; Aporia and Paradox in

"The Outsider"; Is Lovecraft's "Ph'nglui mglw'nafh . . ." a Cryptogram?; *The Dream-Quest of Unknown Kadath*; The Mythic Hero Archetype in "The Dunwich Horror"; Prismatic Heroes: The Colour out of Dunwich; Humour beneath Horror: Some Sources for "The Dunwich Horror" and "The Whisperer in Darkness"; The Thing: On the Doorstep; LOVECRAFT'S POETRY: Lovecraft's "The Unknown": A Sort of Runic Rhyme; On Lovecraft's "Nemesis"; On Lovecraft's "The Ancient Track"; Scansion Problems in Lovecraft's "Mirage"; Lovecraft's Cheshire Cat; Lines of Verse Evoking Close Reading: Acrostic-Formulated Text; Works Cited; Works about Lovecraft by Donald R. Burleson; Index.

Notes. Cover design (incorporating a photograph of Lovecraft) by Barbara Briggs Silbert. The collected Lovecraftian papers of one of the pioneering scholars of recent decades, whose work since the late 1970s has revolutionized our understanding of the dreamer from Providence.

Index of Authors, Editors, and Artists

Numbers refer to item, not to page.

HIPPOCAMPUS PRESS derives its name from H. P. Lovecraft's term of address (used thrice), in unpublished parts of letters to Frank Belknap Long, of which the following (from 6 April 1923) is representative: "be a nice little amethystine hippo-campus, write your Old Grandpa, and prepare to visit Providentia's sequester'd shades when the sun is warm and genial."